MW00830293

This Is
Sanatan Dharma

The Quest for Truth

एष धर्मः सनातनः

This Is Sanatan Dharma

The Quest for Truth

Partho

Title: This Is Sanatan Dharma: The Quest for Truth
Author: Partho

ISBN: 978-93-92209-50-5

First published in India 2023
This edition published 2023

Published by:
BluOne Ink LLP
A-76, 2nd Floor, Noida Sector 136,
Uttar Pradesh 201305.

Website: www.bluone.ink
Email: publisher@bluone.ink

Copyright © 2023 Partho

Partho has asserted his rights under the Indian Copyright Act to be identified as the author of this work.

All rights reserved under the copyright conventions. No part of this publication may be reproduced or transmitted in any form or by any means, electronic or mechanical, including photocopying, recording or any information storage or retrieval system, without the prior permission in writing from the publishers.

This book is solely the responsibility of the author(s) and the publisher has had no role in the creation of the content and does not have responsibility for anything defamatory or libellous or objectionable.

BluOne Ink LLP does not have any control over, or responsibility for, any third-party websites referred to in this book. All internet addresses given in this book were correct at the time of going to press. The author and publisher regret any inconvenience caused if addresses have changed or sites have ceased to exist, but can accept no responsibility for any such changes.

Printed in India

Kali, Occam and BluPrint are all trademarks of BluOne Ink LLP.

धर्म एव हतो हन्ति धर्मो रक्षति रक्षितः ।

Dharma destroys when abandoned.
Dharma, when protected, protects.

To
Maharshi Sri Aurobindo

To
Swami Vivekananda

|| इदं नम ऋषभ्यः पूर्वजेभ्यः पूर्वेभ्यः पथिकृद्भ्यः ||
|| idam namah rsibhyah purvajebhyah
purvebhyah pathikrdbhyah ||
—*Rig Veda*, 10.14.15

We offer our obeisance to the Rishis, born of old,
the ancients, the pathmakers.

...the Sanatan Dharma is life itself;
it is a thing that has not so much to be believed as lived.
—Sri Aurobindo

Contents

The Gita, the Essence of Dharma

Sanatan Dharma and Our Times

Endnotes

Appendix

About the Author   313

Publisher's Note

This book was originally written as brief contemplative notes over a period of several months, and the author has retained the original flow and structure to a large extent, along with certain repetitions or reiterations of concepts, though in somewhat differing contexts.

All English renderings of slokas from the Vedas, the Upanishads, the Bhagavad Gita, and other scriptures quoted throughout this book are by Sri Aurobindo unless otherwise mentioned.

All quotes from Sri Aurobindo and Swami Vivekananda are sourced from the *Complete Works of Sri Aurobindo*, Sri Aurobindo Ashram Press, and the *Complete Works of Swami Vivekananda*, Advaita Ashram, respectively.

Preface

This book was written as a series of reflective notes on Sanatan Dharma from the vedantic perspective, highlighting some of the foundational vedantic concepts of the Dharma.[1] My intention in writing this book was not to provide an exhaustive or encyclopedic span of the Dharma but only to draw some of its broad contours. The Sanatan Dharma, as I have maintained throughout this book, is vedantic in conception but yogic in practice—and this is precisely my leitmotif through the book. There is, of course, much more to Sanatan Dharma than its vedantism, and not all of Sanatan Dharma is vedantic, there is much in it that is dualistic, monistic, even theistic, agnostic and atheistic; there are also pervasive elements of the religious, the symbolic and the ritualistic, as there are of the purely contemplative—but then all of these seemingly disparate elements can be beautifully subsumed and integrated within the overarching vedantic worldview. Once the underlying vedanta of Sanatan Dharma is understood, almost all its other aspects—metaphysical or practical—can be easily understood in that context. I did not, therefore, feel the necessity to go into the more pluralistic aspects of the Dharma, including some dualistic Vedic aspects that I feel are well resolved in the vedanta. In any case, writing on all aspects of Sanatan Dharma in any meaningful way—even if at all possible—would have meant far too much time than I presently have at my disposal. Thus, I have limited the scope of this book to the mystical and the yogic elements in Sanatan Dharma, touching only briefly on some historical and cultural aspects of the Dharma.

---

1 Dharma, wherever it refers specifically to Sanatan Dharma and its correlates, is capitalized.

In writing this book, I have tried to provide, as far as possible, the original Sanskrit descriptors for every concept discussed. I have italicized the Sanskrit words and phrases the first time they occur in the text or for emphasis otherwise, and each of these has been explained, either in the text itself or as footnotes. I have provided the Devanagari script for some of the Sanskrit words and phrases, and almost all of the slokas quoted, for readers who may be particular about pronunciation. I find that most Sanskrit words are difficult to pronounce when read in the English script unless one is proficient in reading phonetically.

As you will discover in the book, I have used Sanatan Dharma and Hindu Dharma interchangeably, as the difference between the two, in most contexts, is nominal. The religion of the Hindus—Hindu Dharma—is, in fact, known as Sanatan Dharma. I must also mention here that Sanatan Dharma, for me and many others, includes Buddhism, Jainism and Sikhism since these three religions are essentially *Dharmic* religions, having originated from the original Sanatan Dharma.[2]

I am, however, aware that some of my readers may question the conflation of Sanatan Dharma and the Indian Hindu civilization in this book; and some may even find the extensive use of Sanskrit in an English book somewhat extraneous. If Sanatan Dharma is indeed universal, then why not speak of it in a more universal, secular idiom? So, why Hindu, why Indian, why Sanskrit?

The first thing that comes to mind, of course, is the inevitability of a geographical and historical context: nothing anywhere can develop without a certain location in spacetime—even if one human being were to initiate a one-person system, they would have to do it somewhere and at some time. What we are referring to as the

---

2 Some modern historians and schools of thought differ on this because there is a widespread postmodern tendency to regard these religions as independent of Sanatan Dharma, with different beliefs and worldviews. However incorrect the historical assumptions for such thinking may be, there is a clear political need in India today to regard these religions as separate.

Sanatan Dharma happened to originate in the Indian subcontinent approximately 4,000 years ago. As Sri Aurobindo said, *this is the Dharma that for the salvation of humanity was cherished in the seclusion of this peninsula from of old.* When the Dharma took birth in the Indian peninsula, those 4,000-odd years ago, there was obviously no India, or any nation, in existence. So the issue of Sanatan Dharma being 'Indian' cannot logically arise. The so-called Indian peninsula happened to be the fortuitous geographical context, and 'India', as a nation, happened to come into existence millennia later in the same geography. Sanatan Dharma is as much Indian as it is Asian and as much Asian as it is human. This whole thing of splitting what is so obviously a human legacy into neat little geopolitical and cultural packets is a childish human habit, and especially ironical when it comes to Sanatan Dharma because this is the one tradition—or religion, if you will—that cannot, by its very premises, admit of any duality or division.

And just as the Indian subcontinent—long before it came to be called 'Indian'—became home to Sanatan Dharma because that is where it originated, the Hindu civilization became naturally conflated with Sanatan Dharma as its first practitioners and proponents came eventually to be called Hindus owing to the simple geographical fact that they had settled on the banks of the river Sindhu or Indus. The Hindus themselves did not use the term Hindu any time earlier than the sixteenth century. In the 2020s, as I write this, many Hindus in India are beginning to question the continued usage of the term Hinduism for their religion or way of life and are consciously reverting to the original Sanatan or Hindu Dharma. Even the descriptor *Hindu Dharma* is a bit of redundancy because the Dharma that this descriptor refers to is *Sanatan* and does not strictly require the *Hindu* prefix.

Therefore, if we remove 'Hindu' and 'India' from our readings of Sanatan Dharma, what would we have? A religion and a civilization that originated in the meditative and philosophical practices of some extraordinary early humans who were natives of the subcontinent that came to be called Bharatvarsha or, later, India; these early meditators and philosophers who lived and worked in complete anonymity claimed no belonging to any community, clan or nation; all that they possessed was their inner light and wisdom, and their only identification was with the Supreme Truth that they had realized, and that was their only lineage and legacy. Thus, all those who claim today to be Sanatanis or Hindus belong only to that lineage of Truth,[3] and that Truth is cosmic and cannot be appropriated by any culture, nation, community, or individual; on the contrary, it is the Dharma that possesses and sustains all life, cultures, nations, communities, and individuals. Dharma cannot belong to you, but you belong to the Dharma—that is how it is. But all those who claim to belong to the Dharma must also learn to uphold and protect the Dharma just as the Dharma upholds and protects them.

A last word about the use of Sanskrit to explain Sanatan Dharma. To begin with, Sanskrit is not mandatory. One can perfectly well understand the Sanatan Dharma without any Sanskrit word or phrase. However, having said that, I must add here that since Sanatan Dharma, as a tradition, was originally transmitted orally in the Sanskrit language, and much of the effective power, beauty, and poetry of the original is preserved intact in Sanskrit, it would be a perfect waste to leave out Sanskrit to make it more palatable for an imagined 'secular' sensibility. And more importantly, the Sanskrit will, in no way, detract from the English. And a pertinent point, in conclusion: there are several concepts fundamental to Sanatan Dharma that simply cannot be translated into the English language, even with contortions worthy of an Ashtavakra.[4]

---

3 Truth, in its absolute and supreme aspect, is capitalized throughout the book, and not capitalized when used in a relative, temporal, mutable, or general sense.

4 A highly revered Rishi of the Sanatan tradition, and a brilliant and forceful teacher of Vedanta. Also known for the eight vikaras or deformations in his body owing to a curse. However, this should not be taken too literally.

Hinduism Is Sanatan Dharma

Though the Hindu religion is the oldest and the third most practiced in the world—with over a billion adherents—not too many Hindus in the modern world, or even in India, the land of its origin and spread, know what Sanatan Dharma really is or its relation to their religion. In fact, most educated Hindus still believe that Sanatan Dharma is some antiquated Sanskritic tradition that has little relevance to modern life. This is precisely what the Britishers believed and systematically imposed upon the Indian psyche for generations till we had young Hindus growing up with the same disdainful attitude towards their own religion and heritage—a clear demonstration of how effectively generations of young Indians have been alienated from their own spiritual heritage, lineage, and even language.

If more proof is needed of this fact, then we have the ridiculous spectacle of Hindus fighting each other over the merits and demerits of a Hinduism[5] largely learnt from English textbooks and perceived through the distorted lens of European and Indian Leftist historiographies. The fact of the matter, which took me more than half my life to understand, is that the Europeans who first attempted to 'explain' Hinduism to the world, the Indian Left-liberals who took it upon themselves to critique it with much zest, and the many Indian intellectuals who faithfully followed the European thinking on Hinduism, were confused and quite out of their depths when it came to Sanatan Dharma. Sanatan Dharma, and its philosophical underpinnings,

---

5 I do not much care for the term 'Hinduism' which I consider an exonym that has outlived its usefulness and would much rather use *Hindu Dharma* or *Hindu religion* instead, though the most appropriate descriptor for Hindu religion would be *Sanatan Dharma*.

are far too multidimensional and protean to make sense to the modern intellectual mind with its either/or thinking and layers of scientific and civilizational biases.

India, post-Independence, sorely needed an education system firmly and unequivocally entrenched in Sanatan Dharma and its philosophical and cultural truths and values in order to quickly and forcefully restore the original civilizational and spiritual heritage of India to the youth of India after centuries of alienation and deracination. And to do that most effectively, the Indian political and academic establishment needed to bring to the fore the thought leaders and masters of the Sanatan tradition, those who truly and deeply understood the Sanatan or Hindu Dharma, those who had fathomed its depths and scaled its heights, the likes of Sri Ramakrishna, Vivekananda and Sri Aurobindo, Rabindranath Tagore and Raja Ram Mohan Roy, or a numberless other sages and seers who spoke and wrote of the Dharma.

But that is precisely what did not happen: these exemplars of the Dharmic tradition were deliberately sidelined by the leadership in the country, with the one clear agenda of keeping the true Hindu Dharma as far away as possible from the young Indian mind. To those worthies, the Sanatan or Hindu Dharma was superstitious, reactionary, a cultural anachronism that had no place in India's secular future. In doing so, they cut off generations of Indians from their own spiritual truth of being, their *swadharma*, leaving them completely at the mercy of the burgeoning influence of Mammon and the Machine, an influence quite clearly foreseen by many of the very thinkers who had been sidelined.

However, fortunately for us, the Sanatan Dharma was not entirely lost. It merely receded into the 'subterranean caves' the Veda talks about—the Sanatan Dharma cannot ever be lost or destroyed simply because it does not exist in any external form or representation and will survive every invasion and subversion as it is the very fabric of our civilization and nationhood; to sever the Sanatan Dharma from India would be like severing the soul from the body: something that cannot be done unless the body itself gives up the soul, willingly or helplessly.

There is a great mantric statement in the Manusmriti— *Dharmo rakshati rakshitah.*[6] This means that Dharma protects when protected. This one statement says it all: we don't need to worry about the future of either Sanatan Dharma or India; we only need to make sure that we uphold Dharma, protect it in all our thoughts, intent, and actions, refuse to violate or compromise it within ourselves, and make our whole lives a sacrifice, a *yajna*, to it so that the Dharma upholds and protects us, our nation, our civilization, and, for those of us who can see that far, this hapless human race itself.

In Sri Aurobindo's words, immortalized in his Uttarpara Speech in 1909—*I say no longer that nationalism is a creed, a religion, a faith; I say that it is the Sanatan Dharma which for us is nationalism. This Hindu nation was born with the Sanatan Dharma, with it it moves and with it it grows. When the Sanatan Dharma declines, then the nation declines, and if the Sanatan Dharma were capable of perishing, with the Sanatan Dharma it would perish.*

What, then, is this Sanatan Dharma which has birthed the Hindu civilization and nourishes it to this present day and age, which is so obviously crucial to our future as a civilization and a nation? To answer this question, we will need to take a long and deep look at the mystical *darshan*, or philosophy and worldview, of Sanatan Dharma and how it continuously affects and shapes the Dharma and the civilization that it engenders and upholds. Amongst the many aspects of the Sanatan Dharma—for this Dharma is an incredibly vast and complex body of spiritual

---

6 धर्मो रक्षति रक्षितः —dharma eva hato hanti dharmo raksati raksitah, tasmad dharmo na hantavyo ma no dharmo hato vadhit: —Dharma destroys when violated, Dharma protects when protected.

knowledge and practice—I consider its darshan to be its inmost core. Without its darshan, its philosophical underpinnings, Sanatan Dharma will not make much sense to anyone, for everything about the Dharma arises directly from its darshan and returns unfailingly to it. All the rituals and rites, metaphors and symbols, poetry and mythology, mysticism and philosophy of the Dharma are overt or occult expressions of its deep and vast darshan, and to attempt any kind of an understanding of Sanatan Dharma without first understanding some of the darshan would be futile and unfair to the Dharma.

An Initial Definition of Sanatan Dharma

Sanatan Dharma, widely referred to as 'eternal religion'—perhaps owing to a mistranslation of the Sanskrit word *dharma* into religion—is not religion, nor even philosophy, but the cosmic principle of order and harmony that binds existence—similar to the electromagnetic forces that hold an atom together[7]—and keeps cosmic existence from falling back into chaos. If cosmos— from the ancient Greek *kosmos* meaning order—is a movement from chaos to increasing order and harmony, then *dharma* is the inherent principle and force molding chaos into cosmos.

The ancient Vedic Rishis were the earliest humans on earth to discover this unifying and harmonizing principle behind the cosmos and cosmic existence—they were, in fact, the first scientists of consciousness who deduced that cosmic reality is best studied internally by contemplating their own consciousness. By ceaseless observation and contemplation, these pioneering scientists discerned the *dharma* and its workings in the universe— from the simplest movements of the sun in the sky, the changing of seasons, the flight of birds, the flow of rivers, to the subtlest movements of consciousness within themselves, they discovered in everything the same underlying truth and order, the same rhythms and patterns, and they discovered too that the order and harmony in all things and beings were not arbitrary or fortuitous but the natural expression or outflow of a still subtler truth or reality that was the very fabric of the universe, the source of their own being and consciousness, and indeed the source of all being

---

7 The electromagnetic force holds the electrons in orbit around the nucleus, while the strong nuclear force binds the protons and neutrons within the nucleus itself. These forces maintain the structural integrity of atoms.

and consciousness; in fact, it was this reality that was everything everywhere. They called this truth *Sat*, which then came to represent absolute reality or absolute being,[8] and because that was the only reality they found everywhere and in everything, they referred to it simply as That One—*tad ekam*. The workings of the cosmic order and harmony, which was an expression of this Sat, they called *Rta*[9]—the right order and expression of Sat. Together they regarded Sat and Rta as *Dharma*—the Truth and Order underlying and supporting all cosmic existence[10]— and because *Sat* was immutable and eternal, so was *Dharma* immutable and eternal, or *sanatan*, if expressed in Sanskrit. The Buddha described this eternal and immutable Dharma as the very truth of the universe, inherent in all things, and always present, whether anyone followed it or not, independent of humanity, transcending time and circumstances, and, therefore, *sanatan*.

The Truth of Sat, and the order and harmony of Dharma, that the ancient Vedic Rishis discovered in themselves they sang and expressed through highly poetic and condensed Sanskrit hymns—or riks—as a poet or kavi would,[11] and these riks grew in volume generation after generation and became their immortalized knowledge-body that came to be called Veda, from the root *vid*—to know. It was through these recited riks, almost magical in nature and intensity, that the eternal, or sanatan, Dharma was brought into human time and consciousness. The

---

8 Sat (सत्), depending on the context, can mean any or all of these: absolute Truth, Reality, Being or Existence, Eternal, Pure.

9 Rta (ऋत) /ɹta/, also *rita*. Pronounced 'rit' with a soft 't'.

10 The etymological root of dharma is *dhri*, which can mean variously to hold, bear, support, maintain, preserve, sustain, and bind. Sanskrit is a polysemic language where words can have multiple meanings simultaneously, all equally valid, across contextual differences. To explain further, *dhri* is the root of many other Sanskrit or Hindi words like *dharti* (धरति), meaning earth or ground, something which upholds, bears; *dharana* (धरण), meaning to hold, support; *dhairya* (धैर्य), meaning steadfastness, forbearance, holding oneself.

11 The Rishi or the Seer is also known as the Kavi, the poet. The Kavi, in the Sanatan tradition, is not merely a poet who composes out of imagination but a Seer who expresses the reality he perceives and knows.

Dharma, thus, came down from its timeless truth-source into time first as awareness, *bodh*, then as *vijnana*, revelatory knowledge, and then as *vak* and *mantra*—inspired utterance.[12]

It was in the vijnana of the Rishis that the Veda, or Sat, was first revealed and, in their mantric utterances, first expressed—perhaps the reason why most Hindus regard the Veda as divinely inspired. Though the Veda that most Hindus know today is not the original 'divinely inspired' *sruti* (that which is revealed) but *smriti* (that which is remembered) and *shastra* (that which has come to be written), the original truth-consciousness and power of the Rishis lie locked in the mantras of the Veda and can again be unlocked and retrieved, without significant loss of transmission, by anyone who can have access to vijnana or the higher knowledge. It is in this way that those of our times who would reach out for the secrets of cosmic existence can connect psychically and spiritually to the forefathers of the Sanatan Dharma.

---

12 *Bodh* in Sanskrit can refer to awareness, understanding, knowledge. *Vijnana* refers to higher knowledge—intuitive, spiritual, supramental.

Dharma and Our Civilizational Future

This Sanatan Dharma of the Vedic Rishis, with its prodigious streams of occult[13] and spiritual knowledge, once understood in the higher sense and context, can become a veritable powerhouse for the future evolution of our society and nation. It needs to be vigorously explored by every Indian who wishes to discover and understand their true spiritual and civilizational identity, their *swadharma*. Sanatan Dharma is not just a tradition but an entire civilizational context that gives India itself, as a nation, its spiritual identity. To be an Indian is to recover India's spiritual dharma in oneself and remold it in the present consciousness and context. India's spiritual possibility and its civilizational future lie locked in its Sanatan Dharma: it is by unlocking the potential of the Dharma that India will gain the strength, the force, and the light to lead the rest of the world towards humanity's evolutionary future, which seems increasingly inevitable as the threat of a technological singularity grows more and more real and potent by the day.

The future of nations, in fact, will have to be civilizational, not political, military, or economic, and this would mean a conscious recovery and restatement of every nation's civilizational and spiritual identity in an ever-widening and converging human or universal context. It is the universal context, the one-world-one-humanity dharma, that will save humanity from itself, its childish religions, schizophrenic politics, and soul-sapping consumerism. And if this does not happen soon enough, the human future, as we know and conceive it, will be over for us—it

---

13 Not revealed, esoteric, secret, or veiled.

will then be either artificial intelligence or the capitalist-military establishment running our lives and our planet while most of humanity slides back into a state of happy stupor induced by mindless acquiescence. While many may not agree with me here, to me, this threat is quite real, and I feel that we need to look up from our daily grinds and games and glimpse something of a higher future, catch hold of some liberating possibility, a new breath, almost.

Sri Aurobindo wrote that *mankind is undergoing an evolutionary crisis in which is concealed a choice of its destiny.*[14] This evolutionary crisis and the human destiny Sri Aurobindo is referring to takes us back to the Sanatan Dharma where we find the key to our crises and our evolution. It is only Sanatan Dharma, spanning many cycles of cosmic manifestation, that gives us an overarching vision and purpose of human existence in this stupefyingly vast universe, for it is in this Dharma alone that we find the answers to the most anguishing queries of the awakened human soul: is there a purpose, do we mean anything at all, or are we insignificant flickers of accidental and ephemeral consciousness? Is there something more to our existence than birth, decay, and death?

But what is so different about the answers the Dharma gives us compared to those our religions have given as well— the grand cosmic design, the triumph of the Good, final Judgment or *Pralaya*?[15] There is one fundamental difference: the answers or insights that come from the Dharma are not credal but experiential and verifiable by anyone willing to take the trouble to find out for themselves. There is no metaphysical speculation or the infallible Word of God— everything can, and must, be personally discovered, lived, validated. This is the inherent strength and beauty of Sanatan

---

14 *The Human Cycle*, Sri Aurobindo.
15 Cosmic dissolution.

Dharma: there is a Truth to be attained, and there are paths to attain that Truth. You only need to choose which one you wish to take, which one resonates with your being, and then, follow it to the very end.

This is precisely what the ancient Rishis did—they explored, pushed the boundaries of their being, probed ever deeper into their consciousness, intuiting that the realities of the vast universe were somehow the same as those deep within. There were no religious scriptures or philosophical treatises back then, and all they had were their own minds to probe and explore. I would think that they were the first serious meditators on earth, and what must have prompted their quest, inspired their lifelong seeking, we will never know, for they left behind no personal records, and in most cases, not even their names. They were the great nameless seekers of truth, and nothing else but truth mattered to them. Most of what they realized and discovered, they shared through intimate dialogues with a few of their chosen disciples, those they knew were most capable of receiving their wisdom, which then those disciples systematically memorized so that the profound insights and wisdom of their masters would not be lost in time. This was the tradition of sruti in Sanatan Dharma. Many generations later, the srutis were converted to shastra, the written scriptures.[16]

When I first delved into the shastras, I was amazed by the depth and extent to which those old explorers, those first maharshis, had gone in their *sadhana*, their spiritual pursuit of truth.[17] I had to keep reminding myself that they were the first meditators, the first great *darshaniks* of our dharma, and they

---

16 *Sruti*, literally, that which is heard, refers to the oral tradition through which the original Vedas were transmitted from the Master to the pupils; *shastra* is the written form that the *srutis* took in the later years and it literally means scriptures.

17 *Sadhana* refers to any concentrated effort of will and mind towards psychological or spiritual attainment; the attainment of the objective of the sadhana is known as *siddhi*. Siddhi also refers to yogic or spiritual powers and capacities of the being that one may develop through the process of sadhana.

had no previous knowledge to build upon.[18] They were literally unravelling the truth, strand by strand, in the fathomless depths of their consciousness. And what they left behind was not just a body of knowledge but a living and dynamic stream of mystical practice, a stream that continues, unabated, to this day. This is the Sanatan Dharma of which I write in this book, and this is the Sanatan Dharma that connects me, directly and psychically, to those great shining ones, the maharshis, of old. It is a profoundly elevating thought.

---

18 *Darshanik*, from the word *darshan*, is a term used for a philosopher or a seer of the Dharma; literally, it means one who has the direct perception (*darshan*) of Truth, but the term is commonly used for a thinker or philosopher.

The Darshan of Sanatan Dharma

The essence of Vedanta is that there is but one Being and that every soul is that Being in full, not a part of that Being, the one central ideal of Vedanta is this oneness. There are no two in anything, no two lives, nor even two different kinds of life for the two worlds. You will find the Vedas speaking of heavens and things like that at first; but later on, when they come to the highest ideals of their philosophy, they brush away all these things. There is but one life, one world, one existence. Everything is that One, the difference is in degree and not in kind.

—Swami Vivekananda

In the remote past, our country made gigantic advances in spiritual ideas. Let us, today, bring before our mind's eye that ancient history. But the one great danger in meditating over long-past greatness is that we cease to exert ourselves for new things, and content ourselves with vegetating upon that bygone ancestral glory and priding ourselves upon it. We should guard against that. In ancient times there were, no doubt, many Rishis and Maharshis who came face to face with Truth. But if this recalling of our ancient greatness is to be of real benefit, we too must become Rishis like them. Ay, not only that, but it is my firm conviction that we shall be even greater Rishis than any that our history presents to us. In the past, signal were our attainments—I glory in them, and I feel proud in thinking of them. I am not even in despair at seeing the present degradation, and I am full of hope in picturing to my mind what is to come in the future. Why? Because I know the seed undergoes a complete transformation, ay, the seed as seed is seemingly destroyed before it develops into a tree. In the same way, in the midst of our present degradation lies, only dormant for a time, the potentiality of the future greatness of our religion, ready to spring up again, perhaps more mighty and glorious than ever before.

You must not merely learn what the Rishis taught. Those Rishis are gone, and their opinions are also gone with them. You must be Rishis yourselves.

—Swami Vivekananda, *The Rishi Tradition*

The Rishi

A *Rishi*, in the Hindu tradition, is one who has attained Truth-consciousness and, thus, can perceive and know Reality directly. The Rishi is also known as a *drashta*, a seer, or a *mantra-drashta*, a seer of thought.

A *Maharshi* (*maha*, great, *Rishi*, seer) is a term of reverence used for the most advanced of the Rishis, those who bring to humanity higher Truths and realizations and open newer pathways for the evolution of consciousness.

In Swami Vivekananda's words—*the truth came to the Rishis of India, the mantra-drashtas, the seers of thought, and will come to all Rishis in the future, not to talkers, not to book-swallowers, not to scholars, not to philologists, but to seers of thought.*[19]

The Rishi has always been given the most revered space in the Hindu religious and philosophic tradition, and it is the Rishi's words that carry the highest spiritual authority for any Hindu.

The *Sanatan Dharma*, the Hindu religion, was birthed and nurtured through the ages by a lineage of Rishis and maharshis who were amongst the first to delve into the profound mystical depths of human existence, and to them, we owe the body of knowledge that has come to be known as the Sanatan, or the eternal, Dharma.

---

19 The word '*mantra*' derives from *manas*, meaning mind, and '*tra*', suggesting an instrument or device (yantra, tantra), therefore, the device or instrument of the mind meant for a specific purpose, often spiritual or occult. *Drashta* derives from *drs* to see, the same root sound for *darshan*, perception of Truth.

An Initial Definition of Darshan

Though I am using the word *philosophy* interchangeably with *darshan*, I must stress at the outset that darshan is essentially different from philosophy as we understand it in the English language. While philosophy is basically an approach of reason and logic to understand reality, and knowledge is its primary objective, *darshan* is an experiential and intuitive verification of reality and its primary objective is not acquiring knowledge but gaining direct insight and realization.

From the Sanskrit root *drs*, (to perceive, see, behold), *darshan* implies direct perception of reality and not thinking and reasoning about it. One sees what is, directly and immediately, and by that, one knows what is—*pratyaksha*. Pratyaksha, in Sanatan Dharma, is direct, spiritual perception and is regarded as the highest proof or *pramana* of truth. Thus, when the young novice Swami Vivekananda wished to assess the authenticity of Sri Ramakrishna as a spiritual Master, he did not ask him what he knew or believed; he asked him point blank—*Have you seen God?* And Ramakrishna, the Master of the Spirit that he was, did not respond in metaphor or riddle: he simply replied—*Yes, I have!* This is the primacy of pratyaksha in Dharma. What is seen cannot be questioned.

Interestingly, both the words *pratyaksha* and *darshan* can be traced to the same Sanskrit roots, *dṛśya* and *drs*, both of which refer to that which is directly perceivable and, thus, knowable. That which we see is what we know. All other means of knowledge are once, twice, or even thrice removed from reality. But pratyaksha is a higher and subtler cognitive order not based on a knower-known duality but on identity, a self-becoming of the object of knowledge. This is, of course, not physical seeing where the observer-observed duality is still maintained: this is seeing inwardly, intuitively, and spiritually where the observer becomes the observed. This is the basis of all spiritual knowing and seeing—one identifies in consciousness with the object of knowledge, thereby becoming the object oneself and, therefore, transcending the knower-known duality.

In other words, the knower becomes, or identifies with, the known. But 'becoming' is itself an imprecise expression because in reality the knower, or the consciousness of the seeker, is always the known. The knower and the known, the subject (self) and the object (truth), are but two aspects of the same reality, and what we just termed a 'becoming' is really a dissolution of a mentally projected duality. All of Hindu darshan moves unerringly towards the dissolution of duality, and what dissolves is not duality but the 'perception' of duality. Therefore, the prime importance of pure, non-dual perception, pratyaksha; and the Rishi, the Seer, is the one in whom the perception of duality has irreversibly dissolved in pratyaksha. Therefore, when the Rishi declares that there is only one truth and reality, *tad ekam*, and everything and everyone is that, he is not using an abstraction but is stating a truth of pratyaksha, that which is literally in front of one's eyes. When one perceives reality thus, one does not reason or speculate, one does not even need to describe or explain: it is there as it is, the real as real: *yatha bhutam*.[20]

Pratyaksha, in Sanatan darshan, is of two kinds: *anubhava* and *smriti*—anubhava is living experience arising from direct and immediate perception, and smriti is remembered perception or that which is relived (though not recreated). The authority of Hindu darshan derives from the anubhava and smriti of the Rishis. What has come down to us as scriptures, or *shastra*, of

---

20 In reality; what is true or real.

Sanatan Dharma are the utterances and expressions, more or less unaltered, of the anubhava and smriti.

But what exactly is the nature of the Rishi's perception? How, and what, does he 'see'? Obviously, the Rishi's 'personal' consciousness itself is a minuscule part of the all-reality he perceives and experiences, and he cannot possibly be stepping outside of reality in order to 'perceive' it. The scientist may still delude himself into thinking that he can study the universe as an objective observer detached from what he observes, but the Rishi knows that there is no way to study reality objectively: he must *become* what he would know, and this self-becoming is an identification of consciousness, like a wave of the sea identifying with the sea because its essential and substantial reality is always the sea: the perception of duality in the wave-consciousness dissolves in the vaster consciousness of the sea. This is the practical basis of what is called *Yoga* in Sanatan Dharma—the realization of the One as self and the self as One, the recovery of the truth of being that all is one single substance and essence, however differentiated the forms and functions of that one reality may appear to be.

Sanatan darshan is, therefore, not monistic as many believe but based on oneness of being in and through all differentiations and diversities, where none of the differentiation and diversity is lost in the oneness. The oneness of Sanatan Dharma is not mathematical but ontological, a spiritual experience and realization of tad ekam.

A human seems to be very different from an elephant and an elephant from a worm, but the human, the elephant, and the worm are all made of the same 'cosmic substance', the same quantum material. This cosmos is a closed system; nothing has evolved here which was not involved in the original potential of the universe—the 'singularity' of physics[21]—just

---

21 If we go by the Big Bang theory, which as of now seems to be the most plausible, then our universe began as a point of infinite gravity and density called a singularity. In Vedic darshan, there is a similar concept, the *bindu*, a non-dimensional point (if it may at all be called that) of infinitely dense consciousness out of which the universe manifests.

as every branch, twig, and leaf of a tree was involved in its
seed-state. Not only that, consider the fact that the seed of
the tree becomes the tree and every part of it simultaneously:
it is the same thing but differentiated, where differentiation
does not affect the sameness. When you see a tree, are you also
not seeing the seed that has become the tree? The difference
between 'seed' and 'tree' is only semantic, in reality, there is
no difference. What you are looking at is both 'seed' and 'tree'
and neither 'seed' nor 'tree'. What it actually is, cannot be
described.

The Rishis speak of *namarupa mithya*,[22] the phenomenon
of the mind imposing its nominal and functional constructs—
namarupa—on form or shape and then assuming the
constructs to be the reality. In the truth-consciousness and
vision of the Rishis, however, all such differentiations of form,
name, and functions are superficial and relative; deeper down,
all is one reality. The seed, the tree, the branches, leaves, and
fruits are one single reality, and for that matter, this whole
universe is one single reality once you have taken away the
nomenclature, the language, and the intellectual constructs.
Think of a person born and brought up on an island forest by
chimpanzees and has never acquired human language—what
kind of reality would they perceive without the filter of words
and definitions?

But the Rishis obviously do not revert to any pre-academic
or pre-intellectual stage, for what is learned cannot be forgotten.
He remembers language, of course, but no longer takes it
seriously, knowing well that it is merely a human convention
and convenience and, in all his inner dealings with cosmic
existence, he doesn't need any of it. The Rishi will observe nature
and all its diverse forms and movements without classifications

---

22 Commonly understood as the delusion of name and form but has a deeper meaning: the
superimposition of name and function on form, and form on the substrate reality. This will
be discussed later in the book.

and descriptions in an inner wordless silence and will therefore perceive a reality vastly more continuous and integral than the schooled mind ever can. In a radical way, the Rishi's perception and worldview are original and pristine, a perception without human filters and distortions. It is this perception and worldview that forms the philosophical basis of Sanatan Dharma, which we term *darshan*.

Knowledge and Immortality

Sanatan Dharma and its workings were discovered, as we have already noted, in the vijnana of the maharshis as they ceaselessly probed the depths of consciousness to unravel there the myriad unfathomed mysteries of existence.[23] Those maharshis were not Hindus—for there was no such designation back then—but simply human beings, and their inner quests were not prompted by any religious compulsion—for there was no religion back then either—but by the innate human yearning for truth and meaning, the yearning that birthed civilizations, science, philosophy, and religions, and continues pushing the human species inexorably towards its final attainment—omniscience and immortality.

Omniscience and *immortality*, though used almost exclusively in religious parlance, are ideas that actually predate religion and science; in fact, these are arguably the two most powerful and all-pervasive human ideas that have been at the root of all human quest for truth and meaning. Most religions claim that their God is omniscient and immortal, but the truth is that omniscience and immortality were the obsessions of the human soul that created the God of religions in the first place: for whatever we project onto our God or Gods is what we most revere in ourselves. Thus, as the maharshis of old discovered the Dharma within themselves, they discovered too the secrets of omniscience and immortality buried in the very depths of existence and knew in their hearts in that very dawn of human

---

23 Consciousness being one, I always refer to it in the singular.

civilization that they and their kind were destined to be deathless, timeless, and perfect in consciousness. And it was these ultimate of discoveries that they embedded in the knowledge-body of Sanatan Dharma.

Thus, these oldest of our human needs—to know everything and to conquer death—are not born of our fallible mortality but of our immortal divinity: these are, indeed, not obsessions at all but 'remembrance' of our eventual future seeded in our distant past. Without this seeding of our eventual future, we would still be monkeys swinging across trees. Our need for perfect knowledge is the first stirring of the higher consciousness in our minds and hearts, and our need to surpass death is the first stirring of the god in our soul: these are the needs that have made us more than animal and will make us more than human. Just as knowledge is the key to humanity, immortality is the key to divinity.

Those many ages ago, when most of humanity was still crude in mind and sensibility, those rare seers of old, refined to an inconceivable degree by their spiritual askesis, were inwardly transformed by their vision and knowledge into a luminous prefiguration of their highest human future—they finally became what they saw and knew to be their evolutionary future. They were thus the very embodiments of the Veda and of the Dharma, and going by the many symbols, metaphors, and myths they left us, they perhaps even knew or foresaw the travails humanity would have to pass through before it would emerge into the luminous day of the gods.

All this was *seen* by the maharshis with more vividness than what you and I can see with our physical eyes—none of it was imagined or speculated. When we read through the records of their inner voyages and discoveries, in the vivid word-images and symbols of the Vedas and the Upanishads, we come to understand just how it all works, how the knowledge unfolds, and what powers and faculties of the human consciousness are needed for this tremendous inner work of the Dharma. These ancient seers and sages, the pioneers of the Dharma, were the first humans to push beyond the frontiers of ignorance and illusion and explore uncharted terrains of occult, scientific, and spiritual knowledge, all of which they left behind in great detail—though in couched, esoteric language for such was the rarity and subtlety of the subject matter—for human posterity, regardless of geographical, racial, or cultural differences.

To insist on Sanatan Dharma, the lore and legacy of the maharshis, being Hindu or Indian would be a disservice to the maharshis as well as the Hindus—Sanatan Dharma is both timeless and universal, born and nurtured in the Indian subcontinent but not limited to it. The sooner the world understands Sanatan Dharma to be what it is and what it was always intended to be—the roadmap of our human future—the better for all, for it is in the Dharma, and its right reading and understanding, that the key to the future of humanity is to be found.

Only One Reality

Almost all of Sanatan Dharma and its darshan may be summed up in a single Vedic phrase, *ekam Sat*—there is only one (*ekam*) reality or truth (*Sat*), though variously described by the seers who have realized it—*ekam sat vipra bahudha vadanti.*[24] This one reality is addressed sometimes as the *ananta* or infinite *Brahman*,[25] sometimes as Self or *Purusha*, sometimes as Atman or Paramatman; and sometimes simply as That One—*Tad Ekam.* However that Sat or Reality is addressed or expressed, it refers always to that which transcends all human conception and perception, that which is the subject of darshan and Dharma but is itself beyond darshan and Dharma, inscrutable, incommunicable—*that which is unexpressed by the word but by which the word is expressed, that which thinks not by the mind but by which the mind is thought.*[26]

But how does this reality come into being? Is there a 'moment of creation'? Is there a 'creator'? The Rishis declare that there is no creation or creator, Sat never comes into being—coming into being and ceasing to be is a human idea, and Sat, absolute reality, is beyond time and causation. One cannot even say of Sat that it was always there because 'always there' itself is a projection of space and time and has no meaning in terms of absolute reality. If Sat is absolute, then 'where' exactly can Sat be, now or forever, except in itself? This *being in itself* is the

---

24 एकम सत् विप्रा बहुधा वदन्ति — There is only one truth though the sages (who realized it) describe it in various ways. —*Rig Veda.*

25 From the Sanskrit root *brh,* which implies vastness, growth, expansion, and becoming.

26 *Kena Upanishad.*

key to grasping the Sanatan concept of absolute reality—Sat exists only in itself, and by itself, there can be no outside or inside, here or there, now or forever, to it: there is only That One, *tad ekam*. This leads directly to the fact that this universe, with all things and beings in it, including ourselves, is that one reality, Sat—not creations or projections of it but Sat itself, without differentiation. The Rishis described this phenomenon as a self-becoming of Sat or absolute being. In other words, this universe and life and consciousness is Sat happening to itself and in itself, an infinite self-becoming of its own essence and substance, *anantam*, without beginning or end.

In the darshan of Sanatan Dharma, the realization and experience of Sat as the one all-comprehensive reality is regarded as *vedanta*, the *anta* or culmination of the knowledge and wisdom of the Veda.[27] Vedanta is not beyond the Veda, or superior to it, as many assume but the essence of the Veda, its distilled knowledge. Therefore, the true vedanta must always be understood in the context of the Veda, the mystic knowledge-body of the maharshis.

This book is an attempt at explaining Hindu Dharma not just in terms of its Sanatan philosophy and worldview but, more specifically, in terms of the vedanta of Sanatan Dharma, which runs warp and woof right through this book.

---

27 The word Vedanta, wherever it refers to one of the six major systems of philosophy in the Hindu tradition, is capitalized, but where it refers to a general 'vedantic' worldview and understanding, it is not capitalized. The 'vedantic' worldview and understanding, of course, arise from the philosophical system of the Vedanta but are not conceptually or practically bound by it.
'Veda' too is capitalized wherever it refers to any of the four Vedas—*Rig, Sam, Yajur, or Atharva*.

Brahman

The whole vedantic quest begins and ends with the realization of Brahman as the one cosmic reality and the one universal Self. Brahman is roughly the equivalent of a supreme God, though 'God' is an Abrahamic construct and does not really apply to Hindu darshan. Brahman is Sat, as we have already seen, absolute reality, and is transcendental—*parabrahman*—in its absoluteness; but Brahman is not limited to its absoluteness, it extends itself into cosmic existence, becomes the universe and all things in it, and is then addressed as the supreme Self, Purusha; but Brahman is not limited even to this dual-status, it even enters more intimately and granularly its self-becoming as the *Atman*, or the individual Self in all beings and things.[28]

What Brahman really is, either in its supreme status or in its all-comprehensive reality, is *anirvachaniya*—inscrutable, indescribable, beyond thought and word. The human mind trying to fathom Brahman's reality is like a two-dimensional ant trying to fathom the reality of the three-dimensional table it crawls upon, without, of course, in any way guessing that its—already difficult to fathom—table happens to be just one amongst millions of other three-dimensional objects in a multi-dimensional universe. This analogy, though effective, would raise a natural question—how would a Rishi then manage to fathom reality? Does the analogy of the two-dimensional ant on a three-dimensional table not apply to the Rishi?

---

28 Though even as the individual self, it is universal for it is the same essence of individuality in all beings.

Let's extend the analogy a bit and imagine the ant on the table to be a Rishi-ant, one who has expanded its ant-consciousness beyond two dimensions and can take in not only the table on which it crawls but the room in which the table is placed, and all the other objects in the room, and the people who come and go, and is perhaps even able to intuit the space outside the room. Such an ant, in terms of its consciousness, would obviously no longer qualify as an ant, and only the outer physical resemblance would persist. But, more pertinently, would this ant be able to 'explain' the reality it perceives to the other ants? Well, if our Rishi-ant were wise, it would not even try.

Therefore, in the lore of the Rishis, there are no explanations or theories, only descriptions of what is seen, touched, experienced, known—*pratyaksha*. This universe, said the Rishis, is a self-becoming of Brahman. There is no actual universe out there, it is Brahman that we see and experience as universe, and that too is an imprecise way of saying it, for 'universe' is only a mental projection—what we actually perceive is Brahman even when we are seeing multiple forms, multiple existences. The analogy often given in the Upanishadic writings to explain this is that of gold and gold ornaments. We can make as many gold ornaments as we want, but we have only one 'gold', the one substance, and whatever the dimensions of the ornaments, the gold in all of them will never change.

Reflect on this: our mind believes that it perceives various gold ornaments, but what it actually perceives is gold in various shapes and sizes. It is always the gold. Likewise, the mind perceives various forms and formulations of Brahman, that one absolute being, but what it actually perceives all the while is Brahman. Brahman itself does not differentiate, just as the gold does not—the differences are only on the surface, in form and description. The Rishis call this phenomenon *namarupa avidya*: the ignorance of form and name. We take the name and form, *namarupa*, to be the real and 'forget' the substance in and behind it all. How many of us can look at various kinds of gold ornaments and see only gold?

But what happens if we do that, if we deliberately, by a reversal of consciousness, look not at the namarupa but at the substance behind and in the namarupa? The 'worldview' will immediately change—we will not see the ornament anymore; we will see the gold in the shape of the ornament. And if we look long enough, even the shape of the ornament will fade, and only gold will remain. In truth, this reversal of consciousness is not too complicated: what we have done is simply remove the mental projection of the particular ornament superimposed on the gold. The ornament itself was never there, it was always gold, but the 'perception' of the ornament was in the mind but superimposed on the gold. In other words, the gold was real, and the ornament was merely a superimposition, *adhyaropa*, and was never really there, it just appeared to be there, a *mithya*. In Sanatan darshan, mithya is an important concept and is used to explain the nuanced and subtle difference between what is real, *satyam*, and what appears to be real, mithya.

This is what Adi Shankar declared in one of his famous—and widely misunderstood—aphorisms,[29] *brahman satyam, jagat mithya*. This sutra, rightly understood, exactly conveys what we are discussing: Brahman is the one true being, satyam, and the world or universe is superimposed on it. It is a projected reality, like a mirage in the desert, and not an absolute one. The Rishis say that the universe is a self-becoming of Brahman, but this self-becoming does not mean that Brahman becomes something other than itself: there is no duality in the self-becoming. Thus, the universe that 'appears' to be is not an illusion, a non-reality, it *is* Brahman, which is all-reality, but we perceive a 'universe' where there is only Brahman. It is our perception, then, that is mithya.

---

29 Known as *sutras* in Sanskrit.

To see the universe without seeing Brahman is a false perception, mithya; and to see always, in all conditions, Brahman alone, even in the multiple appearances without getting bewildered by them, is satyam, the true seeing, or darshan. Shankar completes this sutra with these words: *jivo brahmaiva naparah*, the embodied self and Brahman are not different, they are of the same essence and substance, just as all gold ornaments are gold. In this one single line, Adi Shankar has restated succinctly the secret of the maharshis: Brahman is the one absolute truth, the substratum of all existence, and the self is consubstantial with Brahman, there is no difference. But the secret of the maharshis is not all revealed yet: there are several layers still to be unveiled.

Advaita

Jivo brahmaiva naparah—the embodied self, the individual being, is not different from the universal, cosmic being, Brahman: nothing, for that matter, is separate, like the cells in our body, trillions of them, though all apparently discrete, are all, at the cellular level, one single body, made of the same quantum substance. We may choose to name various cells and tissues of the body according to their location and function, but none of that will change the fact that at the cellular level, all the cells are one single existence. In an analogous manner, we may choose to see a million and one different things making up the universe, but at the quantum level, the universe is one single existence, one single substance. The million and one names and descriptions, including the universe itself, are abstractions of the mind, and once we put them all aside, we will begin to catch glimpses of how our Rishis and maharshis perceived and experienced reality.

The individual *jiva*[30] lives in a fractured reality, perceiving and experiencing reality as so many things and beings, animate or inanimate, small or large, far or distant, but the Rishis lived a non-dual reality, not fragmented or fractured by the sense-mind's abstractions but integrated in a higher supramental consciousness.[31] Such an integrated supramental perception of reality has been termed *advaita* by the Rishis of old.

---

30 *Jiva* refers to the individual soul, or the individual living entity, and represents the eternal, conscious essence in all living beings.

31 Higher consciousness implies a higher-order consciousness necessarily more integrated, unified, harmonized. *Supramental,* as used by Sri Aurobindo, refers to truth-consciousness, a consciousness where falsehood, ignorance, and error are no longer possible, a consciousness one with the Truth.

Advaita is difficult to explain. It is usually understood as non-dual—*dvaita* meaning dual—but that is not a satisfactory rendering of the many-layered meaning of the word. The Vedantic Rishis illustrate advaita by using the analogy of sea waves and the sea. You can perceive the sea and sea waves from four standpoints of reality: as sea waves only; as sea waves in the sea; as sea only; and only as water. The first standpoint, where only waves are perceived and not the sea, may be called *multiplistic* or *pluralistic*; the second standpoint, where the sea waves are perceived as separate formations of the sea, and the sea wave and sea are both perceived simultaneously, may be called *dualistic*; the third standpoint where only the sea is perceived and not the waves may be called *monistic*; and the fourth standpoint where only water is perceived, and neither the sea nor the sea waves are perceived is what may be called *advaita* (beyond duality) in the vedantic sense—ontological non-differentiation, *abheda*. The ontological non-differentiation—determined by the very nature of being—does not negate the standpoints of multiplicity or duality but subsumes and integrates them in a higher-order perception or perspective. This is one of the determining concepts of Hindu Dharma and darshan. It is in this sense that the Rishis declare *sarvam brahmeti*, all is Brahman.

Atman

We are not individuals living *in* a universe, like fish in water; we *are* the universe like sea waves are the sea. When we look at ourselves, we are looking at the universe that has evolved into self-conscious life. Or, to rephrase, we *are* the universe looking consciously at itself; we are, each of us, the self-conscious universe becoming more and more of itself through myriad self-becomings where each self-becoming is an individual eye—or even I—of the universe. There is nothing outside of us, the earth and the heavens and hells, the living, the dead, and the unborn, everything and everyone is within, and going into this fathomless and dimensionless within is going into what the maharshis called the *Atman*; and relative to the Atman, this dimensionless within, there is no outside. Therefore, the exhortation of the maharshis to delve within, except that this 'within' is not a spatial or psychological 'within' but the 'within' of consciousness, the vast interiority of being, the *Atman*.

Just as sea waves all resolve into the sea in the depths, this universe too resolves into Brahman in the depths; and just as waves exist only on the surface of the sea, multiplicity exists only on the surface of being: in the depths, all is the one cosmic self, the one absolute being—Brahman or Atman. To know our own within, our own depths, is, thus, to know ourselves as the one Atman, the one cosmic self, and to know the one cosmic self is to know Brahman. In the end, these are all descriptors of the same reality, and that reality, say the Rishis, is what we are, each one of us, regardless of our circumstances of birth, culture, and religion. This they articulated in a single statement: *ayamatma brahman,* this self within is Brahman,[32] another way of saying *jivo brahmaiva naparah.*

The Atman has a personal and universal aspect in manifestation, for it is the indwelling, essential spiritual self in all beings, and it is also the one universal cosmic self, *simultaneously and seamlessly*—and thus, the essential individual self *is* the universal self; or to rephrase, it is the one same universal self present in all forms of life as the essential individual self. This is the basis for the Hindu belief that all individual selves, all lifeforms, in the universe are essentially or spiritually one: there is no other, no division, and no real differentiation. In the depths, everyone and everything is one. But this oneness is of brahmic substance and does not negate differences and degrees of becoming, as we have discussed earlier in the analogy of gold and gold ornaments. All multiplicity and diversity of namarupa—attributes and form—are but the creative mutations of the one immutable reality of Brahman. Brahman is not uniformly and boringly one, it is dynamically and creatively the many even while, in itself, it is the one.

This advaita of Sanatan darshan goes beyond the non-duality and monism of ordinary philosophy. Neither the non-duality nor monism renders the exact truth of Brahman's oneness in multiplicity and multiplicity in oneness: the maharshis, therefore, declared that Brahman, That One, is beyond even duality and non-duality, being and non-being. What it is cannot be known or described; it can only be lived in the perfect identification of Yoga or spiritual union.

The idea—if one may call it that—of the fundamental or ontological identity of Atman and Brahman is crucial to the

---

32 This is known as a *mahavakya* in Sanskrit, a statement manifesting a profound truth; a mahavakya states the truth but does not elaborate or explain, it is left to the seeker to meditate on it and discover in themselves its truth.
   The mahavakya *ayamatma brahman* is from the *Mandukya Upanishad* of *Atharva Veda* and means this (ayam) Atman (self) is Brahman.

understanding and appreciation of Hindu darshan and Dharma, and puts to rest all the needless noise and debate about Hindu Dharma's multiple gods and goddesses, sages and prophets, for all cosmic forms—infra-human, human, superhuman or divine—is that one Brahman, and it makes little difference if we regard them as so many different entities or the self-becomings of one supreme reality: all finally will depend on the height or depth of consciousness we ourselves have attained.

A Play of Infinite Possibilities

If this universe is the self-becoming of Brahman, and all forms and formations in the universe are Brahman, as the Rishis so explicitly declare, then everything in this universe, from the blind vortices of energy to the stars and the planets, from the first protoplasm and cell to self-conscious life, is the process of Brahman expressing itself as the universe, and eventually then, this universe will become a complete and perfect expression of Brahman in every intricate detail. This, in Hindu darshan, is the idea of evolution: the universe is not hurtling towards a cold death by entropy or dissolution in some cosmic pralaya but is growing endlessly towards perfect being, consciousness and delight, for delight, in the experience of the Rishis, is the very nature of being. In the Vedic conception, cosmic existence evolves towards its own ultimate expression which is the absolute being, consciousness, and delight of supreme Brahman— *Satchidananda.*[33] Satchidananda is said to be the very nature of Brahman. Thus, Godhead—or God, if you will—is not the origin of the universe but its culmination, and as Brahman becomes this universe, this universe too becomes Brahman.

The idea of the evolution of life and consciousness has been crucial in shaping the Sanatan worldview. If all life in the universe is in the process of becoming a perfect expression of Brahman, then there can be no inherent flaw, no intrinsic evil, in existence. There are only stages of evolution, a continuous

---

33 *Satchidananda* (सच्चिदानन्द) a compound of Sat, absolute being, Chit, absolute consciousness, and Ananda, absolute delight of being and consciousness, refers to the triune reality of Brahman. There is nothing in the universe higher than or above Satchidananda.

and progressive unfoldment of the divine potential of existence
and, therefore, no scope for eternal damnation or redemption,
only a timeless self-revelation of perfection already contained in
the infinite possibilities of being, where good and evil, life and
death, knowledge and ignorance are all equal possibilities to be
manifested, transformed, or exhausted, where every single note
of becoming is essential to the overall cosmic symphony.

This leads directly to the *lilamaya*[34] conception of existence
that regards all life as a play of the Divine, and suffering, pain,
and evil as temporary aberrations and anomalies to be vigorously
rejected and replaced by a luminous faith in the Divine's will, or
a higher knowledge and understanding of Truth. Since all life is
a play of the Divine and its infinite possibilities in this lilamaya
conception, there is no final judgment, ultimate reward, or
punishment, at the end of the universe; in fact, there is no need
for an end at all in the play of infinite possibilities of becoming,
and thus, the human soul must keep progressing from lifetime to
lifetime in an ever-ascending and expanding curve towards more
and more truth, more and more consciousness. The highest, and
the inevitable, existential goal for the Hindu who understands
his Dharma is to attain Satchidananda, and here too, there is no
haste, for the soul awakened to its inevitable cosmic purpose can
either rush upward to its goal in a single incarnation or meander
through numberless incarnations, enjoying fully the delight of
being and becoming.

The Hindu's spiritual objective, therefore, can never be to
escape cosmic existence and find God in the rarefied ranges of
a superhuman or divine consciousness but to experience the
divine Lila in its fullness on earth and embody God here, in
matter and mind—this is the ancient Vedic secret of secrets that
the forefathers of Sanatan Dharma left us as their most precious
legacy: that if there is a heaven, it is this earth, and if there is

---

34 Lilamaya (लीलामय), divinely playful; permeated with the bliss of divine play.

God, it is the Self, and if there is a divine perfection of being, it is here and everywhere, in matter, life, mind, and heart, in the very fabric of our cosmic existence. This legacy they encapsulated in a single mahavakya: *Tat twam asi*[35]—that Divine perfection, that supreme delight of being, that one Self in all, you yourself are.

At first sight, this kind of assertion would seem difficult to digest: how can a mere mortal be that divine perfection, that supreme Brahman? But reflect upon this: there *is* only Brahman and its infinite self-becoming; there are no 'mere mortals' to begin with. The 'mere mortal' we consider ourselves to be is our spiritual ignorance, not knowing the truth of our being. This spiritual ignorance, in Hindu darshan, is called *avidya*, the absence of true knowledge, from *a-*(not) and *vid*, to know. Thus, the first thing necessary for understanding the profound truth of this mahavakya is to attain the true *vidya*, the knowledge of the self.

---

35 Tat (that) twam (you) asi (are)—That you are.

Knowledge of the Self and Moksha

Atmajnana, or the realization of the Atman, is the true vedanta—the grand culmination, *anta,* of all human seeking and knowledge, *veda.* The veda, however, exists in two dimensions: outwardly, as the mystical knowledge-body of the maharshis, and inwardly, as the eternal truth in the Atman, of the Atman. While in its outward form, the Veda carries in its mantras and riks the knowledge of the Spirit and its workings, of cosmic existence and Dharma, of life, death, and immortality, the powers and forces of the Divine, the past and spiritual future of the race, in its inward form, the veda is of the Atman and its identity with Brahman. Once the inner veda is known, and the Self realized, the outer Veda becomes redundant—*as much use as there is in well with water in flood on every side, so much is there in all the Vedas for the Brahmin who has the knowledge,* says Krishna in the Gita[36]—because the Self is the source and end of all knowledge, the origin and culmination of all veda. And therefore, we call it vedanta, as the end or culmination of all knowing is in the knower, which is the Self.

But let us not think, when we read the passage above, that the Veda becomes redundant because it becomes useless in any way—this is a common misunderstanding. The Veda becomes redundant because the knowledge of Atman is also knowledge of Brahman—*ayam atma brahman,*[37] as the Upanishadic mahavakya declares—and whosoever realizes Atman becomes thus a knower of Brahman and needs no other knowledge

---

36 यावानर्थ उदपाने सर्वतः संप्लुतोदके । तावान्सर्वेषु वेदेषु ब्राह्मणस्य विजानतः॥ —Bhagavad Gita, 2.46.
37 This Atman is Brahman. See also Footnote 21.

beyond that; as the Upanishad again declares—*yasmin vijnate sarvam evam vijnatam bhavati; yasmin prapte sarvam idam praptam bhavati:* by knowing That Supreme, everything is known; by attaining That, everything is attained.[38] It is in this deeper sense that vedanta subsumes the Veda and atmajnana renders all other knowledge secondary or redundant.

He who attains atmajnana is a Jnani, a knower of Brahman, and is therefore liberated from all ignorance and bondage and attains to what the Hindus call *moksha*. But moksha is not liberation from the endless cycles of birth and rebirth as many erroneously believe, but liberation from avidya or spiritual ignorance and suffering, *dukkha*, that inevitably accompanies avidya. This dukkha is not worldly sorrow or suffering, as again many mistakenly believe, but the fundamental existential angst of not knowing who, what, or why we are. The Rishis refer to this angst as *nirananda*, without ananda or delight of being. *Ananda*, of course, is not the limited transient delight or pleasure of the mind and senses but the absolute fullness of divine being, consciousness, knowledge, and force, which can only be experienced and described as pure, uncaused, and unmixed bliss, perfect delight. The experience of such ananda, obviously, is the very pinnacle of human existence. Moksha, therefore, may best be understood as the condition of being in what the maharshis called *brahmananda*, supreme ananda, or ananda of Brahman.

---

38 *Mundaka Upanishad*, 1.3.

The Nature of the Atman

Atmajnana, as we now know, is the culmination of Sanatan Dharma's ascent to truth, for no spiritual life or higher consciousness is possible without the knowledge of what we are. Atmajnana is the indispensable step towards the ananda of perfect truth-consciousness. To be a Hindu, as Swami Vivekananda once said, one has to be spiritual, and it is in this light that he used the word 'spiritual'. To be spiritual is to be living in the consciousness of the Atman—for the Atman, in the Atman, by the Atman.

What, then, is the Atman? How do the Rishis and maharshis describe the Atman?

It is difficult, the Rishis declare, to explain or understand the nature of Atman—*there sight goes not, nor speech, nor mind; we know it not, nor can we discern how one should teach of this.*[39]

The Atman is the sole knower, the sole consciousness, and force behind all we are and become, it is that in us which makes us active and sentient—*the eyes perceive,* as the Rishis say, *but what perceives through the eyes is Atman; the body breathes, but what animates the breath is the Atman*—were it not for the Atman, no knowledge would be possible, and the universe itself, as we know it in our consciousness, wouldn't exist. Nothing then would exist, no world, no cosmos, no self, for that of which we are not conscious would not exist for us; we

---

39 न तत्र चक्षुर्गच्छति न वाग्गच्छति नो मनो न विद्मो न विजानीमो यथैतदनुशिष्यादन्यदेव तद्विदितादथो अविदितादधि । इति शुश्रुम पूर्वेषां ये नस्तद्व्याचचक्षिरे ॥ — There sight travels not, nor speech, nor the mind. We know It not nor can distinguish how one should teach of It: for It is other than the known; It is there above the unknown. It is as we have heard from men of old who declared That to our understanding. —*Kena Upanishad.*

are conscious only because Atman is conscious in us. And thus, being the consciousness and the knower in all our knowings, the Atman itself cannot be known objectively, for there is none outside of it to know or recognize it. The Atman, as the Rishis have said, is the infinite interiority of consciousness and thus, the yogi who seeks to know the Atman can do so only by realizing that consciousness itself is Atman—*prajnanam brahman*.[40] This kind of knowledge is neither objective nor subjective, it is what the Rishis call *knowledge by identity*—we realize our identity with Atman.

But what, according to the Rishis, does this 'realization' exactly mean? If we already are Atman, then how is it that we do not know or realize it? Because of *adhyaropa*, explain the Rishis. The root of avidya, the spiritual ignorance of true identity, is adhyaropa or superimposition. We superimpose our individual identity as a person and personality, *namarupa*, on the *atmic* self that we are, and we do this unconsciously because we are conditioned since birth to do it. Perhaps the first thing we pick up from our environment is our 'name', and we never really outgrow the name, and this is true even of those who renounce their names because the name inevitably carries the history and identity of our family, society, nation, culture, and religion. The conditioning runs so deep that even in the isolation of our private thoughts, we refer to ourselves by our given names. We completely become the namarupa imposed upon us, we *identify* with it. Once that happens, it becomes nearly impossible to return to our original atmic identity, the 'face we had before we were born'. Try to recall yourself to your mind as you read this—who are you?—and all you will recall is your namarupa, your name and your physical and psychological form. It's like deep hypnosis.

---

40 Another mahavakya from the *Aitareya Upanishad:* prajnanam derives from the word *prajna,* which means consciousness or awareness; it can also mean intuition in some contexts. The identity of Brahman and Atman is already established.

Realizing our true identity, therefore, is realizing what or who we are once we have eliminated who and what we are not—all the superimpositions, the acquired identifications, and influences, the many layers of conditionings of the mind and the vital.[41] The process of elimination usually begins with the yogic practice of self-enquiry, *atma-vichar*: 'who am I' beyond my namarupa, what am I beyond my thoughts and beliefs?

Reflect on this: there is no 'I' that has written this book and there is no 'you' reading this book, it is the Atman, as the consciousness animating and informing the mind, that really writes, reads, and understands; we believe that we are experiencing this world, but it is always the Atman, the consciousness behind all things, that really experiences the world and renders it real to the senses and the intellect. The difference between a living and conscious body and an unconscious and dead body is the absence of the Atman. The common understanding amongst Hindus is that the Atman leaves the body at death, but the truth is that the Atman only withdraws—since it is all-pervading and non-local, the Atman neither leaves nor comes, it always is. It is this permanent *sthiti*[42] of the Atman within a constantly mutating and impermanent universe that gives the consciousness of immortality to the one who realizes his identity with the Atman. Thus we say that the Jnani, the self-realized one, attains immortality. It's not that the Jnani never dies—the Jnani's body, like all other bodies, falls off when the time comes, but the Jnani himself, having realized his identity with the Atman, knows that he cannot die or take birth, he is eternal.

In the Sanatan worldview, Atman is not just the immortal and immutable consciousness in all living beings, it is the only consciousness, *tad ekam*. Therefore, there is none other besides

---

41 Pranamaya, of the emotions, feelings, the life force or prana.
42 Position, established state, or condition.

Atman, and all individual existences are this Atman, non-different. There can be no independent individual consciousness any more than there can be independent individual matter: the body that we claim to be ours is cosmic matter, and the particles that constitute our body are all cosmic matter; the air we breathe or the water and food we consume are also cosmic matter; everything is cosmic, everything is universal, and this is self-evident to anyone who lives in the consciousness of the Atman. And, therefore, the insistence of the Rishis that all being is Atman, one universal consciousness, in spite of all external appearances.

The Real and the Apparently Real

In spite of all external appearances.....and there's the rub: for the Rishis speak from a consciousness where all is truth and only the real is seen and known while we live in a consciousness where everything seen and known is camouflaged or veiled by the outward-turned senses. We are born into *avidya* and *mithya*, and can neither sense nor know reality directly, for what we sense and know all the time is what we believe and imagine to be real—we walk upon a solid earth and see a blue sky above when there is no blue sky or solid matter anywhere outside of our senses; we sincerely believe we are Hindu, Muslim or Christian, Indian or American, white, brown or black, rich or poor, engineer, professor or banker, whereas none of all this is more than skin-deep, and all of these are borrowed, second-hand identities. Reflect on this: if all our identities are taken away from us, will we cease to exist? The so-called reality we live and so passionately defend is all make-believe, and nothing of it exists outside our conditioned and hypnotized minds. If we were only to alter our brain circuitry or chemistry just a bit or wake up one morning with no memory, our so-called physical and psychological realities would be unrecognizably changed or gone.

What relativistic and quantum physics are suggesting is exactly what the Rishis are saying: *there is no objective reality*; our lived reality is subjective, what we perceive and make real to our minds. This power to make real to our minds is known as *Maya* in Sanatan Dharma. Maya is the power to make real. In that sense, this universe itself wouldn't be real to us if it were not for Maya, for it is Maya that makes Brahman appear as this universe of infinite forms and movements. In other words, without Maya, Brahman would remain pure being, unmanifest, *avyakta*.

Let's consider an analogy. There's a rope lying in a dimly lit room, and you happen to enter the room and spot it on the floor. You at once mistake it for a serpent and panic. Then someone comes in with a lamp, and you see that it's a rope on the floor. So, what happens? This is an analogy the Rishis often use to illustrate Reality and Maya. The 'rope' is Reality, the substratum. You perceive a serpent in the rope which is not really there, it's only *adhyaropa*, superposition—your mind superposes the serpent on the rope and then makes that perception of the serpent real to itself, triggering the reaction of panic. The 'serpent' then becomes your dreaded 'apparent reality'. But Maya can create desire as much as dread: by superposing a 'valuable gold necklace'—which is entirely a figment of the mind—on a piece of metal, it can turn the metal into an object of desire. Such is the subtle power of Maya working through the mind's formative and imaginative faculties. It is doubtful that we would find worldly life of much interest if it were not for the workings of Maya.

Maya, of course, goes much deeper than the rope and the necklace. The Rishis knew Maya to be an attribute of Brahman itself, its self-limiting power perhaps, for without Maya, there would be no self-becoming of Brahman. Brahman is infinite being and, therefore, entirely outside the scope of any human experience or knowledge. To become manifest as self and universe, Brahman would need to limit itself, make itself finite, measurable, and thus, experienceable, and mold itself into space and time so that it could become itself in space and time. This is the inscrutable power of Maya, to make finite the infinite and measurable, the immeasurable.

The subjectivity of our lived reality is then an enabling mechanism of Maya, for without that, we would not be able to 'take in' the universe: it would remain unmanifest for us, like the two-dimensional ant, in our earlier analogy, unable to comprehend the three-dimensional room. Imagine experiencing life in the universe without the enabling mechanism of time, for instance, where all existence everywhere would be occurring simultaneously, in a vastly incomprehensible 'eternal now'. Objective reality, then, would be outside the influence of Maya, something only the Rishis could access in highly rarefied states of *samadhi* where the consciousness would withdraw entirely from reality as subjectively experienced—self and the world, jiva and jagat, would both disappear into Brahman.[43]

No one has attempted to describe objective reality to the subjective mind. When specifically asked, the Rishis have declared it to be *anirvachaniya*, something that cannot be explained. Yet, it is the realization of this objective reality that the Rishis exhort us towards, for that reality is Brahman, that reality is Atman. And not only do we need to realize this objective reality of Brahman, but we need to bring that realization into the subjective too, so that we may realize that Brahman is both, the objective and the subjective. Only then will the cosmic experience be complete and justified, and nothing will be omitted, no gap will remain. All that is now experienced as avidya and mithya will be experienced as the same truth of being, and all shall be seen in the light of the Atman. Nothing will dramatically change, the rope will still be there, but the serpent will not appear on it; the necklaces and the bracelets will still adorn our bodies, but we will not be too taken in by them for we shall know that it's all metal anyway. In other words, jagat will go on exactly as it must, driven by its own karmic necessities, but we shall no longer see jagat as jagat, we shall see jagat as Brahman, perhaps veiled ever so subtly by his inscrutable Maya. And, above all, we shall know that in all our objective and subjective experience, it is Atman that alone is, and Atman that alone lives.

---

43 Samadhi (समाधि) has many layers of meaning in Yoga and several interpretations. For our purposes, it is the state of inner absorption in some aspect of Reality; an unmodified state, where the mind is free of all kinds of modifications or *vrittis*. But one can also have waking samadhi, where one is settled in a higher consciousness even while engaged in action.

A Deeper Dive

But the question—why Atman or Brahman can never be known, perceived, or sensed in the lived experience of the universe—returns despite all explanations. Somehow, this seems to be the crux of the vedanta of Sanatan Dharma—if Brahman is the one reality, *tad ekam*, and Brahman has become this universe, *sarvam khalvidam brahman*,[44] then how is it that Brahman is never naturally or directly known? Why would it hide itself in its own self-becoming? What are we missing here? Analogies work up to a point, but beyond that, most logical reasoning fails. For instance, in the serpent and rope analogy, an oft-repeated one in vedantic darshan, what is the origin of the serpent? Where does the perception of the serpent, even if mithya, come from? Where does it arise? It cannot arise from the rope because it is not contained in the rope, and it cannot spontaneously manifest out of nothing; thus, it must arise from the mind of the perceiver, for the mind possesses the power to project and create illusions. But, then, the mind of the perceiver cannot exist outside reality. Going by the premise that all is Brahman, the one reality, the mind of the perceiver is also a self-becoming of Brahman and, therefore, cannot create mithya on its own, following the logic that Brahman is all-truth, *purna satyam*.

Going back to the analogy, we come to the only logical conclusion that the serpent is a self-becoming of the rope and not different from it. This does not mean that the rope actually

---

44 Sarvam khalvidam brahma, all this universe (sarvam khalu idam) is Brahman. From the verse
सर्वं खल्विदं ब्रह्म तज्जलानिति शान्त उपासीत। अथ खलु क्रतुमयः पुरुषो यथाक्रतुरस्मिल्लोके पुरुषो
भवति तथेतः प्रेत्य भवति स क्रतुं कुर्वीत॥ —*Chhandogya Upanishad,* 3.4.1.

becomes the serpent: the rope remains rope, but it becomes the serpent in the mind of the perceiver through the power of Maya. Not only is this reasoning consistent with the vedantic premise that the universe, and all its multitudinous namarupa, is the self-becoming of Brahman, but it is also consistent with the wider Vedic truth of Sanatan Dharma that nothing is false or illusory about the universe as the universe is Sat itself, and what appears to be false or illusory, mithya, itself is a formation of Sat. So, if mithya fundamentally is Sat, then it follows that the universe we know, perceive, and experience is Brahman itself. In other words, we are, at all times, actually experiencing Brahman, but in the mind, we *seem* to be experiencing namarupa, like a person swimming in the sea will experience, in his mind and senses, the reality of sea waves while actually experiencing only the sea and its movements.

Once again, we come to Maya: it is by the power of Maya that our actual experience of Brahman—the sea—in all its namarupa is obscured by the seeming reality of the namarupa—waves—only. The namarupa has an immediate and overwhelming reality that reality itself does not seem to have. If, however, we were to sink deeper into the sea, leaving all the waves, or namarupa, on the surface, the scenario would change entirely: the waves would no longer be real, and it would be only sea. This would be analogous to sinking into Brahman where the namarupa of sansara would no longer be so real.[45]

The universe as we know and experience it, therefore, is Brahman—there is no difference, neither in substance nor in experience. There are many who find it difficult to accept this, for if we indeed are experiencing Brahman all the time as this universe, what of the processes of the Yoga, the lifelong sadhana of the Yogis, to attain to the realization of Brahman? This is

---

45 Do bear in mind that these are all analogies to explain complex points of the darshan, and some analogies are more effective than others. In this particular analogy, we take the deep sea as still, silent, and dark.

a legitimate question, and to explain this subtle point, we will need to go back to the sea analogy. When we are in the sea, what are we experiencing? The sea, the waves, or the moving water? If we still the mind, not allow any conceptual thought to arise, we would experience only the moving water, neither sea nor sea waves. This has nothing to do with the reality of sea or the sea waves, it has everything to do with our own mind and its movements—if we can somehow quiet the mind, withdraw from all conceptualizations and constructs of the intellect, and fathom our own present and immediate experience of reality, we will know, without any scope of doubt, that everything and everyone is that one reality, Brahman, Atman, or Sat—by whatever name we choose to call it: *bahudha vadanti*.

This alone is the process of Yoga, this stilling of the mind and emotions and withdrawing inward into the depths of our own everyday cosmic experience. Nothing else needs to be done: simply the fathoming of what is, for what is, as our Rishis declared repeatedly, is infinite being—where else can one go? Everything is the 'within' of the Atman, the infinite interiority of consciousness. Yoga is nothing but the gentle, effortless sinking into the depths of what we are, the Atman, and what this universe is, Brahman.

Identification, Sayujya

However simple the process of Yoga may be, it does not come easy to most seekers. It takes years of patience and persistent practice to bring the mind out of its habitual identification with its concepts, thoughts, memories, imagination, and all the rest of it. The mind is compulsively busy, always engaged with the occupations and preoccupations of the mundane, even in its sleep, and is likened by the seers to wild monkeys. Because of this inherent difficulty with the mind, many seekers try to kill the mind through enormously difficult and demanding austerities of the mind and body, pushing their wills to an extreme. There is, in fact, a name for this in the Dharma: *manonasha*, literally, destruction of the mind. But, as our seers point out, one seeks to destroy the mind only when one's identification with the mind and its activities is overpowering.

The key to understanding and then mastering the mind is the power of identification, *sayujya*. This is a stupendous power, and every one of us experiences this power intimately—it is this power of identification that makes us cling obstinately to our psychological identities, our namarupa, our bodies and minds, our knowledge and beliefs, our thoughts and ideas; and it is this that makes us die, or kill, for what we believe is ours and of value to us. Almost everything that we fight and struggle for, grieve over, dream about, and pursue with all our energies, even to the point of death, is because of sayujya, identification. It is this power that convinces us that we are the body and mind when the intelligence or buddhi in us knows well that we are neither the body nor the mind.

Yet, sayujya is indispensable for both the practical and spiritual life. Were it not for identification with the body, for instance, a practical physical existence on earth would become extremely challenging, and without identification with the mind and its notions, beliefs, and knowledge, any kind of ordered, coherent life as an individual would become equally challenging. Only a realized Yogi could live without identification with mind or body without going insane.[46] But even the Yogi must first identify with the true self, the Atman, before he can be released or liberated from the lower namarupa identifications. Consciousness can either identify itself with ego and personality, *namarupa sayujya*, or with Atman, *brahmasayujya*. In a fundamental sense, Yoga may be regarded as the transition of consciousness from namarupa sayujya to brahmasayujya.

The Rishis, therefore, exhort us to first understand our identifications through persistent self-reflection, *atma-vichara*, and then, through the knowledge thus gained, gradually wean ourselves away from identification with the mind and body and identify more and more with the true inner self, the Atman. Identification being the power or capacity of consciousness to identify and merge, it can identify with only one thing at a time. We can live perfectly in the inner identification with Atman and still function beautifully in the world; the problems and struggles arise only when we live in the outer and lower identifications. Thus, we don't need to destroy the mind—we only need to detach from it and identify with Atman; the mind is always a useful, even indispensable, instrument for realizing and living the Dharma.

---

46 Think about it: without identification with our bodies, we wouldn't be able to keep our physical existence together; even animals instinctively identify with their bodies to keep themselves safe and healthy. And without identification with our minds and mental processes, we would have no coherent personality or identity, and this is visibly demonstrated in several cases of clinical insanity, schizophrenia, personality dissociations, etc.

Atma-Vichara, Self-Reflection

Atma-vichara, self-reflection, is not a mental process of questioning but a persistent and silent probing into the depths of consciousness, a systematic investigation into the nature of being, our psychological existence and identity, self-regard and selfhood. It reverses our ordinary self-perception and belief, penetrates the many layers of our identifications and projections, and opens the buddhi to the true sense and perception of Atman, freed from the obscurations of the ego.

Sri Ramana, amongst the most revered of maharshis in the Sanatan tradition,[47] taught a simple method of constant and unremitting self-reflection to his disciples—who am I? Who is asking this question? Who is thinking? Who believes? Who comes and goes? Trace every thought back to its source, and you will come to the essential I-consciousness; and then, probe deeper into that. Instead of focusing only on the apparent, try to see out of what the 'apparent' appears, and when you do that, you will see that the 'apparent' appears out of consciousness itself.

Personality is like a refraction of consciousness, an apparent bending of pure consciousness in the denser medium of the sense-mind. But note again that the denser medium of the sense-mind is consciousness too, for it is the Atman that shines

---

47 Ramana Maharshi ('Bhagavan') was a twentieth-century South Indian sage who continues to radiate peace and Self-awareness to the global community of spiritual seekers. You do not need to join any organization, adopt any belief system, or worship anyone or anything to experience this transmission of bliss and clarity. Bhagavan simply points you towards your innermost Self, the unchanging reality underlying all that exists. —*Introduction to Ramana Maharshi*, https://www.sriramanamaharshi.org.

behind the senses and the mind, infusing them with awareness, *chaitanya*, so that the senses and the mind can cognize and experience cosmic reality.

The Atman is the background, the screen upon which the images of self and world appear and disappear. As we trace back the persistent I-thought to its source, we come to this constant background of all thought, activity, knowledge, and awareness, this pure atmic awareness, *atmabodh*. It is then that we realize that there is no personal self at all, there never was—it was always the mind projecting its notion of personality or selfhood on the screen of the Atman. This mental projection, *asmita*, is the root of all sense of me and mine, of egoism, identification, and attachment. It is necessary for every seeker of the Self to distinguish between asmita and atmabodh: whereas asmita rests on identification with objects, persons, relations, events, atmabodh is independent of circumstances, anantam, without beginning or end; while asmita arises from memory and personality, and is ever-changing, atmabodh is an inherent property of consciousness, universal and immutable; while asmita reflects the Atman as the moon reflects sunlight, atmabodh is the direct illumination of the Atman.

Unless we have practiced atma-vichara and are established in the witnessing of atma-vichara, it is very easy to confuse atmabodh with asmita and take asmita as the real self. This is our primary psychological ignorance or avidya. We do not know the real from the apparent self.

The Rishis, therefore, speak of the necessity of the witnessing poise of the self, the *sakshi bhava*—the ability to stand back from the continuous movements and activities of the mind and quietly watch the mind itself. As one watches the mind quietly, not getting carried away or distracted by its movements and activities, one begins to discern the still and silent background of the mind. The thinking mind, with its continuous noise and movements, is like the disturbed surface of a lake, and the background of the mind, once the thinking and the noise cease, is like the deep and still bed of the lake once the ripples have all died down.

With the deepening of atma-vichara, among the first discoveries we make is that we are split into two distinct 'selves' within us—one is the self identified with the movements and activities of the thinking mind, with all that moves in the world and in us, with all the mental noise; and the other is the detached witnessing self, independent of the goings and comings of the world, unaffected by all the ripples and waves of the mind, seated above the play of dualities and multiplicities, *udasina*, in the language of the Yogis.[48] The former is known as *apara* or the 'lower self' absorbed in the play of the mind, and the latter is known as the *para* or the 'higher self', situated above the play of the mind, a detached and impersonal witness.

There is an Upanishadic parable that illustrates this beautifully: two birds, beautiful of wings, close companions, cling to one common tree; of the two, one eats the sweet fruit of the tree, the other eats not but watches his fellow.[49] The bird that 'feeds on the sweet fruits of the tree' represents the self absorbed in mind and senses, the *jiva*, suffering the 'slings and arrows' of its worldly fortunes; the other bird which 'feeds not but watches' represents the higher self, settled in its witnessing poise, calm, conscious, and free, the *purusha*. The two selves that we are, the birds of the parable, are not real entities but two aspects of the one self, and integrating the two is one of the effects of Yoga. Yoga is the union of Atman and Brahman at one level—only in terms of realization, though, for essentially, they are already and eternally one—and the union of the apara and the para at another.

---

48 Udasina (उदासीन) from *ud*, above or apart, and āsīna, seated or situated: thus, seated or situated above or apart from.

49 द्वा सुपर्णा सयुजा सखाया समानं वृक्षं परिषस्वजाते । तयोरन्यः पिप्पलं स्वाद्वत्त्यनश्नन्न्यो अभिचाकशीति ॥ —*Mandukya Upanishad.*

So, what is to be done, asks the seeker, to attain this yoga? How to identify and unite with the purusha? *Nothing*, say the Vedantic seers, *nothing needs to be done except stilling the waves of the mind.* Once the waves of the mind are quieted, the surface self, with all its noise and activities, disappears, and all that remains is the background or the substratum—the purusha, the Atman.

The One and the Many

This universe, according to the Sanatan worldview, is not just a fortuitous play of energy and matter but a self-becoming of an all-pervading, all-encompassing consciousness that at once transcends and contains the manifest universe and is present or immanent in all its movements and forms, vibrations and expressions. The Rishis declare—*isha vasyamidam sarvam yatkinca jagatyam jagat*:[50] all this, whatever moves in this moving universe, is permeated by Brahman, this whole universe is Brahman's habitation, and it is Brahman that has become this universe. This universe and Brahman are not two separate things, Brahman is this universe as it has become this universe. Wherever you see, whatever you see, whatever that moves or appears to move, is Brahman, whatever that lives is Brahman: in fact, there is nothing else but Brahman; what you see is Brahman, what you hear is Brahman, what you feel and touch is Brahman. This is the import of *isha vasyam idam sarvam*— Brahman (*Isha*, the Supreme Ishvara) permeating or enveloping (*vasyam*) all (*sarvam*) this (*idam*). There are, thus, no dualities, divisions, or substantial differences, all apparent differences being those of form and movement only. Brahman is the one existence, ekam Sat, which subsumes all multiplicity—*ekam evadvitiyam brahman*[51]—and there is no other existence besides

---

50 ईशा वास्यमिदं सर्वं यत्किञ्च जगत्यां जगत्। तेन त्यक्तेन भुञ्जीथा मा गृधः कस्यस्विद्धनम् — All this is for habitation by the Lord, whatsoever is individual universe of movement in the universal motion. By that renounced thou shouldst enjoy; lust not after any man's possession. —*Isha Upanishad*.

51 From the *Chandogya Upanishad*. Ekam means one and eva means only, thus, one and only; a-dvitiyam literally means without a second, without duality (a, without, dvitiya, second).

it. Therefore, in Hindu Dharma, Brahman is not a God that creates this universe, and this universe never comes into being: Brahman becomes this universe, and because Brahman is timeless and causeless, so is the universe.

It will perhaps be difficult for the modern mind to grasp the idea of the universe always being there: what about the birth, and therefore death, of the universe, though over eons of time? There is a certain consciousness that the Rishis can access, called *trikala darshan*, or perception of the three phases of time, which is situated above and beyond time—*kalatita*.[52] In this consciousness, everything is happening simultaneously, there is no past, present, or future. It is similar to seeing an event in time-lapse photography: everything happens in a single timeframe. Imagine looking at the universe from this consciousness through trikala darshan—what would you see? Would you see a beginning or end? There is another example the Rishis cite: sometimes we perceive a particular experience in our lives in a single flash, not sequentially, as it actually happened. How does that happen? Unknowingly, we glimpse our own experience in trikala darshan, but because the mind is not familiar with such a phenomenon, we miss it and quickly fall back into temporal or sequential perception. The Rishis admit the relative or *vyavharika* reality of time but do not take it as an absolute: the absolute reality is anantam, without beginning or end. Einstein, I recall, after a lifetime's study of physics, said that 'time does not exist' and the 'distinction between the past, present, and future is only a stubbornly persistent illusion'.

So, in the cosmology of Hindu Dharma, Brahman, the primordial *Purusha*,[53] extends or expands itself into cosmic becoming, and since cosmos is a self-becoming of Brahman, everything in existence is Brahman, without differentiation or

---

52 Kalatita (कालातीत), *kala* (काल) is time, *atita* (अतीत) is beyond or above.
53 Another term for being and consciousness. Brahman is also known as the Supreme Purusha, *Purushottama*.

division. This is a fundamental difference between the Vedic and Abrahamic worldviews: whereas Abrahamic theology stems from the dualistic notion of an extra-cosmic God who creates the universe, Vedic darshan stems from the idea of Brahman, or Satchidananda, expanding itself into the known or manifest universe, becoming everything and everyone, from the quantum to the cosmic, from the plankton to the godhead. It may be pertinent to recall at this point that one of the meanings of *Brahman*, from the root *brh*, is infinite expansion.

But what initiates the self-becoming of Brahman? This is a rather tricky question in Sanatan darshan because Brahman is perfect existence, and being perfect, it is complete in itself— *purnasya purnam*[54]—and thus, can have no need for becoming as becoming would imply incompleteness of being. So, what can move perfect and complete being to become? Perhaps, as the Rishis suggest, our human ideas of perfect being are themselves imperfect, for who is there to determine what Brahman can or cannot do? Or maybe there is no difference between being and becoming except in our very limited temporal sense. A caterpillar, for instance, doesn't 'become' a butterfly at a particular point in its metamorphosis, it is always becoming a butterfly while remaining a caterpillar along a timeless and simultaneous being-becoming curve. Brahman, in the same manner, is perfect being *and* perfect becoming. In Sanatan darshan, there is hardly any either-or, it is always multiple or infinite possibilities.

Thus, the Rishis of old suggest (for none seems really sure) that an original 'desire' or 'will-to-become' arose in Brahman— *ekoham bahushyam*, I am one, let me become many. It is with this will-to-become, a divine *sankalpa*,[55] that the One becomes the Many. This is a possibility, not a fact, of course, since no one can really know what exactly happened—if 'happen' is the word

---

54 Literally, perfect perfection or complete completion (*purna* can be understood as perfect or complete); purnasya means 'of purna'.

55 Sankalpa may mean determination, will, intention.

one can use—inside the Brahmic consciousness prior to the One becoming the Many. Maybe nothing really happened prior to the moment of becoming: Brahman as unity and Brahman as multiplicity is always a simultaneous and undifferentiated reality, two dimensions of the same truth. The difficulty is always in the rendering of absolute truths in the dualistic and relativistic language of the mind.

There is a Vedic hymn about creation, the famous Nasadiya Sukta of the *Rig Veda*, which ends with these hauntingly provocative lines—

But, after all, who knows, and who can say
Whence it all came, and how creation happened?
The gods themselves are later than creation,
So who knows truly whence it has arisen?
Whence all creation had its origin,
The creator, whether he fashioned it or whether he did not,
The creator, who surveys it all from highest heaven,
He knows—or maybe even he does not know.[56]

---

56 अर्वाग्देवा अस्य विसर्जनेनाथा को वेद यत आबभूव, इयं विसृष्टिर्यत आबभूव यदि वा दधे यदि वा न, यो अस्याध्यक्ष: परमे व्योमन्त्सो अङ्ग वेद यदि वा न वेद ॥ —Sukta 129, Mandala 10, *Rig Veda*. Translated by Arthur Llewellyn Basham.

Vasudhaiva Kutumbakam

The cosmogony upon which Sanatan Dharma rests is essentially Vedantic in conception—this universe, *vishwa* in Sanskrit, is not the creation but the self-becoming of Brahman and, thus, all that exists in the universe is Brahman alone, *sarvam khalvidam brahman*. To further emphasize the ontological identity of Brahman and the universe, the Rishis add that Brahman is the great resting place of the universe, the substratum of all being, *vishwa syayatanam mahat*, and that we, as embodied conscious life, are that Brahman—*tattvameva twameva tat*.[57] But then, we do not know it naturally as we are not born in the Brahmic consciousness, which can only mean that the self-becoming of Brahman as this universe is still not complete, and the universe is still evolving towards a complete emergence of Brahman in life and consciousness; in other words, we are still work in progress and not end-products of brahmic evolution.

It is this overarching vedantic conception of the universe as the progressive self-becoming of Brahman that forms the practical basis of the Hindu worldview and psychology. If all life is one reality, and we ourselves are that, *tattvameva twameva tat*, then it follows that there is no concept of otherness, for who or what can possibly be the other? And thus, we have one of the central tenets of Sanatan darshan,

---

57 यत्परं ब्रह्म सर्वात्मा विश्वस्यायतनं महत्, सूक्ष्मात्सूक्ष्मतरं नित्यं तत्त्वमेव त्वमेव तत् — Brahman is indeed the great resting place of the universe and you yourself are it, it is you. —*Kaivalya Upanishad*, 9.16.

vasudhaiva kutumbakam, this whole wide world is one family[58] bound to one truth of being, one dharma, however differently our spiritual prophets and masters choose to describe that— *ekam sat vipra bahudha vadanti*—which is the evolution of life towards perfect truth and consciousness, which would, of course, be cosmic, universal.

And if that is the one human dharma, to evolve continuously towards a perfectly conscious life, then everyone, everywhere, at any point along the evolutionary curve, is imperfection working towards perfection, ignorance working towards truth, selfishness working towards universality, pettiness working towards vastness, self-limiting beliefs and fears working towards cosmicity, cruelty and crudeness working towards divine beauty and love. Nothing then is wrong or intrinsically evil, and nothing needs to be destroyed: the only imperatives are evolution and freedom of being and learning.

If a being is allowed to grow unhindered, it will grow into a beautifully conscious life, though sometimes that may take lifetimes—this is the evolutionary impetus of Dharma: because perfect consciousness is seeded in the very fabric of cosmic spacetime, all its varied forms will eventually and inevitably manifest perfect consciousness. And by the same logic, if the *asuric* or the demonic is allowed to evolve, that too will grow into perfect consciousness in the course of time.[59] So, the essential Hindu mind does not care too much about evil or the devil: everything and everyone is moving inexorably towards Brahman because Brahman *is* everything and everyone and, thus, all things and beings have their place in the cosmic scheme of things.

---

58 अयं निजः परो वेति गणना लघुचेतसाम्। उदारचरितानां तु वसुधैव कुटुम्बकम्, ayam nijah paro veti ganana laghucetasam, udaracaritanam tu vasudhaiva kutumbakam — This is mine, that is his, say the small-minded, the wise believe that the entire world is a family. —*Maha Upanishad*, 6.71–75.

59 From *asura*, a hostile force that opposes or resists the Divine Truth and its manifestation so that the manifestation may become perfect and flawless. As the Mother of Sri Aurobindo Ashram once said, the asura will exist for as long as he is needed for the Divine's work.

This worldview of Sanatan Dharma infuses all existence with a divinity that is hard to explain outside the Dharmic context. Just as a god is considered divine, a beast, worm, or stone, too, is considered divine, for what indeed can be undivine when the universe itself is the unfolding of a perfect divine consciousness? The difference between a god and a worm, or a Rishi and an asura, is not in kind but only in degree of consciousness. The Hindu then would accept all existence, all life, as expressions of Brahman and, therefore, sacred. When the Hindu mind loses the sense of the sacred, it falls from its high and profound Dharmic ground into the mundane, the worldly, the *sansaric*.

All this becomes rather challenging for the Hindu in real-life situations. There are numerous instances of Sanatan Dharma, or the Hindu civilization, being openly attacked, ridiculed, and criticized by those who know little of the Dharma or the Dharmic civilization: how then, in such situations, is one to confront overt or covert aggressiveness when one's Dharma does not admit of any otherness or duality? How is one to stand up to what one knows in one's mind and heart to be wrong, against Dharma, or even common humanity? How does one live in the midst of all the struggles and battles of the modern world without reacting to evil because there is essentially no evil? These are perplexing questions for Dharma. The Hindu epic Mahabharata, whose longest extant version runs into 100,000 slokas, is a provocative and exhaustive study of Dharma and its intractable issues and questions.

There are many teachers of the Dharma who suggest that such challenges arise when we try to live high spiritual truths in down-to-earth practical matters: the oneness of being, the inherent divinity of all existence, the evolution of life and consciousness, the impossibility of otherness and evil, are all high spiritual realities and cannot be applied to practical day-to-day living. There are realities of the spiritual, or *adhyatmik*, plane, and there are realities of the practical, day-to-day *vyavharik* plane; therefore, the realizations of the adhyatmik plane cannot be mixed (at least injudiciously) with matters of the vyavharik plane.

There is much practical truth to this approach—if an angry bull were hurtling towards you, it would be quite foolish not to step aside because all existence is Brahman—but, following the vedantic conception of reality, which, to my mind, forms the practical basis of Hindu Dharma, such a strategic division of reality into the adhyatmik and the vyavharik would contradict the essential darshan of the Dharma. The point of the Dharma is not to live different (and often conflicting) realities but to bring the truths of the higher adhyatmik plane down into the practical day-to-day living of the vyavharik plane so that, finally, the vyavharik world, *samsara* itself, would reflect and express the truth of the adhyatmik. Only then will the Dharma attain its integral perfection, its *purnata*. But such purnata will be possible only when we ourselves live the Dharma in the granular details of our lives and establish ourselves in what the Gita calls *brahmisthiti*—situated in Brahman or the Brahmic condition,[60] and not get perplexed by derived knowledge from scriptures and teachers.

60 एषा ब्राह्मी स्थितिः पार्थ नैनां प्राप्य विमुह्यति स्थित्वास्यामन्तकालेऽपि ब्रह्मनिर्वाणमृच्छति ॥ —
This is brāhmī sthitiḥ (firm standing in the Brahman), O son of Pritha. Having attained thereto one is not bewildered; fixed in that status at his end, one can attain extinction in the Brahman. —Bhagavad Gita, 2.72.

The Godward Endeavor

The most fundamental realizations of Sanatan Dharma—realization of the Self, the realization of Brahman, the realization of the identity of Self and Brahman—are all profoundly personal, and each individual attains to these realizations in harmony with their personal nature and law of being, *swabhava*.[61] The intensely personal nature of Hindu Dharma's highest spiritual attainments makes it an essentially introspective religion, neither bound to any external tradition nor obliged to any collective or social expression. This introspective nature of Hindu Dharma also makes it psychic and spiritual in its orientation, emphasizing self-reflection over scriptures and handed-down beliefs, personalization over systems, and personal experience over teachers and external authority.

This, of course, does not mean that there is no place of honor in Hindu Dharma for scriptures or teachers: the scriptures and the gurus and *acharyas*[62] of the Hindu tradition are highly revered and followed, but none is indispensable—as long as there is an intellectual or even spiritual need for scriptures, acharyas and gurus, they can be sought for and followed; whenever the need is fulfilled, the seeker is free to move on and find his or her own path to Truth. It is this inner flexibility and freedom that makes Sanatan darshan wonderfully eclectic and universal in its scope,

---

61 *Swabhava* has no equivalent expression in English. *Swa*, in Sanskrit, means self and *bhava* implies becoming; thus, self-becoming. But becoming what? What one has always been, one's intrinsic nature, one's truth of being, one's inmost essence. And the divine self is our inmost essence. So self-becoming, *swabhava*, is literally oneself becoming the divine as the divine has become us.

62 *Acharya* is the traditional Sanskrit term for teacher.

embracing every stage and age, aspiration, need, and endeavor of the human soul, denying or rejecting nothing.

Because of the predominant importance Sanatan Dharma gives to self-reflection and self-realization over all scriptural and didactic authority, diverse and even contradictory influences, approaches, and streams of knowledge are seamlessly admitted, integrated, or absorbed into the mainstream Dharma, making it a rich, multifaceted, and continuously growing body of spiritual knowledge and practices. Anyone aspiring for a spiritual life can dip into the myriad streams of Sanatan darshan and take out whatever path or practice that works for them. This is the only religion I know of that gives complete intellectual and spiritual freedom to the seeker to choose and follow their personal path, and there is no central spiritual authority to monitor or censure an individual's inner processes. Every Hindu, essentially, is free to develop their own dharma; and in case someone cannot do so, for it needs a certain intellectual and psychic capacity to develop one's personal dharma, there is always the traditional knowledge systems to seek support from.

The Hindu religion, in Sri Aurobindo's words, *has always been a continuously enlarging tradition of the Godward endeavor of the human spirit.* This is how Sanatan Dharma, as a vast and varied body of spiritual knowledge, has grown over the years: by continuously enlarging itself, emphasizing an uncompromising spirit of enquiry instead of strict adherence to belief, and insisting on truth instead of dogma. Direct spiritual experience has always been valued more in Sanatan Dharma than beliefs and theories. *Sruti,* or what is revealed and heard,[63] and *sakshatkar,*

---

63 Śruti (श्रुति) — hearing; sound; that which is heard. The Vedas are considered to be sruti in Hindu Dharma, referring to the tradition of passing down knowledge orally from generation to generation — 'which has been heard or communicated from the beginning, sacred knowledge that was only heard and verbally transmitted from generation to generation, the Veda, from earliest rishis (sages) in Vedic tradition'. Ref. James Lochtefeld, *The Illustrated Encyclopedia of Hinduism.*

direct seeing and knowing,[64] have always been profoundly important in the Hindu tradition and preferred over any other source or authority.

It must, however, be noted here that sruti, direct intuitive and spiritual revelation, is a dynamic, ongoing process. What is revealed to one Rishi can be superseded by what is revealed to another at a later time or even contemporaneously. The Sanatan spiritual tradition has always maintained that no seer-vision or teaching can be the ultimate: there is always the next step, the next stage. Consciousness is dynamic and ever-evolving, and there can be no single end-product of such a process. No seer or prophet can be the final word, but every seer and prophet of Hindu Dharma is a necessary link, a stepping stone, to the supreme truth. As Sri Aurobindo, arguably amongst the greatest of the maharshis of the Sanatan Hindu tradition, a maharshi who had attained the supreme realizations of the Vedas and the Vedanta, himself remarked on one occasion, when asked by a disciple if his yogic attainment was the final peak, that there was still *an infinite beyond*.

It is true that Sanatan Dharma has many diverse scriptures and teachers, but because it is not bound to any of its scriptures and considers no teacher infallible, it can still remain free of doctrines and traditions to explore ever higher truths and ever newer approaches to truths. Truth is not a one-time given, set in stone: it is a progressive self-revelation and grows as the human consciousness grows. Perfect truth, whatever that may be, would be possible only to a perfect consciousness, and as long as consciousness is human, it cannot be perfect; therefore, as long as one has not become completely identified with Truth-consciousness, one will always be fallible. The only 'infallible authority' Sanatan Dharma acknowledges and reveres is the

---

64 Sākṣātkāra (साक्षात्कार), immediate perception; experiencing, proving, verifying; establishing as true in one's own person or observation; also evident or intuitive perception, realization.

Atman, the indwelling godhead or *Ishvara*.[65] The word of the self-realized being can therefore override the scriptures and tradition.

This is how Sri Aurobindo could take the Sanatan Dharma beyond its scriptural and traditional boundaries and extend its spiritual scope beyond even that which was established by Sri Krishna, acknowledged as an avatar, a divine incarnation, in the Hindu tradition. In fact, Sri Aurobindo's yogic life and work were based on the singular premise that the evolution of consciousness is far from finished, and the work of the avatar, the divine incarnation, therefore continues, with every new avatar building upon the work of the previous one, advancing spiritual evolution to the next level. Several orthodox interpreters and followers of Hindu Dharma still do not accept Sri Aurobindo's yogic work and vision, for to accept that would logically imply accepting that the spiritual work of the great Rishis and Avatars can be surpassed. What the orthodox pundits perhaps fail to understand is that 'surpassing' does not mean negating or downgrading but advancing along a determined spiritual direction, each Rishi or Avatar building upon the work and attainments of the previous ones so that humanity can continue growing more and more towards its highest truth.

I mention Sri Aurobindo in this context because his yogic work specifically demonstrates the inherent nature of Sanatan Dharma: ever dynamic and progressive, eclectic and open-ended, revealing more and more of itself as human consciousness grows upward in what may well be an infinite ascension towards an infinite truth.

---

65 Ishvara, though commonly understood as God (in the theological sense), actually means the indwelling divine Self in the Vedantic sense.

Foundational Aspects of the Dharma

Yoga

Yoga, from the Sanskrit root yuj, meaning union; to unite, to yoke, to become one with; also, complete identification. A Yogi is one who has attained union, or complete identification, with the supreme Self, Brahman. The word 'yogic' relates or refers to Yoga.

Sanatan Dharma, in a fundamental sense, is vedantic in conception—its central tenet being the oneness of existence—and yogic in practice, for without the yogic realization of the vedantic truths of Sanatan Dharma, the Dharma will always remain a belief system, a religion, to be revered and followed but never lived, with no intrinsic value for the spiritual seeker or society, and will, in time, degenerate into ritualism and dogma, as has indeed happened in the past. We can follow a religion as a matter of faith and conform to all its outer rules and regulations but have no inner experience or realization of any of its truths, but we cannot 'follow' Yoga without practicing or living it. In a way, religion can be all theory and belief while Yoga must be practice and realization; religion can be credal while Yoga must be experiential. It is simply not possible to be a believer of Yoga, we can only be practitioners, or sadhakas,[66] of Yoga.[67]

---

66 A sadhaka is one who engages in *sadhana*—spiritual and yogic practice or discipline.

67 Interestingly, Yoga, as a practice of spirituality, applies to all religions. If a Christian decides to personally experience and realize the spiritual truths of Christianity—as the Christian mystics who experienced Christ-consciousness in themselves did—he or she would be engaging in yogic practice, for Yoga is any process that leads systematically to the realization of the Spirit and is as universal as it is Sanatan.

To truly live the deeper truths of the Dharma, one would need to return through Yoga to the original consciousness, Sat, out of which the Dharma arose—it is through Yoga that we would need to recover the path of the Rishis leading back to the supreme Truth, and thus, yoga is also known as the path of the Truth—*ritasya panthah*. It is Yoga that transforms the sadhaka into the Angirasa, the pilgrim of light, that the Vedic Rishis spoke of.[68]

But how exactly does one come to this practice of Yoga? In a general sense, the process of Yoga begins with the turning of one's *dhyana* inward.

Dhyana is our attention or the direction of our consciousness. Our attention is ordinarily turned outward, towards *prakriti*, which is the sense-mind experience of the universe. We close our eyes to prakriti, as it were, and open our inner eyes, *antar drishti*,[69] to the subjective subtler worlds within. As our dhyana stabilizes in the inner mind, no longer running outward with the senses out of old habit, we begin to discern the subtle formations and movements of our inner worlds, our inner preoccupations, the many layers of old conditionings, habits, and tendencies, what the yogis call *sanskaras*—seed impressions, and *vasanas*—seed desires, ever waiting to sprout into thought and action. *The stuff that our dreams are made of.*

And as the Yoga takes the dhyana deeper inward, penetrating layer after layer of our subtler being, our mental notions and beliefs fall away, the sanskaras and vasanas, the desires and fears, all evaporate, and an active peace draws the mind and heart towards the Atman.

The realization of the Atman, or *atmajnana*,[70] is Sanatan Dharma's highest possible spiritual attainment—with atmajnana

---

68　The pilgrims of the light, they who travel towards the goal and attain to the highest, the supreme treasure. —Sri Aurobindo, *Vedic Symbolism*.

69　*Antar*, inner or inward, *drishti*, vision. Through Yoga, one opens one's *antar drishti*, with which one can discern inner realities, inner movements, and formations.

70　*Atman* is the self, and *jnana* is spiritual or intuitive knowledge or direct realization. *Atmajnana* is, therefore, self-realization. Since Atman is Brahman, atmajnana is also the realization of Brahman, *brahmajnana*.

comes the decisive vedantic realization that Atman and Brahman are one single substance, and the whole universe is that one single substance. All the truths and values of Sanatan Dharma then become self-evident; the adhyatmik and the vyavharik are no longer separate, and the realizations of the spiritual can then be lived, without disharmony or conflict, in the mundane. The true spiritual life of Sanatan Dharma is integral and eminently practical, not idealistic or escapist.

The Yogic Approach

Sanatan Dharma, as a darshan and yogic practice, has always been dynamic and evolutionary, growing through its foremost practitioners through the ages, each of its master-seers leading the Dharma higher and deeper through their own spiritual attainments, and as Sanatan Dharma permits within itself a wide range of spiritual and practical divergences and departures, it is not likely to stagnate at any point. Whatever stagnation or fixities we may observe in some of the practices of Sanatan Dharma, casteism, for instance, is not because of the limitations of the Dharma but because of the self-limiting beliefs and superstitions of its practitioners. There are, admittedly, several beliefs and practices in Sanatan Dharma that are not in alignment with its darshan or its vedantic values, and these need to be identified and abandoned vigorously. There is no justification at all if this is not happening naturally or is not being allowed to happen.

There is no central authority or regulating body for the Dharma—as in the religions of the world—and, therefore, there can be no question of any kind of religious heresy or excommunication if progressive Hindus take upon themselves the responsibility of critique and reform. Every religious, quasi-religious, or philosophical system needs constant updating and reform if they are to remain meaningful and relevant for the present generation and the generations to come. The past, however hallowed, cannot, and must not, be carried into the future, and this is especially true for religions and philosophies. If, however, some Hindus still tolerate beliefs and practices which are spiritually wrong or logically inconsistent with the Dharma, then they do so because of their own pusillanimity and lack of true knowledge of the Dharma, yet another form of avidya.

The true Hindu, the Sanatani, must know and understand this. In fact, one cannot claim to be a real Hindu unless he has awakened within himself a degree of spiritual understanding and discernment or what is called *viveka* in Sanatan practice. Swami Vivekananda once said that if a Hindu is not spiritual, he cannot be called a Hindu at all. This is not as extreme as it sounds at first. Being spiritual does not necessarily mean being a perfected yogi or Rishi—anyone who is turned inward, even in the midst of an active life in the world and seeks the truth of the Self in all things and beings is spiritual. Spirituality, for the Hindu, is as much the general attitude of being, *bhava*, as it is the final attainment of life. It is not so very difficult to be spiritual in this sense if one really wants to—what is needed, first of all, is sincerity, then the strength of will and conviction, and finally, wisdom and discernment. These, too, are characteristics of spiritual living.

Swami Vivekananda's statement, therefore, needs to be understood in a deeper and more integral sense—spirituality is not just one of the pursuits of life but the entire orientation and the sole objective of one's existence. One must be spiritual in all things, in all of one's being and becoming: this is the one central and indispensable demand of Sanatan Dharma. Thus, a true practicing Hindu must also be a practicing yogi, one whose life is an unbroken pursuit of the one Self in all. This, indeed, is the core strength and beauty of Hindu Dharma, that it is, first and foremost, a dharma for the Yogi. Wherever and whenever the Yogi has been eclipsed by the priest or the scholar, Hindu Dharma has degenerated into ritual and dogma.

The Hindu, perhaps more than any other, must be aware of this ever-present danger. Spirituality is too high and subtle a thing for the ordinary worldly mind, and a religion or Dharma based on spirituality will always remain abstract and out of mass reach. It is, after all, much easier to catch hold of a subtle truth and turn it into a fixed belief or formula than to follow it to its spiritual source. The advantage of belief is obvious: you don't have to explore, dig deeper and discover the Truth for yourself, everything is handed down to you in convenient formulae of dogmas, and you can go about living your daily life in the world knowing that your religion and your rituals have you covered. But the fact is that belief, however deep and firm, can never be a substitute for experience and realization. Having faith in the Divine is but the first step: realizing the Divine is the next, and living the Divine in the smallest details of one's existence is the final.

Jnana

Jnana, in Hindu darshan, has a wide range of meanings. In the most superficial sense, jnana is intellectual knowledge, jnana of the *buddhi*,[71] acquired through study, reasoning, and contemplation, *swadhyaya, manan,* and *chintan*.[72]

But the jnana of the buddhi, however wide and deep it may be, is still limited and not to be regarded as an end in itself but only a stepping stone to deeper knowledge and wisdom. As the jnana of the buddhi ripens and deepens through contemplation and meditation, *nididhyasana*,[73] the mind begins to shift from its habitual thought-mode to the intuitive, and a deeper level of reality opens up for the seeker.

Intuitive knowledge differs radically from intellectual knowledge: the mind no longer acquires jnana through laborious mental logic and reasoning, which are, at best, fallible, but begins to receive luminous glimpses and insights into the nature of reality—the Zen Buddhists use the term *satori*[74] for such intuitive insight—which rapidly replaces logic and reasoning as the principal method of darshan.

But jnana can go still deeper, into the realm of psychic and spiritual knowing, direct perception and experience of reality, *anubhuti*. It is here that the method and outcome of

---

71 Buddhi (बुद्धि)—Intelligence; intellect. Used here as intellect.
72 Study, reflection, and contemplation, as explained earlier.
73 Nididhyāsana (निदिध्यासन): Fixed contemplation, the absorbed dwelling of the mind on its object.
74 Satori, Chinese Wu, in Zen Buddhism of Japan, the inner, intuitive experience of Enlightenment; Satori is said to be unexplainable, indescribable, and unintelligible by reason and logic —www.britannica.com.

darshan diverge radically from those of Western philosophy and metaphysics. The knowledge then comes no longer through the prism of the knower-known duality but through spiritual identification, where the knower becomes the known. Such knowledge by identity is largely unknown in Western philosophy but the accepted norm in Hindu darshan. It is the direct experiential understanding that turns the thinker-philosopher into a seer, a Rishi, one who possesses the capacity for darshan or pure perception. We may then say that darshan as the pursuit of knowledge and truth culminates in darshan as the direct perception of reality.

Shastras, the Scriptures

Shastra means the written word, the scriptures of Sanatan Dharma. A deep and extensive study of the shastras is an important part of *swadhyaya*, self-study, in the practice of Sanatan Dharma. This study is not meant to be merely an intellectual or academic pursuit but a thorough and systematic intellectual and psychological training of the mind of the seeker to receive and assimilate the higher knowledge of darshan and Dharma. The training proceeds from listening and reading, through discussion and debate, to rigorous contemplation and self-reflection. The training culminates in deep concentration and identification with the subject or object of study—*nididhyasana*.

Such extensive training of the mind through the study and assimilation of the shastras prepares the seeker's buddhi to receive the higher and deeper wisdom of Sanatan darshan. Note that the seeker is not expected to come to the Dharma without thorough preparation in darshan, as darshan paves the way for the true blossoming of Dharma. Without a firm grounding in the darshan and vedanta of the Dharma, the seeker is not expected to live a life of Dharma completely or effectively. A sincere will to live the Dharma is indispensable, but equally indispensable is the knowledge and understanding of the Dharma.

The emphasis on the study of the shastras, however, is not to produce learned pundits but realized seers. Therefore, the shastras, right from the word go, must lead up to *anubhava* or personal realization. In spite of a plethora of metaphysical interpretations and commentaries that exist in Hindu darshan, the unremitting focus remains on anubhava, and the scholar bows to the one with anubhava: this is the inviolable protocol. That which cannot be experienced and realized is not worth knowing. The primary purpose of the shastras in Hindu Dharma is to bring the seeker to an intuitive grasp of the profound truths of the Dharma and to open the mind to possibilities beyond mental logic and reason. The shastras themselves, the Vedas or the Upanishads, for instance, are vast bodies of mystical and spiritual literature that are fully and truly revealed only to an intuitive mind and a psychic approach.

There is a reason why the Vedas and the Upanishads were written in highly arcane, symbolic, or metaphorical language: they were never meant to be understood intellectually but were meant to be deciphered by the intuitive or the spiritual buddhi through dhyana and anubhava. The keys to the Veda and the Upanishads are not to be given by teachers or interpreters but to be found in the deeper recesses of our being. However, there have been many teachers of the Dharma who have explained and interpreted the shastras, which may benefit intellectual seekers or academic researchers but may not be good for those who seek the *paramarthika jnana* of the Dharma, for such jnana can come only through deep and intense personal engagement with the shastras as tapasya of the mind.[75]

---

75 *Tapasya* (तपस्या) is intense, concentrated yogic, spiritual, or mental discipline, askesis, to attain a desired spiritual or worldly goal. The word derives from *tapah* (तप:) meaning heat—attribute of *agni*, fire, the Vedic symbol of the atman or the psychic, that which aspires, and actively reaches, for supreme Truth. Heat is also an attribute of force or energy, concentration, focus, and intensity.

Shastra to Veda

The maharshis, as we know, did not leave any shastra or scripture to carry forth their realizations and revelations; in fact, it was expressly forbidden to note any of their revelations in writing. What they left was their *vak*, the spoken word, with its original mantric force of awakening and transforming the mind and heart of the listener: the key to transformation was in the listening, for listening itself was an act of meditation. The shastras came to be written much later, from memory. Sruti, the heard, turned first to smriti, the remembered, and then to shastra, the written. In this process, much of the original beauty and force of the vak was inevitably lost, but the essential mantric quality was retained as sound embedded in the written word, recreating the resonance of the original vak in the mind and the spirit of the seeker. This meant that the words of the shastra had to be read, enunciated in a certain specific way to awaken the mantra embedded in the sounds and the sound structure. A mental understanding was not needed.

In other words, when we would read the Vedic hymn to Agni, for instance, we wouldn't need to intellectually know the symbolism or metaphor of Agni; we would only need to read aloud the hymn in the right way, and assimilate its sound patterns and resonances, for the truth of the hymn to awaken in us. The mantric force embedded in the sound would awaken the sense of Agni in the mind, and we would intuit or even sense the truth of Agni in ourselves and would then understand the old Vedic hymn in the original spirit of the seers and poets.

I knew of a yogi who could awaken the heat of the Agni in the heart center of the listener by just reciting the hymn, and the listener would immediately understand that Agni signified the inner being seated in the heart, the source of tapas, and that which rose upward as invocation and aspiration, and all this without knowing any Sanskrit or getting any explanation of the hymn.

The shastras that we read, then, are the outer structure, the shell as it were, of the true inner shastra hidden behind the written word, as sound and sense. It is this inner shastra that we must learn to extricate through our own force of understanding, our own intellectual tapas, and when this can be done, even imperfectly at first, the outer shastra begins to recede, and an inner shastra opens itself in the deeper mind and heart. Sri Aurobindo refers to this inner shastra as the *eternal Veda secret in the heart.*[76] Though Sri Aurobindo speaks of this eternal Veda in the specific context of Integral Yoga, the vedantic Rishis also referred to an inner, intuited Veda that would unfold of itself in the depths of the yogi's mind. This intuited inner Veda is the voice of the inner Guru who dwells in every one of us but remains veiled by the incessant activities of our own minds. Once that 'voice'—one speaks here of the silent voice, the wordless voice that carries knowledge in waves of intuition, knowledge without word or thought, the *para vak* of the Rishis—is heard by the inner ear of the Yogi, all need for external knowledge and guidance drops, and the stream of divine inspiration, the Sarasvati of the Vedic Rishis, floods

---

76 The supreme Shastra of the integral Yoga is the eternal Veda secret in the heart of every thinking and living being. The lotus of the eternal knowledge and the eternal perfection is a bud closed and folded up within us. It opens swiftly or gradually, petal by petal, through successive realizations, once the mind of man begins to turn towards the Eternal, once his heart, no longer compressed and confined by attachment to finite appearances, becomes enamored, in whatever degree, of the Infinite. —*The Synthesis of Yoga*, Sri Aurobindo.
Secret in the heart: the word 'heart', in all Sanatan writings, refers to the center of one's consciousness and not the physical heart or even the heart center, *anahad.*

the mind and heart.[77] Thence, the Yogi is led directly by the wordless Veda which is the occult source of the written and recited Veda. This wordless Veda is indeed the direct guidance and inspiration of the godhead seated in the heart of every living being, variously known as *antarguru, jagadguru, Ishvara* in the Sanatan tradition.

The true purpose of the outer shastra, then, is to plough the mental terrain and prepare it to receive the flood of Sarasvati; open the rational intellect, the buddhi, to the suprarational, the mystical, the vak of the Rishis that spreads through *paramam vyomam*—transcendental space—in waves of luminous silence which only the buddhi prepared and purified by Yoga can receive and assimilate.

---

77 Sarasvati is both the river and the goddess. As a river, it is more mythical than real, though first mentioned in the *Rig Veda* as a 'powerful and holy river' that ran through large parts of northwest India; as a goddess, Sarasvati represents divine inspiration and knowledge, or in Sri Aurobindo's words, *She is, plainly and clearly, the goddess of the Word, the goddess of divine inspiration.* —*The Secret of the Veda.*

The Inner and the Outer Veda

The Veda is the highest source of all truth, the knowledge of all that is manifest or not manifest in the universe, of all that is in existence or awaits in the *brahmayoni*[78] as the infinite possibility of existence—but is this the written shastra, the hymns and mandalas that constitute the body of the Vedas or the Upanishads, or is it the veda in the heart? For there is a veda that is vyakta, expressed in sound and word, which forms the written shastra; and there is the veda that is avyakta, inexpressible in thought or word, para vak, that resonates eternally through the fabric of cosmic existence, permeating consciousness as dark energy permeates space.

The intent of the vyakta veda is not so much to inform as to invoke and evoke the avyakta veda inherent in consciousness, seeded in its depths, waiting to be called out to the surface. This calling out to the surface, making vyakta the avyakta, is the essential function of the outer veda and the Upanishads, and mantra is the device that is used for the evocation and the invocation. Sri Aurobindo says of the mantra—*the word is a sound expressive of the idea. In the supraphysical plane when an idea has to be realized, one can by repeating the word-expression of it, produce vibrations which prepare the mind for the realisation of the idea—that is the principle of the Mantra.* The key to reading the shastra is, therefore, in grasping the mantric nature of the shastra, not to read it as mere scripture for intellectual or moral edification but to approach it as dynamic

---

78 Literally, the womb of Brahman: the supreme divine creatrix out of which all existences arise, even Brahman, according to some rishis.

meditation for invoking the Spirit or the Truth within oneself, as if actually reading the words seated in the proximity of the Master, imbibing from the Master not only the import of the word but the living vibrations of the spirit. It is only then that the vyakta shastra, the remembered and the written, reverts to sruti, directly revealed as the inner veda, or 'word of God' as some of the later Vedic sages would say.

This inner veda is no ordinary spiritual knowledge, it does not come clothed in word or thought, it does not come as knowledge of this or that, it comes as pure vibrations, luminous waves, of wordless understanding from the highest supramental ranges of consciousness as *para vak*— transcendental speech.[79] The Vedic Rishis speak of four degrees or levels of speech— from the grossest, the most physical, *vaikhari*, to the subtlest, the most spiritual, *para*. *Para* (pronounced pa-rā) means both supreme and beyond, and so para vak is speech, or sound vibration, that comes from beyond the human realms. Unlike the human vaikhari, para vak is not worded, but it comes through the sovereign power of conscious will, without the vehicle of worded speech—quite easily the most effective way of transmitting and receiving higher knowledge and understanding: as Sri Ramana says, *silence is the eternal flow of language, obstructed by words.*[80]

But not all can receive para vak and know the inner veda, for these demand great purity of mind and heart, and it is the Yoga that prepares and purifies. Purity, or *suddhi*, in Sanatan Dharma, consists chiefly in eliminating dualistic and conceptual thought.

79 Vāk (वाक्) refers to speech, spoken word, and utterance. Para vak (परा वाक्), transcendental speech, the speech that issues forth from the silence of the Atman, *paramam vyomam*, transcendental space.

80 Many of Sri Ramana's closest disciples used to regularly receive his teachings, *upadesh*, from the sage through para vak. *Silence is ever-speaking*, Sri Ramana would say, *it is a perennial flow of language; it is interrupted by speaking…words obstruct the mute language…silence is the eternal flow of language, obstructed by words. What one fails to know by conversation extending to several years can be known in a trice in Silence.* —Sourced by Gabriele Ebert from talks delivered by Sri Ramana at his Ashram.

Thought, the Rishis declared, is the only impurity, *asuddhi*—eliminate thought, and you will need no other yoga or *kriya* to purify, for you will then realize the eternal purity of atman. Atman is eternally pure, *nitya suddha*, is a fundamental truth of vedantic darshan. This will be better understood if we bear in mind that the essential impurity of the mind is not so much thought as it is the I-thought.

Seeing God, the Ultimate Darshan

When Sri Ramakrishna was asked if he had actually seen God, he said yes unhesitatingly and unambiguously. This has been documented in his biographies and widely discussed amongst his disciples. Is it possible to 'see' God physically, as you would see another human? Most do not readily believe that it is. Perhaps, projection and self-suggestion? Or delusion, hallucination? Even Swami Vivekananda, who had asked Ramakrishna the question of seeing God, had initially thought it to be a kind of hallucination. There are others who believe it is possible because someone like Ramakrishna has said so, and beings like Ramakrishna do not lie or exaggerate. But then, again, it all depends on the faith of the person, and it will never be easy to pronounce anything decisive on such a matter unless it is so evidenced by personal experience, anubhava.

But what exactly did Sri Ramakrishna mean when he said that he had seen God? It would be best to recall his own description—*Do you know what I see now?* He had asked. *I see that it is God Himself who has become all this. It seems to me that men and other beings are made of leather, and that it is He Himself who, dwelling inside these leather cases, moves the hands, the feet, the heads. I had a similar vision once before when I saw houses, gardens, roads, men, cattle—all made of One substance; it was as if they were all made of wax.*

Sri Aurobindo, too, had seen God and has described his experience graphically in his famous Uttarpara Speech. *It was while I was walking that His strength again entered into me*, he said, *I looked at the jail that secluded me from men and it was no longer by its high walls that I was imprisoned; no, it was Vasudeva* [the Divine and a name for Sri Krishna] *who surrounded me. I walked under the branches of the tree in front of my cell but it was not the tree, I knew it was Vasudeva, it was Sri Krishna whom I saw standing there and holding over me his shade. I looked at the bars of my cell, the very grating that did duty for a door and again I saw Vasudeva. It was Narayana* [the Supreme Divine, and another name for Sri Krishna] *who was guarding and standing sentry over me. Or I lay on the coarse blankets that were given me for a couch and felt the arms of Sri Krishna around me, the arms of my Friend and Lover. This was the first use of the deeper vision He gave me.*

I looked at the prisoners in the jail, the thieves, the murderers, the swindlers, and as I looked at them I saw Vasudeva, it was Narayana whom I found in these darkened souls and misused bodies… When the case opened in the lower court and we were brought before the Magistrate I was followed by the same insight. He said to me, 'When you were cast into jail, did not your heart fail and did you not cry out to me, where is Thy protection? Look now at the Magistrate, look now at the Prosecuting Counsel.' I looked and it was not the Magistrate whom I saw, it was Vasudeva, it was Narayana who was sitting there on the bench. I looked at the Prosecuting Counsel and it was not the Counsel for the prosecution that I saw; it was Sri Krishna who sat there, it was my Lover and Friend who sat there and smiled.

What Sri Ramakrishna and Sri Aurobindo both describe is undoubtedly 'physical'—how much more physical can one get? But then, many would ask if these were not projections of their minds? After all, no one else around or with them was seeing God while they were. And this brings us to an important point: Sri Aurobindo did not *project* Sri Krishna onto the people around him in the jail or onto the walls, the tree, the bar and the blanket of the jail: it was Sri Krishna, omnipresent, permeating all existence, who revealed himself in the substance of the walls, the tree, the bars, the blankets, the people. Sri Ramakrishna, too, did not project anything on people around him nor did he hallucinate: again, it was the Divine that revealed itself in all beings and things to Sri Ramakrishna. In both cases, it was the will of the Divine, and, of course, the spirituality of the seers that made possible the divine vision or darshan.

The potential for divine darshan is in every living and conscious being who wants such a darshan or whom the Divine chooses for such a darshan, for it works both ways. Sri Ramakrishna, by his own accounts, intensely and persistently wanted divine darshan, especially of the goddess Kali whom he would address as 'Ma', while Sri Aurobindo, again by his own accounts, was chosen by the Divine for its darshan. And both, may I point out, were considered Avatars, or divine incarnations, by their closest disciples. And both went on to attain a stage of their yogic work where divine darshan was no longer needed, for they had themselves become the Divine—complete identification, *purna sayujya*.

But what about the rest of us, those who are not avatars? Can we, too, attain divine darshan? If we go by Sri Aurobindo and Sri Ramakrishna's teachings and writings—absolutely yes; anyone who wants it sincerely enough can have the divine darshan, even the purna sayujya, simply because of the one sovereign fact that we already are the Divine in our depths, we only need to realize that in our consciousness. *Tat twam asi*, as our Vedic maharshis had declared.

Atman, Purusha, Ishvara

Tat twam asi—that Brahman, the Divine, you yourself are, and if you yourself are that Brahman, everyone is equally that Brahman. This is the great legacy of the maharshis of Sanatan Dharma. But how to realize this mahavakya in our life and mind? Again, the maharshis say that we do not need to go to any cave in the forest to realize this or any other truth of the Dharma: it is all in the cave of the heart, in the depths of the consciousness—find the Atman, and you will attain the truth of Brahman.

Brahman reveals itself in its infinite self-becoming as Atman, the inmost universal self in all, as Purusha, the pure conscious being, and Ishvara, the Divine immanent in all existences. Finding one, we shall find the others, for these three are the modes of Brahman through which he becomes manifest to us. The Vedantin seeks Brahman in his self, the Atman, while the Yogi seeks Brahman as Purusha, the universal witnessing self behind all phenomena of mind and nature, and the devotee, the *bhakta*, seeks Brahman in Ishvara, in the personal God. But impersonal, personal, or universal, it is the attainment of Brahman that is the *anta*, the completion and culmination. But these are three modes of realizing the same Divine because the Divine manifests according to our swabhava and *sraddha*.[81] In whatever form

---

81 *Sraddha*, at one level, is deep-seated and compelling faith, a driving force of the being; and at a deeper level, it is the soul's intuitive knowing that percolates into the mental and the vital substance of our being, transforming their movements and activities, precipitating the realization.

the disciple seeks the Divine, in that very form, the Divine appears or manifests to the disciple.

The most natural and intimate form in which the disciple can seek Brahman is as oneself. It doesn't matter if the self is personal, one's ego-self, the I. This is the beauty of the non-differentiation or *abheda* darshan of vedantic Sanatan Dharma: there are no real differences once we understand the mystery of namarupa. If we follow the atma-vichara of vedanta, we can trace the I of the buddhi and prana to the essential I, the *aham* or ego, and further down (in subtlety) to its source in the self-awareness behind the namarupa.[82] Once we have come to this self-awareness behind the namarupa, we are at the threshold of the Atman. Anyone who follows through sincerely and persistently with atma-vichara will come to this threshold sooner or later. Sri Ramana used to teach only this method to attain self-realization.

It is our personal self, then, that first reveals the true Self to our inner gaze. It is when we begin to see our own personal self and personality as a veil at once concealing and revealing the true Self, and regard our very act of perception as the conscious gaze of the Atman seeing through the physical senses and knowing through the mind, that we begin to see through all the other faces and façades, and glimpse the same Atman gazing outward through all physical forms and embodiments. It is then like seeing in a different light: the face of the other becomes transparent, and we begin to see the Atman behind every face.

But the true face is not really 'behind' in a physical sense; it is, in fact, more as an expression or a presence shining through the façade of the outer face: the outer face, the rupa, is still there, but the true presence is so clear in the background that we no longer pay attention to the outer face. The outer face is a mask that becomes increasingly transparent to the growing inner

---

82 The I-thought, *ahankara* (literally, the *akara* or form/formation of the I) is present in the buddhi as the mental (*manomaya*) identification with aham, and in the prana, the life force and vitality, as the vital, *pranamaya*, identification with aham.

vision of the Atman in all forms. This is what the seers call the *atmabhava*, the sense of oneself in all and all in oneself, the final and irreversible reconciliation of multiplicity, and it is this bhava that forms the practical basis for living the Sanatan Dharma.

When the Hindu therefore says *ahimsa paramo dharma*, non-violence is the supreme dharma, he does not mean it as a moral injunction or an intellectual idea: he means it practically and concretely—since he sees the one Divine in all forms, how can he not be non-violent? The Hindu does not seek to propagate non-violence as an ideal: he seeks to eliminate the last tendency of violence, from the grossest, the most physical to the subtlest psychological, from all parts of his being; in other words, he seeks to embody *ahimsa*. Likewise, when he speaks of truthfulness and sincerity, it is not from the moralistic or intellectual standpoint at all; in these, too, he seeks to embody truth not because he has an intellectual conception of it but because he lives it in anubhava: these are facts of integral experience he lives in his everyday life.

To know Atman as this universe, in all its details, and to know the self as Brahman, and to know all other forms as the same Atman, the equal self-becoming of Brahman, is the threefold Dharma of the Hindu. This is the Dharma that was given to every human to discover and realize integrally in their being. This Dharma is the actualization of the Divine in humanity's mind, life, and body. Thus, the Sanatan Dharma knows no outsider, no alien; none can be permanently hostile to the Dharma, for in all, even in that which appears antithetical to Dharma, there dwells the same Divine Truth. Therefore, the Hindu, standing firm on the realizations of Sanatan Dharma, can say that Truth or Dharma will finally prevail—*satyameva jayate*.[83]

---

83 सत्यमेव जयते नानृतं सत्येन पन्था विततो देवयानः । येनाक्रमन्त्यृषयो ह्याप्तकामाम्म् यत्र तत् सत्यस्य परमं निधानम्म् — It is Truth that conquers and not falsehood; by Truth was stretched out the path of the journey of the gods, by which the sages winning their desire ascend there where Truth has its supreme abode. —*Mundaka Upanishad*, 3.1.6.

Those then who choose to walk the path of Dharma, not merely profess to be religious, those who can free themselves of the gravitational pull of their egoistic consciousness and give themselves in mind, heart, and body to the demands of the Dharma, those who can boldly walk the Vedic path, the *panthah ritasya*, ascending peak upon peak of human consciousness in their relentless quest for truth, knowledge, and bliss are the ones who will emerge victorious in this timeless battle of Dharma against the forces of adharma raging worldwide, in various forms and guises, even as we read this.

The Soul, Self, and Atman

We have used *Atman* extensively in this book as a foundational concept in Sanatan Dharma. Though the most common rendering of the Sanskrit *atman* in English is soul, we have used the word *Self* for atman, following a well-established convention in Vedantic writings. Note, *Self* is used with an upper-case S to distinguish it from the *self* of everyday usage in the normal psychological sense. While the English *soul* has multiple connotations, *Self* refers specifically to the essential or pure individuality behind the ego or the apparent individual, often called the true or the authentic self; it refers to the essential self-awareness behind the mental personality and identity and is not the product or fabrication of the mind's experiences and memories. This Self, or Atman, is realized when all psychological identifications and sensorial, cognitive, intellectual, and emotional distractions are systematically eliminated from the consciousness through varying depths and intensities of inner contemplation and concentration. The Atman is realized not as an object in one's consciousness—like thought, feeling, or memory, for instance—but as one's own essential being.

One realizes the Atman because one is that Atman much more intimately than one is the mind or even the body. In all spiritual and mystical literature, the Atman, or Self, is known as pure subjective consciousness free from absorption in sense, mind, and matter. Self-realization, therefore, differs radically from any known psychological or cognitive state and is not easily described in the language of the mind.

The remarkable fact about the universal belief in the Atman is that it does not, in its origin, derive from any conceptual construct. The belief expresses, in various cultural vocabularies, some of the deepest and most intense personal experiences known to human consciousness. In all cases, the experience of the Atman has been a peculiarly individual one, yet in all cultures that have a record of such experiences, there has also been a remarkable consistency of the experience. Several individuals widely separated in time and space have recorded and expressed exactly the same kind of experience in almost the same symbols and metaphors. This is interesting because it indicates that the reality of the soul is as compellingly individual as it is universal, an intensely subjective and yet completely objective realization.[84]

The *Spirit*, in the widely used words *spiritual* and *spirituality*, refers to the Atman, the Self. True spirituality, at least in Sanatan Dharma, is living in the consciousness of the Atman. In other words, one is truly spiritual when one knows the Atman and lives in its consciousness. The Atman, of course, is not so abstruse or remote that it cannot be known: it is perfectly knowable and realizable, provided one follows the right path to it.

---

84 Part of this explanation is from the author's previous book on integral education.

The Atman and the Psychic

The Atman, though one and indivisible, projects itself into the manifestation in various forms and poises—as *jivatman*, it is the central being presiding over an individual existence, poised above the evolutionary sansaric play, not descending into time, neither taking birth nor evolving, immutable and one with the supreme Brahman. As jivatma, it supports the individual manifestation from above by extending itself into a mental, vital, and physical formation known respectively as *manomaya*, *pranamaya*, and *annamaya koshas*—bodies, sheaths, or layers. Though the mental, vital, and physical sheaths are its own formations that it puts forth into the manifestation, it does not enter the evolutionary play but stays above and beyond it.

The portion of the Atman that descends into the manifestation to inwardly support the being in the material play is the *antaratman*, the Divine presence in all living beings. *Antara* means inner, so *antaratman* would mean the atman inherent in the being. But it is as the *chaitya purusha*, the psychic being, that it descends into the evolution and consents to participate in the material and evolutionary play of existence, learning, and growing as the human learns and grows through lifetimes of experiences and realizations.[85] As the psychic being,

---

85 The 'psychic being' is a term Sri Aurobindo and the Mother use for the soul so that all the cultural and religious connotations of the word 'soul' can be avoided. The psychic is the unifying and integrating center, the seat or core of our psychological being, and the eternally present spark of the Divine in the individual. When Sri Aurobindo was asked for an appropriate Sanskrit expression for the psychic being, he suggested *Chaitya Purusha*, a term already used in the Veda. However, Sri Aurobindo prefers to explain the psychic being in terms of the Vedic *Agni*, the symbol flame of the Divine, itself a godhead leading humans towards the Supreme Truth, an eternal spark of the Divine Fire in the heart of all living beings.

though timeless, beyond birth, decay, or death, it travels with the individual through its spiritual odyssey across lifetimes till it can eventually cast off its various veils and stand revealed as the divine truth of the individual.

The psychic, though the very core of the human individual, remains veiled or obscured by the activities, influences, habits, and desires of the mind, vital, and body—or the surface personality of the individual—and carries the individual upward and inward through all its experiences good, bad, or ugly, fortunate or unfortunate, pleasant or unpleasant, for in the psychic sense, every experience can be used for the growth of consciousness. As the psychic is evolutionary, it grows through lifetimes, becoming stronger and more intense: *it is the divine spark that grows into a Fire, evolving with the growth of the consciousness.*[86] And as it grows, whether through several lives or in a single life, it becomes progressively capable of coming to the front of the being and taking over the mind, life, and body entirely.

Since the psychic is beyond the processes of physical birth and death and carries all its learnings, realizations, and essential experiences across lifetimes, it becomes the single most important instrument for human evolution. Intellectual knowledge, however vast and subtle, does not have the power to bring about a lasting change of nature, a widening or deepening of the consciousness, but the psychic consciousness has the decisive, direct, and immediate power of effecting profound and irreversible changes in perception, belief, and the quality of consciousness. The psychic is the ultimate evolutionary secret that Sanatan Dharma reveals to the awakened human mind. This is the secret that the Mother and Sri Aurobindo discovered in themselves and made the pivot of their integral Yoga.[87]

---

86 Sri Aurobindo, *Letters on Yoga.*
87 See also *Atman, Jivatman, and the Psychic* by Sri Aurobindo in the Appendix.

Purusha, Prakriti, Buddhi

The concept of *purusha* and *prakriti* are of fundamental importance in the practice of Sanatan Dharma.[88] Purusha is the witnessing, conscious self behind all our psychological activities, all personal, natural, and cosmic phenomena, and prakriti is phenomena at all levels—personal, natural, and cosmic. Everything of which we are aware, everything that we can know and experience, is prakriti—the word itself means manifestation—and that in us which is aware, the conscious being behind the multitudinous play of prakriti, is purusha. Purusha, in its *para* or higher aspect, only observes prakriti but is not involved with it, while the purusha in its *apara* or lower aspect is identified and involved with the play of prakriti.[89] The bird that feeds on the bittersweet fruits of the tree in the parable of the birds represents purusha in prakriti, and the other bird that watches represents the independent, impersonal purusha,[90] and both these aspects are present in all of us, though the purusha in most of us is obscured by the ceaseless movements and activities of prakriti, just like the bottom of a lake is obscured by its surface movements.

To grow in inner consciousness, it is indispensable to learn to distinguish between the action of prakriti in us and the awareness of the purusha. In more yogic terms,

---

88 Prakriti means manifestation; purusha means self. Prakriti is referred to in the feminine as it represents an aspect of Shakti while purusha is referred to in the masculine as it represents an aspect of Ishvara.

89 'Higher' and 'lower' here refer to a hierarchy of consciousness, a higher and a lower order of consciousness.

90 See the chapter — *Atma-Vichara, Self-Reflection.*

prakriti is the field of manifestation, *kshetra,* the dynamic, ever-changing field of the mind and body, and the self—purusha—is the knower of the field, *kshetrajna.*[91] In the Gita, Sri Krishna declares the body to be the kshetra and purusha to be the kshetrajna, the knower of the field. The kshetra, being the field of prakriti or manifestation, is ever-changing and impermanent, while the purusha, as the knower of the field of manifestation, is the unchanging in the ever-changing. Thus, behind the mind and its workings is the mental or the *manomaya purusha;* and behind the vital-emotional being and its activities is the vital or the *pranamaya purusha;* there is also a physical or annamaya purusha behind the physical consciousness. But these three are the outer poises of purusha supporting the workings of the outer being—body, vital, and mind—from behind; there are also the inner purushas: the *vijnanamaya* and the *anandamaya.* The inner purushas are, however, inaccessible to our ordinary outer consciousness and can be experienced only in deeper yogic states.[92]

Prakriti binds purusha to herself by the mind's power of identification, but prakriti herself has no inherent power of binding. As long as the mind in us is identified with prakriti, purusha will be in her thrall, playing as she plays with him, a puppet moved by her strings. And here too we must understand that prakriti herself is not an inherently conscious entity: she is the constant interplay of her three gunas—*sattva, rajas,* and *tamas.* These three gunas constitute and determine all action and reaction in prakriti. What we believe to be 'our' desire or

---

91 Kshetra (क्षेत्र), field; kshtrajna (क्षेत्रज्ञ) root *jna,* to know.
इदं शरीरं कौन्तेय क्षेत्रमित्यभिधीयते । एतद्यो वेत्ति तं प्राहुः क्षेत्रज्ञ इति तद्विदः॥ महाभूतान्यहङ्कारो बुद्धिरव्यक्तमेव च । इन्द्रियाणि दशैकं च पञ्च चेन्द्रियगोचराः ॥ — This body, O son of Kunti [Arjuna], is called the Field; that which takes cognizance of the Field is called the Knower of the Field by the sages. The indiscriminate unmanifest Energy; the five elemental states of matter; the ten senses and the one (mind), intelligence and ego; the five objects of the senses. This is the constitution of the Kshetra. —Bhagavad Gita, 13.2, 13.6.
92 See the following chapter on the koshas.

'our' fear is but the automatic play of the gunas reflected in the purusha consciousness. Which guna dominates at what moment and in what manner determines our state of being: happy or sad, elated or depressed, angry or loving, generous or greedy. Nothing that we believe to be ours is really ours—all is prakriti's play: ours is only the identification.

To break purusha's identification with prakriti, the mind will need first to step back from prakriti and her play of gunas. This stepping back, or psychological disengagement, from our own processes will create a distance between the action, the field of action, and the knower of the field.

The action, which can be anything that happens in daily life, any thought, feeling, sensation, incident, or reaction to the incident, would be the action of prakriti and her gunas; the field of the action would be the consciousness of the purusha involved in prakriti; and the knower of the field and the action, the kshetrajna, would be the purusha—the witness of the action, the field of the action, as well as the effects of the action on the field. Thus, the awareness of the purusha, as kshetrajna, would be triplefold and finely nuanced, a detailed perception or witnessing of the workings of prakriti in oneself and in others.

As the yogi stations himself in the purusha-awareness, which we have also called witnessing or sakshibhava, he grows increasingly detached from prakriti and her workings and more and more aware of himself as purusha. He grows aware too of the ego as nothing more than a centralizing and self-organizing tendency in prakriti and regards the personal and universal play of the ego with growing unconcern, *udasina*, and *nirapeksha*.

As the purusha-awareness deepens, and the ego-consciousness dissolves in that deepening awareness, the yogi becomes conscious of his true identity with purusha behind the workings of the mind and the heart and grows aware simultaneously of the presence of the same purusha behind all other 'selves' in the world.

All that is in prakriti or the manifestation, all that belongs to the field of experience, everything that can be cognized, perceived, or conceived is not the Self or purusha—for the purusha is always beyond cognition and conception. The purusha itself, being the awareness within and behind prakriti, can neither be perceived by the senses nor known, conceived, or imagined by the buddhi. At best, a pure, enlightened buddhi can intuit it. Therefore, it is necessary for the yogi to cleanse, purify the buddhi, to enlighten it so that it can intuit the truth of purusha. As long as the buddhi is clouded and deluded by its sense of duality and continuity—the inherent dynamics of prakriti that keep the purusha bound to its play—the buddhi is said to be impure, *asuddha*.

In yogic practice, purification—known as *suddhikaran*—is always a cleansing of prakriti's influences from the buddhi and the prana, the intellect, and the emotions. In its asuddha or contaminated state, the buddhi is conditioned and layered by prakriti and sees and knows whatever prakriti determines in its workings—it has no identity of its own; once purified, in its suddhi, the buddhi becomes aware of purusha as the true presence behind its workings and turns towards it with growing clarity. Once the buddhi is firmly identified with purusha, instead of with prakriti, it becomes the *prakashmaya*, or enlightened, buddhi.

The prakashmaya buddhi dwells in purusha, fully aware of prakriti and her workings but no longer identified with any of it, transparent to itself, regarding all things and phenomena— events, objects, people, relations, and the world itself—as they are and not as determined by prakriti and her gunas. While in its deluded and unenlightened state, under the yoke of prakriti, the buddhi is driven by a craving for continuity and permanence, in its purified and enlightened state, the buddhi, united with purusha, is aware of the immortality of purusha and is, thus, naturally free of any kind of need or craving. In the language of the yogis, the buddhi is no longer *brastha*— gone astray, corrupted, ruined: it has returned to its source in *dhi*, the subtle, the refined intellect, the understanding that holds and organizes, where *viveka*, or spiritual discernment, replaces error and confusion, and *pratibha*, intuitive perception, replaces thought and reason.[93]

---

93 *Dhi*, in the Veda, refers to intuitive vision or inspiration through which one gets the knowledge of transcendent truth or reality; it also means visionary insight, intense thought, or reflection.

The Koshas

In Dharmic psychology, the human being is not one whole but a composite of the spiritual, psychic, mental, vital, and physical layers, or *koshas,* as known in Sanskrit.[94] Each kosha has its distinct function, capacities, and character, and each performs its own part in the complete manifestation of the human being. However, most humans are conscious of and engaged only with the outer layers or koshas of the physical, vital, and mental; very few are aware of or engaged with the inner psychic and spiritual layers.

The physical is known as the annamaya kosha, *anna* meaning food but representing matter in general. The annamaya kosha is what we are conscious of as the physical body and the sense organs, most concrete and tangible to our immediate experience. The physical consciousness occupies a major portion of our attention and concerns. But subtler than the physical and far more critical to our human existence is the vital-emotional layer, the pranamaya kosha. Prana means both life and breath, and it is the force, *prana-shakti*—literally life force—that animates the being. When a person dies, Hindus often refer to it as *prana-tyaga,* the giving up of prana. The popular yogic term *pranayama* means the control or mastery of breath.

The vital is the closest English rendering of pranamaya. It is the vital being, the pranamaya, that is the seat of all our emotions, the source of our likes and dislikes, attractions and aversions, attachments and indifferences, pleasures and

---

94 In some contexts, the *kosha* is also known as *sarira* or body. For most purposes, kosha and sarira are interchangeably used.

displeasures, excitements and depressions, enthusiasm and discouragement, hope and despair. The vital is also the source of all our ambitions, desires, self-will, and passion. Most of our creative pursuits originate in the vital-emotional being. Whenever we are conscious of our emotions, feelings, reactions, desires, or fears, we are conscious of the vital or the pranamaya, the first of the subtler sheaths we possess.

Subtler than the vital is the mental, the *manomaya kosha*. Manomaya derives from *manas* or mind. The manomaya, or the mental being, is the seat of our mental existence and activities and determines our thoughts and the functioning of the mind; this is the kosha associated with sensory perceptions, emotions, desires, memories, and thoughts. It includes the conscious and subconscious aspects of the mind and determines the quality and direction of our experiences and perceptions. Sri Aurobindo divides the mind into three differentiated functional parts—the thinking mind, dynamic mind, and externalizing mind. *The former is concerned with ideas and knowledge in their own right, the second with the putting out of mental forces for realization of the ideas, the third with the expression of them in life (not only by speech but also by any form it can give).*[95]

In the psychology of Sanatan Dharma, the mind is divided into four components—*manas, buddhi, chitta,* and *ahankara.* These four components, taken together, constitute what is known as *antahakaran,* the inner (*antar*) instruments (*karan*). In this classification, manas represents the receiving and processing aspects of the mind—all external information cognized through the senses is taken in and stored in the manas. The manas then generates thoughts, impressions, and responses to the 'perceived' world. This is typically a lower-order function of the mind. The *buddhi* represents the intellectual and discriminative aspects of

---

95 Sri Aurobindo, *Letters on Yoga.*

the mind, the typical higher-order functions. When it possesses a higher spiritual understanding, it is known as the prakashmaya, or enlightened, buddhi. *Chitta* is the repository of memories, impressions, and tendencies; it is the subconscious mind that retains all accumulated experiences and impressions from the past and perceptions and experiences of the present. *Ahankara*, literally the form or forms (*akara*) the I (*aham*) assumes in us, is our sense of individuality, our personality. Ahankara is the seat of our personal identity and the source of all our inner and outer identifications. It is only by going beyond ahankara that one can move towards the deeper realizations of the Dharma.

The teachers of the Dharma hold that the buddhi, especially the enlightened buddhi, is the instrument that leads from ignorance and ego—avidya and ahankara—to Truth and Dharma. It is for this reason that the buddhi needs to be cultivated, honed, and raised in its inherent quality of reasoning and intuition.

The *Katha Upanishad* equates the human body to a chariot pulled by horses which represent the senses and, therefore, need to be reined in by the charioteer; the mind represents the reins, and the buddhi is the charioteer; the passenger of the chariot represents the Atman, the Self.[96] This analogy clearly illustrates that the true self, Atman, is separate from the body, senses, and mind, and it is the buddhi that must be the master of the senses and the body. In the words of the Upanishad—*But the man who has a discriminating intellect for the driver and a controlling mind for the reins, reaches the end of the road, that highest place of Vishnu, the Divine.*[97]

---

96 आत्मानँ रथितं विद्धि शरीरँ रथमेव तु । बुद्धिं तु सारथिं विद्धि मनः प्रग्रहमेव च ॥ इन्द्रियाणि हयानाहुर्विषयाँ स्तेषु गोचरान् ।आत्मेन्द्रियमनोयुक्तं भोक्तेत्याहुर्मनीषिणः ॥ — Know the body for a chariot and the soul for the master of the chariot: know Reason for the charioteer and the mind for the reins only. The senses they speak of as the steeds and the objects of sense as the paths in which they move; and One yoked with self and the mind and the senses, as the enjoyer, say the thinkers. —*Katha Upanishad*, 1.3.3-4.

97 विज्ञानसारथिर्यस्तु मनःप्रग्रहवान्नरः। सोऽध्वनः पारमाप्नोति तद्विष्णोः परमं पदम् ॥ —*Katha Upanishad*, 1.3.9.

Subtler and higher in consciousness than even the prakashmaya buddhi is the *vijnanamaya kosha*, the knowledge-body. The knowledge of the vijnanamaya is not intellectual but supramental. In the vijnanamaya, one possesses the Truth-consciousness, Rta-chit, of the Vedic Rishis. Subtler than the vijnanamaya is the *anandamaya koshu*, the bliss or delight body, representing Satchidananda.

The annamaya kosha, being the grossest, constitutes the *sthula-sarira* or the gross body, while the manomaya and pranamaya, being subtler than the annamaya, constitute the *sukshma-sarira* or subtle body. The subtlest vijnanamaya and anandmaya koshas constitute the *karana-sarira* or causal body. Though classified differently, these sheaths or layers are continuous and progressive, a kind of gradation of consciousness. Sri Aurobindo describes it thus—*There is in fact no gap in man's sheaths. It is a gamut or scale ascending from the lowest to the highest plane; and the principle of each is repeated in all. Thus all is in each. Otherwise the world cannot go on.*[98]

---

98 Sourced from the *Evening Talk with Sri Aurobindo* by A.B. Purani.

The Truth and the Vast

The simple mantra for all those who would live a dharmic life on earth is expressed in one line—*satyam vada, dharmam chara.* Speak the truth and abide in Dharma. But this is not as simple as it may sound. Before we speak the truth, we must know the truth; and before we abide in the Dharma, we must know the Dharma.

At a very preliminary level, perhaps for young children, satyam vada can simply mean speak the truth, do not lie; and dharmam chara can simply mean do the right thing. But as life gets increasingly complex, the questions of truth and right action also get equally complex—what is truth, and what is right action? At one level, truth is as simple as self-evident and obvious fact: what you see and feel is what you express, and right action is doing what you feel is the right thing to do.

But when situations and circumstances are no longer simple and obvious, and when truth itself gets too nuanced, complex, and subtle, then how does one know what truth to speak and what right action to undertake? The whole of the Mahabharata revolves around such questions, and no one seems to have the final answer, perhaps because the final answer is not in mentally knowing what truth to speak or what right action to follow in which circumstance, but in the realization of Truth itself, of growing into what the Rishis call Rta-chit, Truth-consciousness. But this Truth is absolute and immutable and must first express itself in terms of the manifestation for it to be grasped and followed. At its transcendental heights, it cannot be known or possessed.

Thus, in the cosmic manifestation, this absolute Truth, Sat, becomes *Satyam-Ritam*, absolute Truth expressing itself in terms of cosmic existence and evolution. While Satyam is the pure and exact expression of Sat, Ritam is the actualization of Satyam or Satyam in action. As Ritam, Satyam becomes dynamic and creative and possesses the power to impose the law of Satyam in the manifestation. But Satyam-Ritam, by their own expression and action, are still not enough to attain Rta-chit. Rta-chit is the consciousness and power of the Supreme Truth. To attain the Truth-consciousness, we must also grow in consciousness, break out of the limits of ego and personality, time and circumstance, and become as vast as the Truth we seek to possess—for Truth is vast, and so the knower of Truth must be equally vast.

This vast is known as *Brihat* in the Veda and is the third term of the triune Vedic formula of ascension to Truth: Satyam-Ritam-Brihat.[99] Brihat shares the same etymological root, *brh*, with Brahman—both represent vastness, an infinite expansion. Vastness also means height. With the expansion of consciousness, there also comes a heightening of consciousness. The higher we climb on the scale of consciousness and being, the more Truth we see and know.

Satyam, then, is the expression of Sat, absolute Reality or Truth, in the cosmic manifestation and is therefore evolutionary, not immutable. It grows—widens, heightens, and deepens—as the consciousness grows. To express satyam in our thought, speech, and action then is not immediately possible. What is known and felt to be true today may not be the truth of tomorrow: what we perceive and believe to be real here and now

---

99 Satyam-Ritam-Brihat, सत्यमृतंबृहत् or सत्यम्-ऋतम्-बृहत् —*Atharva Veda*, 12.1.1. The original verse is सत्यं बृहदृतमुग्रं दीक्षा तपो ब्रह्म यज्ञः पृथिवीं धारयन्ति — Truth (satyam), the cosmic order (ritam), and the Vast and mighty (brihat) initiations, austerities, and sacrifices (yajna) to the Divine (Brahman) by the Sages have sustained Mother Earth for ages. (Author's rendering.)

will inevitably change in another setting and time. The more our consciousness grows, the more of truth we shall perceive and know. The more our knowledge and understanding grow, the more nuanced and subtle our truth-perception grows. Thus, as the teachers of Dharma always say, we have to keep expanding our horizons, perception, and our knowledge. We have to grow larger in ourselves, vaster in our being. This is the dimension of brihat, the vast. Unless we grow vast in our being, we cannot possess or express much of Truth. The truths of a small consciousness will inevitably be limited, while the truths of a higher and wider consciousness will always be more comprehensive and more nuanced. Sri Aurobindo once wrote, *till all is known, nothing is known*. This beautifully sums up the issue: an all-comprehensive consciousness alone can have all-knowledge and possess the whole Truth. Till then, we are all wayfarers to Truth.

When we possess the vaster consciousness, then we have the vaster knowledge and understanding of Truth, and then whatever we think and do is right, in alignment with Dharma. When we possess the brihat, action proceeds directly towards satyam, which is the exact working of ritam, for ritam is the right action that flows from undistorted or unobstructed satyam.

It is thus that Sat and Dharma grow in our being through the action of satyam and ritam in a consciousness ever expanding, ever deepening. Or rather, it is not Sat and Dharma that grow but our capacity for Sat and Dharma.

Only when we have attained the Truth within ourselves, when we have known Sat and Dharma intimately, as movements and extensions of our own consciousness, will we truly be able to fulfill the simple injunction of the Vedic rishis—*satyam vada, dharmam chara*—without any complexity or confusion. Satyam will no longer need to be 'practiced', it will be as natural to us as breathing; and Dharma will no longer need to be followed, we ourselves will be embodiments of Dharma, perfect living expressions of Satyam-Ritam-Brihat.

Dharma and Moksha

The Vedic Rishis laid out for the seekers of Truth a fourfold aim of life, known in Sanatan Dharma as the four *purusharthas*—*kama*, *artha*, *dharma*, and *moksha*. These are not four developmental stages but simultaneous objectives of human life. Kama is related to desire, fulfillment of desire, the fullness of vital-emotional existence, expansion of self through the pursuits and fulfillments of worldly existence, and the celebration of beauty, love, and companionship. Without kama, life would be a dreadful chore and burden, and thus, kama is considered to be the *rasa* of human life. Unfortunately, there is no English word for rasa: think of delight, sweetness, flavor, or enjoyment, and you have an approximate sense of rasa. When you deeply enjoy music, art, poetry, the beauty of the human form, and the beauty of nature, you are experiencing rasa. Hindu Dharma considers the pursuit of rasa as essential to the fullness of life on earth, and even spirituality would be an incomplete thing without the experience of rasa, or *rasanubhuti,* as we would say in Sanskrit. Rasanubhuti is the essence of kama.

But the rasa of life would be incomplete without *artha*, the second purushartha. Artha refers to wealth in all its forms—material, physical, intellectual, emotional, and spiritual. Wealth, of course, is not just money (money is a particular symbol of wealth) but integral wellbeing, prosperity, the sense of fullness and fulfillment. The true Sanatan Dharma does not reject wealth or glorify poverty, as commonly and erroneously believed: it celebrates wealth in all its forms, and what it rejects is the poverty of consciousness. One can live frugally, like a monk, but there need be no sense of poverty in that, it is the consciousness that must be full, overflowing with life force, beauty, generosity, and joy—this is the meaning of artha in Hindu Dharma. To be wealthy is to live in wealth-consciousness, a consciousness of prosperity and well-being, and it matters little whether or not one possesses the visible trappings of wealth.

But the secret of fulfillment and fullness of existence is in living the four purusharthas simultaneously—kama and artha in the constant pursuit of Dharma, the truth of being and becoming, and moksha, unalloyed freedom in the highest bliss. It is Dharma that gives the higher orientation to kama and artha, for without Dharma, kama can easily degenerate into lust and selfish pleasure-seeking and artha into crass consumerism and greed. It is Dharma alone that orients life to moksha, the ultimate end of human existence. Moksha, as the final end of human existence, does not mean self-extinction but a liberation into the eternal and immutable bliss of Brahman—*ananda*.

In a truer Dharmic sense, therefore, kama, artha, dharma and moksha blossom finally into ananda.

Sat, Chit, Shakti, and Ananda

Sat, as the Vedic Rishis have revealed, is absolute Reality, the sole Self-existent on which all other existences stand. *All things*, declares the Rishi, *stand upon Sat, but Sat stands upon nothing.* All things in existence refer to Sat, but Sat exists only in reference to itself. But Sat, to refer to itself, even in its absolute sense, must have the inherent attribute of self-consciousness. If existence were not conscious of itself, it would need to depend on some other reality besides itself to make it real to itself. But this, as the Rishis say, is not so—Sat is self-illumined and, therefore, Sat is also *Chit*, absolute consciousness, and the primary term of existence is therefore Sat-Chit and not Sat or Chit alone.

But consciousness is not static but dynamic, not immutable but evolving—it possesses an intrinsic *shakti*, or creative force, that evolves and expands; and therefore, it is Chit-Shakti, creative consciousness and force. Thus, we now find that our primary reality is Sat and Chit-Shakti, existence and dynamic, omnipotent creative consciousness—*Sat-Chit-Shakti*.

The Vedas declare Sat to be the ultimate, the supreme, beyond which there is nothing. For anything to be beyond Sat, it must pass out of Sat or existence and become *Asat*—non-manifest. Asat, though commonly understood as non-real may not inevitably be non-real: it is also non-manifest, avyakta. That which is not manifest is not real, therefore, *asat*. In the simple Vedic scheme, then, there is Sat, the Real, and there is Asat, the not real or not manifest. Between these—*Sat* and *Asat*—lies the spread of our entire cosmic and psychic experience. Asat, being not real or unmanifest, is known only by the absence of Sat, as darkness is only known by the absence of light. But light and darkness are relative to perception; in the absence of perception—or the capacity to perceive—darkness and light would both lose value. So, it is for Sat and Asat—these are relative to consciousness; consciousness alone lends value to Sat and Asat. Therefore, it is said that Sat is Chit, or being is also consciousness of being.

There is then the higher and subtler reality of *Satchidananda*—a continuum of Sat, absolute being, Chit, absolute consciousness, and Ananda, absolute bliss or delight. Chit being creative, dynamic, and evolutionary, leads existence ever upward, through endless evolutionary spirals, towards Satyam and Sat. It is this upward ascent of existence through consciousness, Sat through Chit, that gives this manifestation its third fundamental term, *ananda*. *Ananda* in Sanskrit means bliss or delight. Ananda is the natural expression of existence ascending through consciousness towards its own highest summits. The very movement upward is one of delight, just as any movement downward, away from the heights of consciousness, is one of shrinking, misery, *nirananda*.[100]

---

100 Without delight, the absence of ananda.

Satyam and Its Knowledge

Satyam is the expression of Sat in the manifestation. Sat by itself is absolute and unknowable and can only be known by its manifest expression as Satyam. All that exists in the universe are terms, derivations, and gradations of Satyam. All things in existence are known and defined by Satyam. Thus it is said that all things are made manifest in the light of Satyam.

But Satyam too is an abstraction, a representative term for something that cannot be directly or objectively known or comprehended by the mind. When we use the word truth, we usually associate it with the truth of *something*. But Satyam is not a truth of anything, it is Truth itself, absolute. Absolute Truth, like absolute Being, is unknowable to the objective mind. In other words, as long as there is 'knower' wanting to know Truth, it cannot be known.

The logic is simple: all things are made manifest in the light of Satyam, but Satyam, being an expression of Sat, is not made manifest, nor known or defined, by anything outside of itself. How then can any 'knower' know Satyam? Satyam therefore is said to be beyond objective knowledge, beyond the duality of knower and the known.

However, Satyam can be known subjectively. If we accept the Dharmic dictum that all is Satyam—*sarvam satyam*[101]— and Satyam alone exists, then it implies that consciousness is Satyam and the conscious mind seeking Satyam too is Satyam. This then changes the equation: Satyam is no longer

---

101 All (sarvam) is Truth (satyam).

out there, high and mighty, remote and inaccessible, but it is what we are, intimately, through and through. *We are Satyam.* To know Satyam, we only have to know ourselves. This is the profound import of self-realization in the Dharma—realize the self, and you will realize Satyam. There is nowhere to go, no temple or pilgrimage is needed, and no teacher or scripture can take you there: it is all about how deep you delve within your consciousness. All Dharmic scriptures and philosophies, all gurus and their revelations, serve only one purpose: to point the way to the Truth. Truth, itself, is pathless.

But not all of Satyam is at once revealed or knowable. The knowledge or realization of Satyam is progressive. There are two aspects of Satyam—*avyakta* and *vyakta*. *Vyakta* literally means that which is manifest or expressed. Therefore, *avyakta* is that which is not manifest or expressed. But this needs to be understood. Not-manifest does not necessarily mean nonexistent. Truth, manifest or not, never ceases to exist: by definition, it is always and everywhere. Truth that ceases to exist, even for the tiniest fraction of time, wouldn't be Truth at all. Therefore, avyakta Satyam is that which is not expressed in consciousness, it exists in a state prior to consciousness. In other words, it exists, but there is no one conscious of it. The manifestation of Truth is necessarily the consciousness of it. If I am not conscious of something, it is not manifest for me. If I am not wholly conscious of it, it is not wholly manifest for me. Therefore, the evolution of consciousness is the unfolding of Truth, Truth becoming more and more manifest.

Karma, Death, and Rebirth

The concepts of karma, death, and rebirth are fundamentally important in Sanatan Dharma, and no discussion on the Dharma can be complete without understanding these in some depth. There has been much debate amongst scholars and philosophers about these concepts, and no one seems to know for sure what the facts really are.

Most Hindus grow up believing that the human soul, atman, is eternal and indestructible, but it takes multiple births in an endless cycle of reincarnations, also known as the *wheel of samsara*. There is no escaping this wheel of samsara as long as one's karmas are not all exhausted or one understands the whole karmic machinery and gets out of it by attaining moksha through personal sadhana. Attaining moksha through sadhana does not mean short-circuiting karma but accelerating it till all of it, or almost all of it, is quickly exhausted, for there is karma accumulated over lifetimes and brought to surface in the present lifetime—*prarabdha* karma—that cannot be avoided or exhausted, but perhaps somewhat mitigated by divine Grace.[102]

Accumulated karma is what drives the wheel of samsara. As we live and act in this lifetime, so we determine our next— intentions and actions in harmony with Dharma lead to

---

102 There are four kinds of karma: *sanchita,* which is karma accumulated over several lifetimes, *prarabdha,* which is karma ripe for exhaustion, *kriyamana,* which is karma still in the process of formation, and *agami,* karma which is still to be formed. The analogy used by the teachers of Dharma is that of the *tarash,* the case in which arrows are accumulated, and the arrows of karma. Tarash represents the sanchita; the arrow that is ready for discharge represents the agami; and the arrow which has already left the bow and must strike the target represents the prarabdha.

'good karma' in the present or future lives, and intentions and actions violating Dharma lead to 'bad' or 'negative' karma in this or future lives. At least, this is the popular understanding of karma and karmic cycles. This, however, seems a superficial understanding as it raises a pertinent question: where and how does it all begin? If my present life is the result of the karmas of my past lives, and I'm living a 'good life' because of 'good karma' in past lives, and another is living a 'bad life' because of 'bad karma' in past lives, where would it all have started? At what point in time or causation would the one and universal soul divide itself along two divergent directions of evolution and progress along the lines of good and bad karma? This is something no school of darshan has managed to resolve satisfactorily, and different teachers and sages have taken different approaches, ranging from an entire acceptance of the law of karma to an entire rejection. The Charvaks, for instance, did not accept karma or rebirth—*punarjanma na vidyate*, they declare;[103] while Krishna states emphatically to Arjuna—*na tvevaham jatu nasa na tvam*—it is not true that at any time I was not, nor you, nor these; nor is it true that any of us shall ever cease to be hereafter.[104] And both these approaches are equally accepted by Sanatan Dharma. Is there a perspective that reconciles these two?

A resolution to this issue is found in the deeper vedantic darshan of Sanatan Dharma—that we are neither the body nor the mind but Atman in essence and substance, and the whole purpose of existence is to realize the Atman and not to seek escape routes from karma and samsara. Whoever understands this will neither accept nor reject karma and rebirth but concentrate solely on self-realization, atmajnana, for he would know that it is in atmajnana that the true resolution of karma and samsara is to be found, and when self-realization comes,

---

103 पुनर्जन्म न विद्यते — rebirth does not exist.
104 The Bhagavad Gita, 2.12.

it liberates not from karma and samsara but from the ideas of karma and samsara—one realizes that the Atman is, and has always been, free and pure—*nitya-mukta, nitya suddha*[105]— one neither needs to remain in the cycles of birth and death nor escape from it. There is, indeed, nothing to escape from: there is no samsara, no cycle of birth, death, and rebirth in the final analysis, for the Atman, being eternal and immutable, neither comes nor goes, is neither born nor decays or dies, is above and beyond time and causation, eternally free, exactly as Sri Krishna explains to Arjuna. As Swami Vivekananda once asked: *How can there be mortality when there is no birth?* Finally, then, all these ideas of karma and rebirth are concepts of the mind and disappear once the truth of the atman is known. This is the crux of the Dharma.

Those who believe that the Atman leaves, or transmigrates, when the body dies have only grasped a partial and relative, vyavharika, truth: the paramarthik or spiritual truth is simpler— the soul does not leave the body for it was never *in* the body—it was the body or the body-idea that was a formation in the soul. When death, or what we humans believe to be death, occurs, the body drops off, as it were, resolves into its fundamental elements, the *panchbhutas*, while the individual mind and the vital being resolve into the universal mental and vital substance, much like a river merges and dissolves into the sea. The interesting thing to note is that nothing really remains of the individual to actually 'die'. The Atman, being beyond matter and time, neither takes birth nor dies, and the physical, mental, and vital sheaths simply disintegrate and return to the universal.[106]

---

105 *Nitya* means eternally, *mukta* means free, and *suddha* means pure—this is a fundamental thought in Sanatan Dharma, that the soul is eternally free and pure.

106 This is, however, not universally true. Yogis and Rishis may have highly integrated mental or vital bodies that do not disintegrate at death but can be carried consciously to the next birth. However, such matters are beyond the scope of our present discussion.

The Four Stages of Life

Sanatan Dharma divides human life into four stages or *asramas*—*brahmacharya*, when one is a student, *grihasta*, when one is a householder, *vanaprastha*, or the stage of the forest dweller, and *sannyasa*, the stage of complete renunciation. Each of these stages or asramas is estimated to last about 25 years, with brahmacharya starting about the age of five when the child is ready to leave family and home and live with the Guru in his or her ashram, known traditionally as the *Gurukula*, literally, community or family of the Guru. This is at least the generally understood and accepted tradition though I do not know of any modern-day Hindu who follows or wants to follow this tradition anymore. However out of fashion this tradition may now be, I strongly feel that it needs to be understood in its deeper context and brought back into popular practice. The division of human life into the four asramas is an eminently pragmatic and intelligent system that, if followed widely, can restore balance and sanity to our presently chaotic, crowded, and stressful social order.

Let's start with the first asrama of brahmacharya. This stage is usually from the age of five, when the child is ready to live with the Guru in his community or home, to about twenty-five, when he or she is ready to commence their worldly sansaric life, the life of the grihastha or the householder. Brahmacharya, in its original and deeper sense, is not just a period of academic study but an intensive and extensive integral training in all aspects of human life—physical, vital-emotional, intellectual, and spiritual. Physical training would include learning and mastering various physical skills like gymnastics, athletics, martial arts, dance, swimming, climbing, boating, and charioting. It would also include manual skills like carpentry, weaving, stitching, cooking, pottery, and drawing. Remarkably, this kind of integral training was never gender-specific, and all the arts could be learnt by anyone regardless of gender or social background.

The vital-emotional training would include awareness and mastery of emotions, the practice of self-control, strengthening of the will, leadership skills, organization and management, managing interpersonal relationships, arts and music, dance and theatre, and the experience of the rasas and aesthetics. The aim was always to make young men and women of noble character prepared for a full experience of life and oriented to a higher spiritual or Dharmic objective in all spheres of life.

The mental and intellectual training would include intensive study of all disciplines—the Vedas and the Upanishads, sciences and mathematics, grammar and linguistics, language and literature, mythology and psychology—and the aim again was a comprehensive education of the mind and heart. The students were trained in self-reflection and contemplation, reasoning and analysis, discussion and debate, and sustained enquiry into the meaning of existence.

Spiritual and yogic training would begin early and would progressively deepen with the years. There would be strict yogic regimens to develop austerity, self-control, and purity in every student, regardless of gender and background. Intellectual training of the mind would also deepen in all aspects into spiritual training, and the students would learn the psycho-spiritual disciplines of concentration, meditation, and detachment under the direct supervision of the Guru or his advanced disciples.

Here, too, what is remarkable is the fact that spiritual and intellectual training was given to everyone, whether brahmin, kshatriya, vaishya, or shudra. There was no rigid birth-based caste system in the original Sanatan Dharma: after a comprehensive integral education, the student could choose any mode of life or activity in accordance with his or her swadharma and the guidance of the Guru. Every occupation, profession, or mode of life was equally respected.

Obviously, by the time the student completed their brahmacharya stage, they would be highly proficient, self-conscious, disciplined, and focused individuals—perhaps, the best of their kinds—integrally prepared for a noble and dharmic life as a grihastha. The grihastha, or the householder, was expected to live the purusharthas of kama and artha—desire and wealth. This was the stage meant for marriage and family, though that was always optional. If a grihastha was keen enough to continue developing spiritually, he or she would have the freedom to opt out of marriage and family and return to the Guru for sadhana.[107]

But the grihastha who would choose to live the householder's life would then be expected to marry and raise children, build up wealth and prosperity for self and community, and work in the spirit of Yoga towards personal excellence and social well-being. The object of work was never to earn a livelihood, as it is now, but to add value to oneself, to one's community, and to all humanity—the true aim of all works was *jagat kalyana*, universal welfare. There was a reason for such expectations: the spiritual guardians of society, the Rishis and the acharyas, knew well that it was easy to lose oneself in the mazes of samsara; greed and possessiveness, ambition and attachment, come too readily and easily to the grihastha. In order to safeguard themselves from the obvious pitfalls of sansaric life, the grihastha was always reminded to keep their eyes always on the larger picture, the

---

107 It was, of course, not mandatory for a *brahmachari*, or student, to leave the Gurukula at all if they chose not to. There are numerous instances of young men and women who would stay on at the ashrams of their gurus and continue with spiritual and yogic training. There would also be students who would take the vow of brahmacharya—lifelong austerity—and go on to become gurus in their own right.

cosmic scheme, and the higher goals of Dharma and Moksha. To live the sansaric life with one's vision narrowed to the immediate was not an option; the aim was always the higher and the highest. This was essential to prepare the grihastha for the next stage of life—vanaprastha.

Vanaprastha is the stage of the 'forest dweller', one who departs into the forests, but this need not be taken literally. The forest is a metaphor for the ashram, the hermitage, which represents detachment. It is, in fact, a metaphor for detachment. At the vanaprastha stage, the grihastha is expected to progressively give up their worldly duties and obligations and start weaning themselves away from home and family. It is not renunciation yet but gradual withdrawal. Everything about this stage is gradual and progressive. To give up our emotional attachments to family and friends, to detach from all that was of value and significance for so many years, is never easy, even for the best of us. Our strongest attachments are to our children and grandchildren. Yet, this is the stage where we have to let go of these attachments and step back from active life, turn more and more to solitude and meditation, to the study of the shastras and self-reflection—in many ways, a return to the brahmacharya years. This is the stage where the husband or wife, father or mother, becomes increasingly the patriarch or the matriarch, in the background, more of a witness than an active participant, learning detachment the only way it can most effectively be learnt—in the experiences and events of everyday family life.

If all goes well, the vanaprastha gradually moves towards the final sannyasa, and there comes a time when the vanaprastha-grihastha realizes that they are no longer too involved with home and family, friends and society, desires or ambitions, that they are free of the old bonds and attachments and have attained a certain degree of stable detachment and peace. This is the stage at which sannyasa happens naturally and effortlessly. And this is an important point—sannyasa must happen naturally and effortlessly; it cannot be forced, rushed, or precipitated artificially. Sannyasa should be like the falling off of dried leaves from a tree—one shouldn't even notice it is happening.

Sannyasa itself, as a stage or state of being, is widely misunderstood or understood very superficially. It is not as simple as walking away from the world, for however far one walks, one can always carry the world with oneself. The real sannyasa is the inner renunciation of ego and possessiveness, of ahankara and asmita, the dissolution of personality and identifications, and the transcendence of the dualities. The sannyasi is one who is firmly established in samata and no longer regards the play of the world as real; all attention is given to moksha, to liberation from avidya and mithya, and finally, to atmajnana.

If one can attain this state within oneself, it matters little whether one continues to live in society or retires to the forest, whether one eats the food of the grihastha or the diet of the renunciant, whether one wears the garments of the grihastha or the garb of the sadhu. In fact, to the real sannyasi, nothing of namarupa matters.

The Ten Attributes of Dharma

Dhṛtiḥ kṣamā damo'steyaṃ śaucamindriyanigrahaḥ |
Dhīrvidyā satyamakrodho daśakaṃ dharmalakṣaṇam.[108]

Manusmriti—also known as *Manav Dharma Shastra*, teachings on human dharma—speaks of *dashakam dharma lakshanam*, the ten attributes of dharma: *dhriti, ksama, dama, asteyam, saucham, indriyanigraha, dhi, vidya, satyam,* and *akrodha*. Whoever possesses these ten attributes of dharma, embodies Dharma.

Dhriti is the first. From the same root *dhri* as in Dharma, it means fortitude, forbearance, steadiness or *dhairya*, the capacity to bear or hold. *One who possesses dhriti*, Manu declares, *is set on the path of Dharma*. But dhriti is a yogic quality, similar to the equality—samata—of the Gita, and one would need first to develop the qualities of contentment, *tripti*, and detachment, *vairagya*, in order to establish dhriti in one's being.

The first requirement to develop all these inner qualities is to slow down the being. One of the implications of dhriti is an absence of agitation, restlessness, and impatience; all agitation and impatience arise from either desire or frustration of desire. Thus, a firm control over desire would be eminently desirable for the disciple of the Dharma. The Bhagavad Gita, of course, develops this further into complete desirelessness, *naishkamya*, as a necessary condition for spiritual life.

Kshama, forgiveness, is the next attribute. The opposites of kshama are hurt, anger, and resentment, whether expressed or

---

108 The ten attributes of dharma — धृतिः क्षमा दमोऽस्तेयं शौचमिन्द्रियनिग्रहः। धीर्विद्या सत्यमक्रोधो दशकं धर्मलक्षणम् । —Manusmriti, 6.92.

suppressed, and all of these arise inevitably from the hurt ego. If we have internalized the truth of oneness, the non-duality of vedanta darshan, then the hurt ego is no longer possible; in fact, no egoism is possible. The state of kshama then arises effortlessly: what is there to condemn or punish when there is no one to blame?

Sri Krishna tells Arjuna in the Gita—*prakritim yanti bhutani nigrahah kim karishyati*[109]—all beings are driven by their own natures, what then is the use of coercion, resistance, reaction? This, if truly understood and internalized, can liberate us in a trice from all personal reactions of hurt, anger, resentment, self-righteousness, and all the rest of negative emotions that we bear for others; and then alone the mind becomes imperturbable, even when wronged or hurt. Kshama then complements dhriti.

Once kshama and dhriti are firmly established in the being, we can develop the attribute of *akrodha*, freedom from anger.[110] Anger, in fact, would be impossible once the quality of kshama develops in the being, for anger always arises from the hurt ego, frustrated desire, or fear. The qualities of dhriti and kshama destroy the very seeds of anger in the mind. However, there is also the self-righteous anger we experience against perceived injustice, wrongdoing, adharma[111]—should one let go of that too? Dharma is not static or dogmatic, therefore, such questions are difficult to answer. The whole epic of Mahabharata revolves around the nuances and subtleties of dharma and its attributes.

But dhriti, kshama, or akrodha are not possible without *dama*, self-control, which is yet another attribute of Dharma. Dama, self-

109 सदृशं चेष्टते स्वस्याः प्रकृतेर्ज्ञानवानपि। प्रकृतिं यान्ति भूतानि निग्रहः किं करिष्यति। —Bhagavad Gita, 3.33.
110 In the verse from Manusmriti quoted at the beginning of the chapter, *akrodha* is mentioned as the tenth attribute, following satyam.
111 The absence of dharma (a-, used as negation, dharma).

control, often begins in the mind and the vital and involves self-discipline, self-denial, and austerity, but progressively it deepens into spiritual mastery and understanding. Dama is the ability to hold back the outgoing impulses and energies of the vital and the movements of the mind. In a deeper sense, dama involves *brahmacharya*—the in-gathering of mind and heart, the retention of the life force within, and the inner concentration on Atman.

Asteyam, literally, non-stealing, goes beyond the mere act of stealing and implies the non-appropriation of what does not belong to ourselves. But it does not stop at that: asteyam also implies not taking for entirely selfish ends. Nothing in the universe belongs to us, not even our own physical bodies or the air we breathe: everything comes from Brahman, is Brahman, and returns to Brahman, thus whatever is given to us or taken by us must be done in a spirit of giving, sacrifice, yajna. The asteyam then develops into *aparigrah*—nothing is looked upon as a personal belonging, no grasping, no greed. Sri Krishna says clearly in the Gita—*fostered by sacrifice, the gods will grant you all the desired enjoyments of life; but those who enjoy what is given to them without offering to the gods, he is a thief.*[112] Asteyam, then, leads to the profound Vedic concept of cosmic existence being an endless yajna—as the gods foster the human by sacrifice, the humans too must foster the gods by sacrifice.

And then is *saucham*, purity. In the simplest sense, saucham is physical and environmental cleanliness, both indispensable conditions for spirituality in Sanatan Dharma. But deeper than that is purity and cleanliness of mind and heart, purity of attitude and intention, purity of thought and speech. Whosoever works towards inner purity will inevitably be outwardly pure as well. But saucham is also yogic, spiritual—an absence of desire, fear, and repulsion; freedom from duality, freedom from asmita and

---

112 इष्टान्भोगान्हि वो देवा दास्यन्ते यज्ञभाविताः।तैर्दत्तानप्रदायैभ्यो यो भुङ्क्ते स्तेन एव सः॥   —Bhagavad Gita, 3.12.

ahankara. In the deepest Dharmic sense, purity is transparence, and complete purity is complete transparence.

Indriyanigraha is another important attribute of dharma. If aparigrah is non-possession, non-grasping, indriyanigraha is non-attachment to the objects of the senses, non-attraction to the external, and withdrawal of the senses into the buddhi. This is essential for any kind of spiritual progress as the chief obstacle in the inner journey is the habitual distractions of the sense-mind. Without indriyanigraha, neither saucham nor asteyam would be entirely possible.

But none of these attributes is really possible without viveka, clear discrimination between the real and the apparent, true and the false, and the many shades between the two. *Dhi* is the attribute of dharma that represents clarity of mind and perception, clarity of intelligence, discrimination, and right understanding. Dhi is pure intelligence, unclouded by desire, fear, prejudice, and ego. Once dhi is developed, the disciple can attain complete clarity of perception and understanding, whether in the transactional vyavharika world or in matters of the higher adhyatmika.

With the development of dhi, we can progress to the next higher attribute of Dharma, *vidya*. Vidya is spiritual knowledge, self-knowledge, *atmajnana*. With vidya and dhi, the disciple passes beyond all incomplete and imperfect knowledge and judgment, all stumbling and errors, all perturbations of mind and heart, and comes to peace which is itself the attribute of jnana and vidya. Purna or complete vidya results in *purna shanti*, perfect peace that nothing and none can disturb. It is in that state that the disciple can attain the *purna samata* and the condition of *sthitaprajna* of the Gita.

And then comes the attribute of *satyam*, the integral expression of Sat in life, mind, and body. Whatever we do then is right, just, and good. All our thoughts, speech, and actions are in perfect harmony with Rta, and our very existence becomes an embodiment of Dharma.

The Yugas and the Stages of Dharma

Kaliyuga, in Sanatan Dharma, is the last of the four ages of Dharma. There are four stages of the rise and fall of Dharma, each corresponding to a *yuga* or epoch. The first yuga is known as the Krita[113] or Satyayuga, the epoch of Truth, where Dharma stands on the four pillars of austerity, purity, compassion, and truth—*tapas, saucha, daya, satya*. These four pillars give Dharma its fullness of strength, stability, and completeness. In the rich Vedic symbology, Dharma is visualized as a bull, symbolizing life force and virility, that stands on all four legs in the Kritayuga and loses its legs one by one as time moves entropically towards the Kaliyuga, where it manages to stand on only one of its legs. The loss of the legs is symbolic as well—in each epoch or stage of the decline of Dharma, the four driving Dharmic values diminish progressively and eventually disappear from mass consciousness.

The Krita or Satyayuga is when Dharma shines at its fullest, like the midday sun. In fact, the Sun, *surya*, which represents the highest Truth, is indeed the symbol of this truth-age. The Dharmic values of austerity, purity, compassion, and truth are dominant in human nature, and it is that stage of Dharmic civilization when humanity is at an apogee, closest in spirit to the gods or the *devas* who represent the fullness of Dharma. The Dharma at this stage resides in the head of humanity, which represents its higher mental consciousness, and shines through its radiant knowledge of truth or satya.

---

113 Literally accomplished, completed.

In the second phase, the Tretayuga, as the Dharmic force begins to wane and the devas recede, the spiritual and moral stature of human beings begins to diminish. Symbolically, the human of this epoch loses some of his height and grows a bit smaller, shorter. The Dharma now descends from the head to the heart, representing the higher psychic-vital body of humanity, marked more by devotion and intuition than pure knowledge.

In the third or the Dvaparayuga, Dharma has lost much of its shine and vigor and the human being has shrunk even further, grown smaller in spiritual and moral stature; the devas have almost completely receded, and civilization has degenerated to an extent where *adharma* has become powerful enough to precipitate a *dharmayuddha,* the great battle for Dharma. It is this dharmayuddha that forms the kernel of the Mahabharata legend. At this stage, Dharma descends further into the vital-emotional being of humanity, marked by emotional and moral devotion, passion, ambition, and valor.

As the great Mahabharata war ends, the Dvaparayuga passes into the fourth and the ultimate stage of its decline and enters the *Kaliyuga,* the age of the demon, the *asura.* Dharma, at this stage, descends into the physical-material consciousness of humanity. It is here, in the physical-material, that the final battle for Dharma is to be fought, for it is here that we find the densest darkness of Tamas, and the roots of greed and discord. The word 'kali', pronounced with the short vowel sound of 'a',[114] means discord or quarrel and represents the present age characterized principally by strife and discord, disharmony and imbalance— the core characteristics of the asuric forces. This is the age when adharma will dominate the human mind and heart and the Light of Dharma will recede.

Yet, because of the extremity of adharma, this is also the age which will be marked by the decent of Kalki, the tenth avatar of

---

114 कलि

Vishnu. But Kalki, more than the mythological avatar who shall come on a white horse to destroy falsehood with a sword, is a symbol of the Divine incarnating in a new form and embodying a new consciousness, entering directly into the evolutionary play on earth and precipitating, perhaps even actively establishing, an entirely new creation, a new world order, which will mark the end not only of this Kaliyuga but of the present spiral of evolutionary time.

Time does not move cyclically, with Kaliyuga always returning to Satyayuga, as commonly believed by Hindus, but in spirals, each spiral a level of evolution of consciousness. The next spiral, therefore, will not lead again to the old Satyayuga but to a higher Truth, a higher Dharma.

We must remember that the Vedic patriarchs were not philosophers or scholars but seers and poets and what they perceived or grasped intuitively they expressed, most readily and felicitously, in the language of mystical poetry, metaphors, and symbols. The mysteries of time and evolution too will best be understood in that spirit.

The Divine in Sanatan Dharma

The Forms of the Divine

Brahman is *Sat* and *Chit*—absolute being and consciousness, and in its absoluteness, beyond form and attributes—*nirakara, nirguna*. How this universe arose out of Brahman, none knows but Brahman, and what Brahman knows in the eternal, fathomless depths of its being cannot be known even by the great Gods and the Maharshis. Such is the unspeakable mystery of Brahman. Yet, this universe is, you and I are—how then did it all come about? How did it all arise? The old Vedantins say that none of all this really is; what is seen, known, and experienced as self and universe is only appearance created by Brahman's inscrutable power of Maya, and Brahman itself is immutable, inactive, beyond any becoming. Yet the Vedic seers assert that Brahman itself becomes the universe while remaining beyond it, as it is both—immutable and inactive as *avyakta brahman,* and mutable, active, and dynamic as *vyakta brahman*. Brahman does not need to become one or the other, it is simultaneously both. As vyakta, the formless Brahman assumes multiple forms and formations and enters into its own cosmic self-becoming, veiling itself from itself. It is perhaps this self-veiling that the Vedantic Rishis refer to as Maya.

Brahman is ananta, infinite, and needs to limit itself in order to manifest. This is what self-veiling means. By veiling or limiting its infinitude, it becomes finite and, therefore, manifest or vyakta. In the cosmic manifestation, Brahman makes itself vyakta first as its own higher representations in consciousness, and these are the various forms and formations of the Divine, the higher gods and goddesses. In these forms and formations, it makes itself 'visible' and 'tangible' in the manifestation. If this were not so, Brahman would always remain the transcendental *Parabrahman*—non-manifest.

Narayana-Narayani, Shiva-Shakti are the first and supreme emanations of Brahman in the manifestations. Please note that Narayana is also known as Vishnu, Vasudeva, and Krishna, as Narayani too is known through her multiple names, forms, and emanations. Neither Narayana nor Shiva are 'gods' in the theistic sense. More accurately, they should be called godheads, powers, and personalities of Brahman. We should not think of Narayana or Narayani, Shiva or Shakti, as separate in any way from Brahman—think of them as various personalities, manifestations or emanations, self-extensions, of the one Brahman, the one Divine being.

Nor are the personalities or self-extensions of Brahman limited to the great godheads of Narayana, Narayani, Shiva, or Shakti. There are numberless other divine emanations, personalities, and powers that manifest in the evolutionary play of the universe. Anyone who wishes to understand the bewildering pantheon of gods and goddesses of Hindu Dharma must know first that Brahman is the one all-pervading existence and nothing and none exists besides Brahman. This is the central principle of Sanatan Dharma. Brahman, therefore, pervades all forms and movements—cosmic, terrestrial, gross or subtle, visible or invisible, divine, human, subhuman or demonic; all are the various forms, motions, or vibrations of Brahman.

We must remember too that every one of these gods and goddesses, these various powers, personalities, and emanations of Brahman, live and move in our universe, though in forms too subtle for our human vision, to participate in the evolution of life and consciousness, to aid and support the human aspiration for Truth and Perfection, to bring down higher possibilities into the dynamics of evolution. These godheads, these powers and presences, are, therefore, collaborators and partners in evolution.

It is not always possible for the human disciple to directly approach Brahman, attain to the Brahmic consciousness, or even meditate on it because Brahman is beyond form, attribute, and description. The ordinary mind needs a recognizable and relatable form, a personal approach to the Divine, and a personal connection. Sanatan Dharma allows its devotees and followers to approach the Divine in whatever way and form it comes naturally to them, according to their swabhava or bhava, and the disciples know full well that whatever divinity they worship, their devotion and prayers go inevitably to the one Divine, the One Self in all. Whatever the namarupa of the divinity, behind all namarupa is the same reality, ekam Sat.

The Symbol and the Symbolized

We have already established that this universe, with all its forms and formations, is the self-becoming of Brahman. The Vedic seers categorically state, through several of their mahavakyas, that Brahman is everything that exists—from the subtlest to the grossest, from the atomic to the galactic, from the single cell to the body of mammoths, from the first quivers of nervous energy in matter to the cosmic consciousness of the maharshi. To the Hindu, therefore, there is nothing in the whole universe that is not Brahman, not sacred—the whole universe is the Divine's sacred ground and all life an unending *yajna*, or self-offering, to the Divine. Thus, the Hindu regards all forms, forces, and movements the same as Brahman—*sarvarupa-sarvagati brahman*—and bows in reverence to all, big or small, significant or insignificant, high or low. In fact, one of the chief injunctions of the Dharma is equality of being at all levels: to see no difference, to sense no difference, to accept no difference, and, thus, to exclude none from one's worldview—bird or beast, animate or inanimate, king or peasant, learned or ignorant, virtuous or sinful, noble or ignoble, human or divine—and hold all beings and things as the same Brahman.

This vast and all-comprehensive sense of oneness is the practical basis of Sanatan Dharma: either all is the Divine or nothing, even the *asura* and the *rakshasa*, and those who oppose the Dharma, all are divine, however seemingly distorted; there is no such thing as implacable evil or irredeemable hostility to the Divine, no such thing as original sin. If at all there is any sin in Sanatan Dharma, it is the error of duality, of separation.

The Hindu equivalent of the Christian 'Fall' is the fall from the unified consciousness to division and separation, and all that is inimical to Dharma is born of this fall. Conversely, the one thing desired, the highest virtue of the Dharma, is equality of vision and understanding, where one sees only Atman, hears only Atman, and knows only Atman.

The true disciple of Hindu Dharma, therefore, does not regard even images and idols as lifeless objects—every idol, image, and totem is symbolic of something divine; the human body itself represents Brahman. Brahman—formless and beyond qualities, nirakara and nirguna—lives and vibrates in every animate and inanimate form and can only become tangible to our senses, however approximately, in living forms or forms created by the living. When the Hindu erects an idol of a god or goddess, he first infuses life force—*prana shakti*—into it, as prescribed by tradition, before the image or the idol assumes 'divinity' and can be worshipped. This infusion of life force, through an occult Yogic process, is known as *prana pratistha*, literally, establishing the life force or prana. Once this is done, the idol or the image assumes a vibration of divinity and becomes like a live wire connecting the aspiring human consciousness to the Divine or to that aspect of the Divine that the external form represents. Those open spiritually or intuitively can sense and feel the divine vibrations in these forms.

The Mother, perhaps one of the most accomplished spiritual beings of the twentieth century, a remarkable occultist, mystic, Yogi, widely regarded as a divine incarnation by her disciples,[115] and Sri Aurobindo's spiritual collaborator, explained it thus: *All this idol worship is based on the old idea that whatever the image— which we disdainfully call an 'idol'—whatever the external form of the deity may be, the presence of the thing represented is always*

---

115 Technically, the feminine of rishi is *rishika*, and therefore, the Mother should be called a *maharshika*.

there. And there is always someone—whether priest or initiate, sadhu or sannyasi—someone who has the power and (usually this is the priest's work) who draws the Force and the Presence down into it. And it's true, it's quite real—the Force and the Presence are there; and this (not the form in wood or stone or metal) is what is worshipped: this Presence.

The presence of the Divine in forms—invoked or latent—is the key. If the presence can imbue even one form anywhere on earth, it can imbue all forms.[116] Thus, whether it's a block of stone or granite or an entire mountain, a carved wooden statue or tree, a lake or river, sun or moon, a photograph or an object of daily use, in everything one can sense the divine presence and force if one is open in heart and spirit. The animating force is not in the object of adoration but in the consciousness of the one who adores it.

Sri Aurobindo once visited a temple in Karnali, on the banks of the Narmada, near the end of his stay in Baroda (1904–06). At that time, he was quite an atheist. As he shared in one of his evening talks: *Once I visited Ganganath (Chandod) after Brahmananda's death when Keshwananda was there. With my Europeanized mind I had no faith in image-worship and I hardly believed in the presence of God. I went to Kernali where there are several temples. There is one of Kali and when I looked at the image I saw the living presence there. For the first time, I believed in the presence of God.* Regarding the same experience, he wrote to Dilip Roy, one of his disciples—*You stand before a temple of Kali beside a sacred river and see what? A sculpture, a gracious piece of architecture, but in a moment mysteriously, unexpectedly there is*

---

116 Physics can better explain this idea. Matter is finally reducible to energy (in fact, matter is energy), and what we are calling 'divine vibrations' are also vibrations of shakti or energy. What physics calls pure energy, the yogi calls divine energy because the yogi experiences all energy as divine. Therefore, the presence of divine energy or vibrations in material objects and idols is not unscientific at all. Further, the Vedantin experiences the entire cosmic existence as Chit-Shakti or Consciousness-Force, and so, at the quantum vibrational level, it is all one undifferentiated reality.

instead a Presence, a Power, a Face that looks into yours, an inner sight in you has regarded the World-Mother.

The presence of the Divine can be felt and touched anywhere, in a piece of stone or a single leaf, if the consciousness is open, wide, and receptive. The modern intellectual mind does not grasp this, not half as well as the savage mind instinctively used to, because it lives in concrete structures of thoughts and prejudices. There are many, including Hindus, who regard idol worship as superstitious and primitive, and there have been Hindu reformers as well, like Dayanand Saraswati and Ram Mohan Roy, who tried to rid Hinduism of idol worship, as well as ritualistic worship.

The idol worship of the Sanatani Hindu, however, must be understood in the context of Hindu mysticism and religious symbolism. For the Hindu, the idol is a symbol, and the symbol is inseparable from that which is symbolized. All things and beings are symbols, and each symbol is a little bit of that which is symbolized. The Vedic Rishis regarded the human body itself as a living symbol of the supreme Purusha. *Living symbol* is a mystical phenomenon that explains many of the practices and beliefs of Hindu Dharma.

When Ramakrishna stood before the clay idol of Kali, he did not just see the symbol of the goddess, he experienced the Divine Mother herself in that symbol and thus transformed the symbol-idol into the living presence—the symbol thus revealed the symbolized, the image of the Mother revealed the Mother.

That which is symbolized is always Sat, the Real, and the symbol is always the representation, *pratika*, of the Real. Interestingly, idol in Sanskrit is *pratima* and pratima in Sanskrit also means symbol, pratika. When the Real behind or within the symbol is forgotten or recedes from consciousness, the symbol loses its spiritual significance and is reduced to an ordinary object, a symbol without its spirit—when the Real is no longer expressed in the external, the symbol is no longer the symbolized.

This applies equally to several other important aspects of Hindu Dharma.

The mystical significance and beauty of temples, the profound symbolic significance of sacrifices and offerings, the tremendous significance of the devas and the asuras, and the spiritual significance and power of mantras are all aspects of the Hindu religion that need to be restored to their inner significance, reconnected with their spiritual and mystical source and revived in contemporary forms and formulations.

The Mystery of Ganesha

Of all the divinities of Sanatan Dharma, Ganesha is perhaps the most mysterious and mystical of all. All important religious rituals, sacrifices, and offerings begin with a customary obeisance to Ganesha, who is known as the remover of all obstacles, without whose blessings and grace, no auspicious event can happen. Ganesha is the mystical opening to the divine Omnipresence, and none can cross the threshold into the spiritual life without a 'nod' from Ganesha. Ganesha is neither earthly nor divine but a blend of both, a perfect dynamic equipoise between the two.

Ganesha is known to us as *achintya*, beyond thought, *avyakta*, beyond expression, and *ananta*, without end—and thus, he has no form, attribute, or existence as you and I know it, for that which has no form or attribute is practically nonexistent for us. And because Ganesha manifests but with no form—a formless manifestation is when the godhead appears to the devotee simply as a felt emanation of the Divine or as a bhava inwardly known and felt—he is addressed as the *parabrahman svarupa*, the very own rupa, form, of supreme Brahman.

The nirakara or the formless is not really formless: our human consciousness can only comprehend the material—*bhautik*—or the subtle—*sukshma*—rupa, that is, the rupa that we perceive outwardly or feel inwardly. But there is a form beyond these, an essential self-nature, or true form, that we call svarupa, *an essential figure of Truth, which we cannot know with the intellect, but only with a higher faculty. And every swarupa is itself only a symbol of the one essential existence which can only be known by its symbols because in its ultimate reality it defies logic and exceeds perception.*[117] So, if Ganesha is the svarupa, the self-nature, of supreme Brahman, how to give him a visible form, how to approach that which exceeds our perception?

Therefore, something totally illogical—or totally symbolical—like an elephant form. And why not? The thing is to get the essence. And to get the essence, and sense, of Ganesha, we will need to go into the details of his incarnation as a god. Like all gods in Sanatan Dharma, Ganesha has a mythological origin. He is the son of Shiva and his consort Parvati, an incarnation of the divine Mother. It is said that during Shiva's absence, Parvati felt lonely and wanted a child. So she created a child out of her own body matter (dust of her body, as the story goes, but obviously, that is symbolic of earth and earthly matter). Parvati's loneliness, too, is entirely symbolic of the divine Mother's aloneness, *ekanta*, when the divine Self is eclipsed.

One fine day, while Parvati was having a bath, Shiva came home, and when he tried to enter the house, he was met by the young boy Ganesha who did not allow him to pass—another reference to Ganesha being the portal to the Divine. Shiva did not recognize him, got angry at not being allowed into his own house, and promptly chopped off Ganesha's head. When Parvati discovered this unfortunate accident, she obviously told Shiva who Ganesha was. Shiva immediately went out and brought back the head of an elephant to replace the boy's head, and that is how Ganesha got the elephant head.

Was he actually beheaded? The old story says that Shiva, because he couldn't recognize Ganesha as his own son, beheads him with his trishul for obstructing his way to Parvati. On the face of it, it doesn't make sense because Shiva being what he is, he couldn't not have known the reality. There is symbolism here, too, then. The head represents the mind and its faculties—*manas, chitta, buddhi, ahankara*—including the ego, and is,

---

117 Sri Aurobindo, *Record of Yoga.*

therefore, the root of all our problems, symbolically speaking. So beheading Ganesha signified the destruction of the root of all problems, the destruction of the personal ahankara or egoism, and the trishul with which Shiva beheads Ganesha represents the three gunas of nature.[118]

This then, is a 'heady' mix of symbolism, poetry, and a lot of poetic license. The poets who compose these stories are seers, and they do not mentally conjure the symbolism, but they see or intuit the truth of a thing and express it in terms of symbols and metaphors that would make it easier for the mind of the devotee to understand.

So, why an elephant's head as a replacement? Besides the obvious symbolism again—an elephant's head being symbolic of strength, power, wisdom, and knowledge—it is a deliberate poetic device of the seer to show that the severed head that represents the human mind and ego cannot be replaced with another head because it is the pattern that must be broken, the very template that must be shattered. Therefore, an elephant's head—seemingly nonsensical and provocative. But here is the deep and compelling import of the symbolism: the head must go and go permanently, no replacement, no substitute. This is a symbolic suggestion, a poetic device, and not to be taken too literally.

Symbolism of this kind would appeal to certain minds and temperaments to focus on the divine attributes of the god which would otherwise be too abstract to grasp—the single tusk of Ganesha, for instance, which would signify one-pointed concentration or the broken tusk which would signify the capacity to eliminate the unnecessary, the large ears would signify deep and universal listening, the small mouth would signify austerity of speech, and the huge stomach would signify the ability to take in and hold everything within oneself, the *ankusa* or the axe

---

118 See the chapters on Shiva.

that he carries in his hands would signify self-reflection because of its ability to cut off all the knots of bondage and ignorance, and the *paasa* or the rope would signify control, as any deep spiritual awakening needs deep control as tremendous energies are released during the process of awakening.

But beyond all the symbolism is the deeper spiritual truth that the formless just cannot be represented in form; the best poetic or artistic representations may convey the spiritual truth but will, in time, degenerate into mere formalism and ritualism. Those who do not have the subtle understanding will eventually cling to the form and forget the essence, the truth.

Purusha and Shakti

Brahman, in its self-becoming, manifests first as *Adi Purusha*, the primordial cosmic being, the first conscious Self. In Sanatan Dharma, both Vishnu and Shiva are considered Adi Purusha, the original being. But the Vedic maharshis regard Adi Purusha as Brahman's first emanation in the manifestation. *Adi*, in Sanskrit, means the first, the original, and *purusha* means conscious being or self. Adi Purusha is so called because he appears prior even to cosmic existence, when there was nothing, *the hour before the gods awake*,[119] prior to being and non-being.

Adi Purusha, in that indeterminate dawn before the birth of time and space, called forth the universe from Brahman's infinite play of possibilities. There was no divine fiat commanding Light or Life to be,[120] there was only a vibration, *spandan*,[121] of the divine will-to-become, wordless, fathomless—*ekoham bahushyam*: *I am one, may I become many*—and out of that divine vibration or spandan, there arose the primordial consciousness-force, *chit-shakti*. This primordial consciousness-force, known as Adi Shakti—*shakti* meaning force or energy—brought forth the universe from Brahman's transcendental space—*paramam vyomam*.

Mark the all-important distinction: Adi Purusha *calls* forth, invokes, Adi Shakti *brings* forth, manifests. Purusha

---

119 The evocative opening line from Sri Aurobindo's epic *Savitri*. The line, though, occurs in a somewhat different context.
120 Referring to the Biblical fiat, 'Let there be Light and there was Light...'
121 Also trembling, quivering, pulsation.

represents the will-to-become, Shakti represents the power-to-become. Without Shakti, Purusha cannot manifest, and without Purusha, Shakti cannot arise—but even as we speak of Purusha and Shakti as two, they are one and inseparable in essence—*tattva*—and existence—*sattva*. They are one as fire and heat are one, and as heat is the inherent attribute—*dharma*—of the fire, so is Shakti the inherent attribute—*dharma*—of Purusha. This was the divine mechanism of self-becoming, the arising of the universe out of *brahmayoni*, the cosmic womb of Brahman.

And as cosmic becoming unfolded, Adi Shakti poured out of Herself multitudinous forms and formations, infinite forces and movements, space and time, life and consciousness. As Purusha stood back, observing from His heights of consciousness, Shakti shaped the universe out of Her divine vision and will. And thus, were the gods born, the shining devas of the higher planes who would then embody in the lower planes as conscious selves, as jiva; and Purusha Himself entered the hearts of every living being and established Himself there as atman, the one divine, immortal Self in all beings, permeating all existence, holding all things and beings together.

And thus, Purusha and Shakti reside in each of us as the conscious being and the conscious force so that every living being may return, through the endless spirals of time, to the divine source, for if that were not to be, then the divine will-to-become would remain incompletely and imperfectly realized.

This is the deep metaphysical truth revealed by our Vedic forefathers: as the One becomes the Many, the Many must become the One. Every conscious being is Purusha in essence and, therefore, must realize itself as Purusha in existence. In that manner alone would Purusha, the Eternal One, become Purusha, the Eternal Many. This is the creative spiral of cosmic existence—as the divine Purusha has become the human

Purusha, the human Purusha must become the divine Purusha. This is the mystic significance of the Vedic *Yajna,* for it is through the Yajna that this spiral is completed. Yajna is that which raises the lower human Purusha, by the askesis and creative force of Adi Shakti, the eternal Mother, to the highest divine Purusha— or *purushottama,* in the language of the Vedic Rishis.

The Divine Mother

Shakti, the eternal Feminine, the Divine as Mother, is unique to Sanatan Dharma. Though Brahman is formless and, therefore, beyond masculine and feminine, in the multiplicity of the manifestation, Brahman is as much feminine as it is masculine. The pure Vedantin approaches Brahman as formless, free of attributes; the bhakta approaches Brahman as Ishvara, the personal Divine, and the *shakta*—the worshipper of Shakti or Consciousness-Force—approaches Brahman as the feminine, the Mother. There is also the approach of some of the Vedic Rishis who place Shakti, the Divine Mother, even above Ishvara and Purusha, as the firstborn of the Eternal, the primordial Womb, out of which even the gods come forth. Thus, Shakti is the consciousness-force out of which Purusha himself arose.

The Hindu reveres the Divine as Brahman, or Krishna, or Shiva, as Ishvara or Purusha—all male manifestations, and yet, as a constant undercurrent, right from the realizations of the Vedic Rishis, the Divine Mother has been running through Sanatan Dharma, like the invisible, mythical Sarasvati, influencing and shaping all its darshan and civilization. The universal Mother, *Adishakti*, the creative-dynamic Force of the Divine, contains within herself the infinite potentiality of Satchidananda and brings forth into manifestation all that is seen and shaped in her infinite vision and will.

The Divine Mother is the root and branches of this universe, the creative force that weaves the fabric of spacetime, the One who dwells equally in the emptiness of the atom and in the inmost self of the human, the One who spins the cosmos around the invisible axis of Her divine being, and the One who lies coiled and involved in the heart of matter as the Supreme Light of Truth, *jyoti-parasya*.[122] She, whose very substance is the Light of Truth, is also the *Agni* of the Vedic maharshis burning deep, as a flame, in our hearts and minds. It is when we, in our inward plunge, grow aware of our Atman that we also grow aware of the presence of the divine Agni within.

As Purusha is the embodiment of pure consciousness, the Mother is the embodiment of love, not human love but the love that vibrates through the universe and through all life and being, the love that makes Yajna possible, the love that holds everything together, raises everything to the highest Light. Without her as the embodiment of love, this universe as we know it would fall apart. It is out of her love that she keeps the universe cohesive and coherent, from the quantum to the cosmic levels, from the tiniest spark of life in the single cell to the vast consciousness of the mighty Gods—she alone is the love that binds and wields.

When the physicists contend with the powerful forces within the atomic nucleus and stand back, amazed at the sheer potency of the very small, they are but countering just a minuscule fraction of the Mother's immense Power and love. When the astronomers look upon the incredible cosmic vastnesses, into the farthest reaches of space and time, and stand bewildered by those appalling immensities, they are but catching just the faintest tantalizing glimpses of the Mother's inscrutable power of creative formation or Maya. As the possessor and wielder of Maya, the divine creative power of infinite formation, she is known as Mahamaya.

As Mahamaya, she sustains, at multiple levels, from the invisible to the supracosmic, the grand appearance of the universe, for the universe is not really a thing out there but one of her formations that she holds in her infinite consciousness;

---

122 *Jyoti* is light, *para* is the supreme; thus, the light of the supreme.

and there are numberless such formations and universes that the
Divine Mahamaya weaves out of her infinite creativity—and all
these are not out there in some objective space but deep within,
as we discover on entering the inner layers of her manifestation,
layers subtler than the subtlest, so subtle, in fact, that these
appear almost void to our ordinary gross consciousness.

Therefore it is said that the Mother as Mahamaya holds all
conscious life in her inscrutable spell, and none—not even the
great gods and seers—can escape her spell without her grace
and consent. She is known to her ardent devotees as the One
who grants all the capacities and powers of consciousness—
sarvasiddhidayini.[123] It is by her divine love that she liberates
the soul from the ego; it is by her love that she liberates the
mind from mithya and avidya—she is, therefore, also the One
who grants all liberation and freedom, *sarvamuktidayini*.[124] For
all souls caught in the spell of cosmic Maya, her love is the Light
of hope, for not only is she love, she is also the source of Light,
she herself is the Light of the highest, jyoti-parasya, that Yogis
through the ages have invoked and revered, the Light without
which there would indeed be no Yoga or Sanatan Dharma.

The Divine Mother is truly the heart of the Dharma.
Whoever, wherever, gives himself to Dharma gives himself to the
Divine Mother. When one stands for Dharma in this universe of
perplexing duality and confusion—for all evil is but confusion
and duality—and protects Dharma, he is protected directly by
the power of the Divine Mother.

There are those who feel, perhaps rightly so in the confusions
of everyday life, that the Sanatan Dharma is in grave danger,
under threat by hostile forces, but they forget too easily perhaps
the deeper truth that the Sanatan Dharma is the manifest
field of the Divine Mother's Yogic work upon earth, and while

---

123 One who gives, or grants, all siddhis or capacities and attainments.
124 Mukti is freedom or liberation, thus one who grants all freedoms.

earth herself may be destroyed, the luminous seeds of Sanatan Dharma will survive, concealed eternally in the Mother's bosom, awaiting its time of revival and rejuvenation in the endless spirals of evolutionary Time. The ones who have known even an infinitesimal portion of the Divine Mother's consciousness also know that the Mother is vaster than this earth of ours, and a million earths—nay, a million universes—can arise and dissolve in the infinite consciousness that she is.

The Mystical Shiva

Shiva represents the pure non-differentiated consciousness of Brahman: he is both Sat, the eternal reality, and Chit, the eternal consciousness. Widely known and revered as *Maheshvara*, the Great Ishvara, Shiva is the infinite Unmanifest, *avyaktam*, out of which arises all manifestation through the infinite creative force of Shakti. Shiva, thus, is the infinite potential of existence, and Shakti is the infinite force that manifests this existence as the multitudinous universe of name and form, this vast, eternal Prakriti.

Shiva, then, is the mystical Darkness out of which the creative Light, *prakasa*—the pure luminous Light of consciousness by which everything is known and made manifest to itself—emerges and spreads as subtle vibrations of energy-matter.

Shiva is like the blackhole, infinitely dense and packed with energy but invisible as no light escapes its infinite gravitational field. From the outside, if there could be any outside to Shiva, Shiva would appear void, empty, nothing—in other words, avyakta. Yet within, in its own absolute interiority, Shiva is everything and everyone; all possibilities of existence teem within Shiva, all space and time lie coiled within him like an elemental serpent still to awake. Shiva holds in his absolute stillness the infinite expansion of universes, waves upon waves of consciousness-energy pouring out into the universe, manifesting the infinitely rich playfield of Prakriti.

This darkness of Shiva is not the absence but the infinite concentration of light as pure consciousness, prakasa. To know Shiva as the divine Dark is to transcend the universe of ordinary light and darkness; Shiva's divine Dark is the formless non-duality that can only be known when the physical eyes are closed in what the Yogis know as *samadhi*, the perfectly unmodified state, and the third, the occult eye, opens, the self-luminous eye that needs no external source of light, the eye of Shiva in which the seer and the seen are one.

Shiva is the primordial Chit, consciousness, which holds within itself infinite dimensions of life and existence. It is in this timeless and fathomless trance of Shiva that the first divine spark of becoming is lit, that first desire to become the Many, and with this spark manifests *tapas-shakti*, the fierce creative force of Shiva's concentration, and out of that tapas-shakti, Shiva appears to himself as the universe, his own radiant reflection in the mirror of his infinite consciousness. As the self-effulgent Light, he remains in his sovereign *Shiva-tattva*, his eternal essence out of which all manifestation arises and into which it subsides; and as Shakti, the eternal feminine, the divine creatrix, he becomes the universe and all beings and things in it. There is no duality here, Shakti is to Shiva what heat is to fire, two attributes of the same reality. Shakti is Shiva manifest when Shiva opens his eyes and turns his gaze outward, and Shiva is Shakti held within, in potential, when Shiva closes his eyes and turns his gaze inward. The Yogi who possesses the truth-vision sees Shakti as Shiva in movement, and Shiva as Shakti coiled up in eternal quiescence.

As Shakti, the eternal feminine and the divine creatrix, Shiva becomes the universe, he does not merely project it out of his creative consciousness but becomes it. Thus, the Yogi knows that all that exists, all that can be seen, known, felt, and touched, is Shiva as Shakti; and even that which is conscious in himself as himself, the Atman, is Shiva. Shiva is Brahman, Shiva is Atman, Shiva is Ishvara. *Shivoham*—I am Shiva—therefore becomes the chief mantra of Yoga, and as this mantra penetrates and fills the consciousness of the Yogi, all differences and dualities fall away, and Shiva alone stands revealed as self, world, and cosmos.

Yet, though Shiva permeates all existence, none can know him as Shiva himself is the sole knower and the seer of all, the witness of all that is. I perceive, I experience, and I know only because Shiva in me, as me, perceives, experiences, and knows. The I is merely a reflection that falls from Shiva and dissolves into him. The highest attainment of the Yogi is the realization of his identity with Shiva, when he can hold within himself, in full and resplendent self-knowledge, the identity *Shivoham*.

But this identity must be understood. Shiva is perfect non-duality, in him all dualities and divisions of the knower and the known dissolve, there is no knower left to know, and thus is Shiva known as void, *shunya*. But Shiva is not really void, he is simply beyond the reach of all dualistic human consciousness and knowledge. Like the blackhole, Shiva is invisible and inaccessible and, therefore, *shunya* or void to our consciousness. But Shiva is this universe and everything in it, he is the substratum of all being, and when all is dissolved in the endless spirals of time, it is Shiva's void that remains, immutable, unfathomable; when the Light, prakasa, in which existence appears to itself is withdrawn or extinguished, all that remains is the shunya of Shiva.

To enter Shiva's divine shunya is to enter the heart of his supreme mystery, for it is in that shunya that one knows oneself in the starkness of being as the pure and the one. It is in that inmost cave of the mystic heart that one becomes Shiva in a supreme ecstasy of spiritual union, when Shakti, as Prakriti, the eternal feminine, returns to Shiva, the Supreme Ishvara, and resolves herself in him. This is not some distant one-time supracosmic event but an intimate yogic experience that repeats itself endlessly through all humanity, wherever and whenever a human soul realizes its identity with Shiva and dissolves into his unfathomable vastness. Dissolution in Shiva is the highest nirvana, the utter liberation, *purna moksha*.

The Manifestations of Shiva

Most Hindus regard Shiva as the destroyer, the God of pralaya or cosmic dissolution, but Shiva does not destroy, as there is no necessity of destruction in Shiva's scheme—Shiva only dissolves and absorbs his own manifestation back into himself once the cosmic evolutionary afflatus is exhausted, much like a spider withdrawing its web back into itself; the Many return to the One, multiplicity collapses back upon non-duality or singularity. In withdrawing existence back into himself, Shiva does not destroy; he transforms. Pralaya is a misunderstood idea: it is not the final destruction of the universe, it is the dissolution of the false universe and the false self in Shiva's Truth. Thus, the Yogi knows Shiva as the godhead of transformation and not destruction. In Shiva's auspicious presence, death itself ceases to be an individual pralaya and turns into a spiritual metamorphosis for the realized Yogi.

Shiva's play of manifestation and withdrawal of manifestation, oneness and multiplicity, projection and dissolution, does not happen only over yugas or aeonic spans of time but through the individual human consciousness in human time. Transformation of consciousness is the natural outcome of all Yoga, and as the *Adiyogi*, the first, the archetypal Yogi, Shiva presides over all transformation of consciousness: it is Shiva that leads human evolution through the ages. Shiva, therefore, is known as *Yogeshvara*, the Lord of Yoga. The ancient seers who had known Shiva intimately in their consciousness had said that whosoever surrenders to Shiva sincerely and entirely is led by Shiva himself, the Adiyogi and Yogeshvara, to the supreme heights of self-realization in a single lifetime. Shiva's compassion and generosity to whoever invokes him sincerely and persistently are legendary.

Shiva is also known to mystics as *Swayambhu*, self-manifested. He manifests all existence out of himself, but he himself has no source, no origin. This is a profound mystery. If existence itself arises in Shiva, Shiva must be beyond existence; and that which is beyond existence cannot exist. That which is beyond existence, the maharshis tell us, is Parabrahman, beyond being and non-being, beyond manifestation and non-manifestation, the all-transcendent, unknowable, and indescribable; and those who know Shiva in their inmost hearts know him as Parabrahman.

But then these are some of the most profound mysteries of existence, and the Yogi learns to rest with such mysteries and not try solving them; the way to Shiva's secrets is through profound passiveness and surrender where the mind and heart fall into deep silence and the gaze turns inward, knowing that it is within that Shiva resides. To meditate on Shiva as Swayambhu is one of the most powerful ways of transcending the dualities of consciousness and entering the silence of the soul.

But Shiva is also known as *Ardhanarishvara*, literally, Ishvara who is half feminine. As Ardhanarishvara, Shiva symbolizes a deeper ontological non-duality, the perfect blend and balance of the creative force of Ishvara, regarded as the masculine, and the sustaining and nurturing force of Ishvari, regarded as the feminine.[125] As the divine consciousness-force, Chit-Shakti, Shiva, as Ardhanarishvara, represents the non-separability of the masculine and the feminine. The masculine-feminine duality is the primary polarity of our human universe. To meditate on Shiva as Ardhanarishvara is a powerful way of transcending this primary polarity of our existence and restoring the original

---

125 Perhaps the first appearance of the Ardhanarishvara was in the *Brihadaranyaka Upanishad* as the archetypal creature which was of the same dimension as a man and woman closely embracing, which then fell apart into two aspects out of which were born man and woman.

dynamic equilibrium of meditation and action, freedom and order, evolution and assimilation, the outer push and the inner pull. Whoever transcends these primary polarities comes closer to the repose of a perfect identification with Shiva as the Formless, nirakara.

Worshipping Shiva, in the Sanatan tradition, is an act of consciousness, an inner consecration and offering of body, mind, and heart, a constant invocation of his mystical and spiritual aspects through an elaborate system of external symbols and mantras. Shiva can be easily propitiated if one understands his deepest and perhaps best-kept secret, that he is the indweller, the one who is seated within; the one who searches for Shiva in the universe of form and name is sure to be confounded, and the one who can renounce form and name and invoke Shiva within is the one who will be granted the boon of higher consciousness.

Thus, many smear ash on their bodies, metaphorically or actually, renounce homes and families, become mendicants and ascetics, and even practice harsh austerities but come no closer to Shiva's inmost mysteries, for Shiva eludes them like the horizon. But those who understand that Shiva is the inwardness of being are the ones who unravel his mysteries in their hearts and souls. They are the ones who understand that Shiva's asceticism is not physical but psychological; Shiva's *tapasya* is the tapasya of Truth and purity. Shiva's devotee must descend into the caves of the heart and there find the eternal Light.

Shiva is commonly depicted as an ascetic with ashes of corpses smeared on his body. This is a stark symbol of Shiva, the Adiyogi as a *tapasvi*. Tapasya, from the word *tapah*, heat, is the fire that burns delusion and ignorance. The form of the ascetic represents the inner detachment of the tapasvi who lives in the mortal world, amongst all its attractions and distractions, but is constantly aware of its impermanence; the ash— *vibhuti* or *bhasma*—of corpses—*shava* in Sanskrit—symbolizes impermanence, death, and dissolution, ash being the final residue of the mortal body. Thus, holding always in one's mind and heart, in constant inner remembrance, the ascetic smeared in the ashes of corpses, the Yogi can rapidly transcend his identification with the body and the material world and attain the detachment and freedom of Shiva in his being.

The archetypal Yogi and tapasvi, Adiyogi Shiva, is also the Mahadeva who is known as *Neelkantha*, the One with the blue neck, the blue symbolizing the effect of the poison that Shiva takes within his own body as an act of supreme compassion to protect the universe from the effects of evil. The symbol goes back to primordial times when the ocean of existence was being churned in a great battle between the devas and the asuras. This great churning, *mahamanthan*, releases destructive toxins in the atmosphere that threaten to destroy all life. Shiva drinks the poison out of his divine compassion to save and protect existence, but the Divine Shakti that eternally dwells in Shiva stops the poison from entering the body, and the poison remains in Shiva's throat, turning his neck blue.

This is profound and powerful symbolism. The churning is the eternal evolutionary process in the human universe that releases forces of good and evil, forces that strengthen the evolution of consciousness and forces that oppose it. Shiva takes in the poison that symbolizes the evil or anti-divine forces and holds it in his throat: he does not consume it nor does he expel it; he instead holds it in abeyance and transforms its effect to permanent good. Meditating on this aspect of Shiva, invoking him as Neelkantha, the Yogi can transcend the duality of good and evil, of devas and asuras, and collaborate in this timeless cosmic battle to transform all forces of evil and destruction to the ultimate good of life in the universe. This, indeed, is the ultimate aim of Mahadeva: to transform everything, every form and force in the cosmos, to the ultimate Good.

Shiva is also depicted with his hair coiled in matted locks and adorned with the crescent moon. This further adds to the rich tapestry of symbology woven around Shiva. According to mythology, Shiva stopped the descent of Ganga from the heavens and broke her fall on earth by absorbing Ganga in his hair and reducing her torrent to a trickle. There is obvious Yogic symbolism in this: Ganga is not the river but the symbol of a higher consciousness descending to a fragile earth plane in a torrent that would have flooded the earth. The matted hair symbolizes the higher crown or chakra that alone could contain the descent without cracking. Releasing the flow of Ganga in trickles is symbolic of how the Yogi, in complete control of Prakriti, releases the higher consciousness, chakra by chakra, into the mind, heart, and body. Meditating on this aspect, the devotee can open their own mind, heart, and body to the descent of the higher consciousness through Shiva.

Shiva is also known as *Trayambakam*, the three-eyed One. The two eyes of Shiva represent the ordinary dualistic perception, the sense-universe, with the right eye representing the sun or the solar influence and the left eye representing the moon or the lunar influence; the third eye, which opens when the other two close, represents fire, *Agni*, which is the Yogic or spiritual vision, direct perception of Truth which 'burns away' all dualities. This third eye, when open, brings direct perception by destroying the mind's powerful identification with duality. This is the reason it is said that the third eye can destroy when focused on the outer world: what it destroys is the delusion of duality. By meditating on this aspect, the devotee can ascend to the non-dual direct perception of Shiva.

The crescent moon that Shiva bears on his head symbolizes time and the measure of time; in the Vedantic sense, the measurement of time, or any measurement, is an attribute of Maya. In wearing the crescent moon on his head, Shiva represents complete control over time and the Maya of time. Shiva is eternal—beyond time—and thus, he wears the crescent moon as the symbol of time itself, as an ornament that can be taken off at will.

The serpent around Shiva's neck, Vasuki of mythology, represents the vital force of the ego and the deep-seated fear of death. Ego and the fear of death are deeply related and intertwined. The serpent around Shiva's neck symbolizes complete victory over both ego and fear of death. Shiva wears the serpent as an ornament which is itself symbolic of mastery. Some devotees regard the serpent as symbolic of the eternal cycles of time, *kala*. By wearing it thrice around his neck, Shiva represents complete control of kala, time. Time represents mortality. So, control of kala is control of mortality.

In a deeper sense, ego, time, mortality, and the fear of death are all entwined. By meditating on this aspect of Shiva, by bearing Shiva's representative form in the consciousness, the Yogi can transcend ego and conquer the fear of death. Remember that the *mrityunjaya*[126] mantra, the occult key to conquering the forces of death and decay, was given as *beej*, or seed, mantra by Shiva.

The *trishula* or trident that Shiva carries as a weapon represents the triune reality of Shiva as the one who manifests the universe out of himself, preserves it in his consciousness, and finally absorbs it back into himself. To some devotees, the trishula represents the perfect equilibrium of the three *gunas* of nature—*sattva*, *rajas*, and *tamas*. Through sattva, Shiva manifests the cosmos; through rajas, he sustains or preserves the cosmos, and through tamas, he reabsorbs the cosmos into his divine Darkness. Some others regard the trishula as the triune powers or faculties of the human consciousness: volition, *ichha*, knowledge, *jnana*, and action, *kriya*. With this triune power in hand, anything in the world may be accomplished. Meditating on this aspect of Shiva, concentrating on Shiva with this trishula, the Yogi can master the three gunas in his own nature, master the powers of his consciousness, and work towards accomplishing the highest good, even as Shiva himself.

---

126 From mrityu, death, and jaya, victory: mrityunjaya, that which conquers death.

Shiva also carries the *damaru*, a drum, in one of his hands in a symbolic gesture or *mudra* called *damaru-hasta*. This is yet another profound mystic symbol. The damaru, or the drum, represents the *Shabda Brahman* or the primordial sound of *Aum*. When the damaru is played with the right concentration and in the right inner state, it produces the sound of Om, rising to *Nada*, the primeval cosmic vibration of A-U-M. The Yogi meditating on Shiva with the damaru can enter that consciousness-space where he can merge his being with the Nada and bring something of that divine vibration into his own psychic being.[127]

One of the most popular symbols associated with Shiva is the *Linga*. With the linga, the devotee comes to the purest and most powerful of all symbols of Sanatan Dharma. The linga is the symbol of the infinite, formless Shiva. It is also the most ancient of symbols, going back to times when the now-accepted representations of Shiva in images or idols did not exist. The word linga itself means symbol or mark. Swami Vivekananda once described the linga as the symbol of the eternal Brahman.

In certain mythological references, we find that Shiva's abode, Mount Kailash, which is itself a symbol of the highest consciousness transcending the cosmos, is represented by the linga as the center of the universe, the central axis around which the cosmos revolves. The linga is not just a block of stone but a mark of the great avyakta, the Unmanifest, and simultaneously, it is the most profound mark of the vyakta, the manifestation, a symbol of the perfect equilibrium of the masculine and feminine, of the visible and the invisible. It stands silent, lone, absolute, evoking in the devotee a silence beyond thought and speech. One who meditates on the linga, understanding its profound Yogic and occult significance, can transcend all duality of manifestation and taste the rarest bliss of the Unmanifest in the Manifest. Through concentration on the linga, one can

---

127 See chapter 'Om, the Imperishable Word' for further explanation.

merge one's consciousness in that pillar of Shiva's pure light, the *jyotir-linga*. The legend goes that Shiva once appeared as a pillar of Light, jyotir-linga, to Brahma and Vishnu, the other two mahadevas—or supreme godheads—of Sanatan Dharma, and asked them to find the extreme ends of the pillar. Neither of the great Gods could find the end—and how could they? Infinity has no dimension, no end.

Shiva's linga is the symbol of the unknowable in the known, the unmanifest in the manifest. To meditate on the linga is to meditate directly on the supreme mystery of Shiva.

However, even after all these descriptions and interpretations, one is aware that one has only scratched the surface of a fathomless mystery. Shiva cannot be known, understood, or explained by the human mind, however vast and profound be its understanding. Our attempts to describe Shiva are like a child's attempts to describe deep space. The deeper one delves, the more one realizes the vastness and profundity of Shiva's mystery: Shiva is neither God nor person. Shiva never was, never will be. He is, and he is not. All forms are his, but he is formless. He is nearer than the nearest, more intimate than our own breath, yet he is everywhere and everything. Where indeed to find such a one? For Shiva is dark and void to those who look for him outwardly, in forms and symbols; for those who can penetrate the symbolism of the symbols and the formlessness of forms, he reveals a bit of himself, just the first glimpse, to lead the soul farther and deeper. But to those who are willing to give themselves inwardly to him, as a moth to the flame, knowing that he is all there is, he gives of himself, freely and with overwhelming generosity. Shiva's Grace is the Grace of the Divine Mother. To invoke him is to invoke her. He is the one ever-present, indwelling, and luminous in our consciousness, as Ishvara and Ishvari.

Sri Krishna

Krishna as a godhead is the Lord of Ananda, Love and Bhakti; as an incarnation, he manifests the union of wisdom (jnana) and works and leads the earth-evolution through this towards union with the Divine by Ananda, Love and Bhakti.

—Sri Aurobindo on Sri Krishna

If Shiva is the austere, inconceivable, vast impersonality of Supreme Brahman, Sri Krishna is the adorable Divine Personality supporting the eternal play of existence as Vishnu, the archetypal sustainer and nurturer, and himself entering into it as a friend, lover, intimate guide, and Guru. Invoking Shiva to descend to our earth plane to support or aid evolution is a near impossibility, but Sri Krishna is a constant presence amidst the world-play as the incarnate Divine and the World Teacher, the Avatar and the *jagat guru*, leading humanity towards its highest consciousness. It is his assurance to the human soul that he would be born upon earth, age after age, whenever the burden of unconsciousness would threaten to disrupt the evolutionary balance of the universe.

If Shiva is the archetypal ascetic, the ash-smeared Adiyogi with matted locks and serpents, Sri Krishna is the cowherd with the alluring flute, playmate of the *gopis*, king, statesman, and warrior who understands the intricacies of the world as much as he understands the most profound mysteries of the universe, is as much at home with politics as he is with metaphysics, can fight and destroy as skillfully as he can play the flute and dance.

If Shiva is the silence of the Infinite, the shunya in which floats all existence, Sri Krishna is the music of the spheres, he is the manifest universe brimming with life and energy, the radiant godhead of Ananda—the divine bliss of existence and consciousness. If Shiva is non-duality, the absolute Alone, Sri Krishna is the delight of the One playing amidst the infinite Many, the Lord of Love and the *rasa* of the Divine's all-becoming. The seers declare that this whole existence is Sri Krishna's blissful play, *Krishnalila*. Of him indeed the Upanishads say, *raso vai sa*—verily, he Himself is Delight.[128]

Hindu Dharma has two faces: one, Shiva, the ascetic, the tapasvi, seated on Kailash, symbolic of the supreme peaks of Yogic consciousness; and the other, Krishna, the delightful, the *anandmaya*,[129] the one sporting with the gopis in a *Raaslila* symbolic of the eternal play of the Divine and the human, the play of the spirit in matter, the play of love drawing the soul ever closer to the incomparable delight of union with the Divine. Shiva is the consciousness-source of existence, and Krishna is the delight-source: we arise out of consciousness and delight, and we return unto consciousness and delight. This is the mystery at the heart of Sanatan Dharma. Whichever route we take, through consciousness or delight, it is the same consummation we reach—for consciousness is delight, delight is consciousness. We say Shiva is that all-consciousness and Krishna is that all-delight out of which arises this universe—all beings and things are manifestations of Shiva, of Krishna. But these, too, are human expressions limited by human consciousness. The truth, as our Rishis declared trenchantly, is absolute oneness—Shiva and Krishna are two aspects of the same Parabrahman.

As the *Yajur Veda* declares categorically—*Shivaye Vishnu rupaye, Shiva rupaye Vishanave; Shivasya hrudayam Vishnur, Vishnuscha*

---

128 रसो वै स: —*Taittiriya Upanishad.*
129 Of ananda, filled with ananda, the ever-blissful; Sri Krishna is the godhead of Ananda, thus, *anandamaya.*

hrudayam Shivaha; yatha Shivamayo Vishnuhu, yevam Vishnu mayah Shivah: Shiva is the manifest form of Vishnu, another name for Sri Krishna; Vishnu is the manifest form of Shiva. Vishnu dwells in Shiva's heart as Shiva dwells in Vishnu's. Wherever one finds Vishnu, one will find Shiva; and wherever one finds Shiva, one will find Vishnu. Realizing the one is realizing the other.[130]

Thus, existence is consciousness, and consciousness is delight—Satchidananda. Where there is existence, there will be consciousness, and where there is consciousness and existence, there will be delight. To be, therefore, is to be conscious, and to be conscious is to possess the bliss or delight of being.

The moment one understands this triune reality, one understands as well the purpose and meaning of existence— to grow in consciousness towards the perfect delight of being. In fact, it is not even so much a question of one's growing in consciousness; it is more a matter of understanding that consciousness grows by its very nature towards more being and more delight. This is what is known as *brahmagati*—the movement of Brahman into its own vastness and bliss.

Shiva, then, is the expansion of consciousness into its own vastness, and Krishna is the deepening of consciousness into its own infinite depths of truth, knowledge, and delight. Together, for one who can fathom the experience, this is the whole of the *rasamaya* anubhava—and there is still an intenser bliss of knowing that Shiva, seated in the mind's pinnacle, opens the consciousness to the Truth above, the vast expanse of Brahman; and Krishna, seated in the inmost heart, opens the consciousness to the one Self in all and the eternal delight of being. The true devotee of the Sanatan Dharma is, thus, neither a *Shaivite* following Shiva as the one godhead, nor a *Vaishnavite* following Sri Krishna as the one godhead; he

---

130 शिवाय विष्णु रूपाय शिव रूपाय विष्णवे । शिवस्य हृदयं विष्णुं विष्णोश्च हृदयं शिवः । यथा शिवमयो विष्णुरेवं विष्णुमयः शिवः ।

is the Yogi in whose consciousness the two are eternally and integrally one.

It may be enough for some seekers to aspire for Shiva's perfect non-duality within themselves, and some seekers may be content aspiring for Krishna's perfect knowledge, action, and bliss, but for the complete Yogi who aspires to realize the very heart of the Sanatan Dharma, neither is sufficient: he must aspire for *purnata*, integrality and completeness, which is realizing Shiva's fierce purity in Krishna's delight and Krishna's bliss in Shiva's fierce purity. Can one even begin to conceive of such a realization? For this is a Yoga of a different dimension: austerity, asceticism, and impersonality merge blissfully into love and delight of the Personal Divine; non-duality revels in the variegated opulence of multiplicity, and multiplicity resolves back, moment to moment, into an indescribably profound unity. Everything comes together, all diverse streams converge, and the Yogi dissolves into the perfect ananda, only a thumb-sized portion of his inmost being remains to partake of the timeless Anandmaya Purusha, the Being of Bliss. This is the experience of the supreme, the most excellent rasa of all existence—*paramam rasanubhuti*.[131]

It is this *paramam rasanubhuti* that is at the heart of the Sanatan Dharma. All other experiences and realizations, all other processes and attainments, are only preparations for this supreme rasa, for it is in this rasanubhuti that existence is finally justified and validated in the most profound possible way. All existence arises out of Ananda and into Ananda subsides. Sorrow, pain and suffering, birth and death, delusion and ignorance, falsehood and evil are all steps along the way, processes of an infinite evolution of consciousness that even the vastest human mind would fail to grasp.

---

131 *Paramam*, supreme; *rasanubhuti* (rasa and anubhuti), realization and experience of delight.

This consummation of the Sanatan Dharma is a state of perfect and permanent absence of sorrow and disturbance; the Vedic Rishis called this the *anamayam padam,* the sorrowless state. This is the brahmanirvana that Sri Krishna holds as the highest good in the Bhagavad Gita. This nirvana is not an extinguishing or extinction of self—it is the consummation and ultimate fulfillment of the human soul in perfect union with the Divine.[132]

Anyone who understands this understands too that this universe and our human existence in it is not just maya and mithya, it's not just delusion and ignorance, not just pain and suffering, not just meaningless extinction in death, nor an eternity of heavenly reward or hellish retribution, nor even an ever-circling round of karmic processes from lifetime to lifetime. It is none of all this. Existence is a vast field of Lila, of divine delight and play; human life is a journey of consciousness from one peak of light and delight to another, ever higher, ever more fulfilling. It is not evil or falsehood that stands opposed to the godhead; it is our own spiritual ignorance and unconsciousness. It is an obvious thing—the antithesis of consciousness is unconsciousness, not evil. If anything, evil and falsehood that so bewilder the human mind exist only to serve the spiritual purpose of awakening the human soul to higher light and truth.

This is the truth of Sri Krishna: that all is his play, do not be bewildered, do not be dismayed by appearances; look deeper, look with more love and understanding, and you will see Sri Krishna, you will see Shiva, and you will see your own highest and deepest self, the Atman, and you will know that there are no divisions or differences. To realize one's own existence as the

---

132 कर्मजं बुद्धियुक्ता हि फलं त्यक्त्वा मनीषिणः । जन्मबन्धविनिर्मुक्ताः पदं गच्छन्त्यनामयम् ॥ — The sages who have united their reason and will with the Divine renounce the fruit which action yields and, liberated from the bondage of birth, they reach the status beyond misery. —Bhagavad Gita, 2.51.

Divine's play of consciousness and delight is the crowning glory of the devotee and the Yogi.

As Sri Ramakrishna once remarked, equating the Divine with honey—*I do not wish to become the honey; I want to taste and savor the honey.* This savoring of the divine honey is the soul of the Sanatan Dharma. Why else would one consent to be born as mortal on earth?

The Historical Krishna

So much about Krishna comes down to us through legends and folklore that it becomes difficult to sift facts from mythology or fiction. Did he really live as a man, albeit an Avatar? And if yes, what kind of a man must he have been to grow into such an extraordinary legend? And did he really do all those things ascribed to him—like killing the demons Trinavarta and Putana, vanquishing the serpent Kalia, lifting the hill Govardhana to protect the villagers and all that? Did he really have eight wives, and did he really sport with all the *gopis*? Where does one draw the line between historical fact and fanciful fiction?

True, it is difficult to know much about the real, historical Krishna. The real Krishna is in the background, a mystical figure known only to a select few and unknowable to most. What the world knows is Sri Krishna the myth and the legend, and through the myth and the legend, we catch glimpses of the extraordinary phenomenon that was Sri Krishna, as the eighth avatar of Vishnu, as a Mahayogi, a profound philosopher, a statesman, king, and warrior extraordinaire. Interwoven through all this are also the stories of his prophesied birth, childhood, and youth, the escape on an impossibly stormy night from imminent death, the exile from his own family and kingdom, his childish pranks and early miracles, his youthful romances and fierce conquests—all of which constitute some of the most fascinating mythologies of old.

Mythology is always a bit of history and a bit of poetry, a heady mix of fact, invention, and collective imagination, a blend of recorded events and metaphor. One needs a certain familiarity, perhaps even intimacy, with a person to write or say anything definitive or authoritative about them. There is no way any of us can travel back 5000 years to meet the historical Sri Krishna and pronounce anything definitive about him, but we have something as good, if not better, than that—the testimony of one who was a maharshi and had lived in Sri Krishna's consciousness through almost all his yogic life, one who knew Sri Krishna intimately in all the aspects and dimensions of his being—Sri Aurobindo.

Thus, in Sri Aurobindo's words—*The historicity of Krishna is of less spiritual importance and is not essential, but it has still a considerable value. It does not seem to me that there can be any reasonable doubt that Krishna the man was not a legend or a poetic invention but actually existed upon earth and played a part in the Indian past. Two facts emerge clearly, that he was regarded as an important spiritual figure, one whose spiritual illumination was recorded in one of the Upanishads, and that he was traditionally regarded as a divine man, one worshipped after his death as a deity; this is apart from the story in the Mahabharata and the Puranas.*

Om, the Imperishable Word

Om is this imperishable Word, Om is the Universe, and this is the exposition of Om. The past, the present and the future, all that was, all that is, all that will be, is Om. Likewise all else that may exist beyond the bounds of Time, that too is Om.[133]

Om is the quintessential signature of Hindu Dharma. No sacred task, no holy sacrifice or yajna, no worship, prayer, or invocation can begin without Om. Om is the first invocation and the last benediction. All mantras and hymns, all prayers and salutations to the Divine end on the note of Om. The Mother, Sri Aurobindo's spiritual collaborator, called Om *the signature of the Lord,* and the supreme invocation.

Whether one recites Om quietly within oneself or sings it in a group, it has the same beneficial effect of spreading the vibrations of peace and calm, of concentrating the mind and heart in the deepest or highest consciousness. Om is the sound that rises ever upward, from the lower chakras to the higher, from the lower nature to the higher, from our earth plane, the so-called *Mrityuloka* or the plane of death, to the highest *Anandaloka*, or the plane of Divine bliss. Om is the ascending path of Light from death to immortality, from unconsciousness to Truth-consciousness. It is believed in Sanatan Dharma that the right understanding of Om can open the passage of the mind to the highest realizations.

---

133 ओमित्येतदक्षरमिदँ सर्वं तस्योपव्याख्यानं भूतं भवद्भविष्यदिति सर्वमोङ्कार एव । यच्चान्यत्त्रिकालातीतं तदप्योङ्कार एव । —*Mandukya Upanishad.*

In Sri Aurobindo's words, *Om is the symbol, and the thing symbolized. It is the symbol, aksharam, the syllable in which all sound of speech is brought back to its wide, pure indeterminate state; it is the symbolised, aksharam, the changeless, undiminishing, unincreasing, unappearing, undying Reality which shows itself to experience ın all the change, increase, diminution, appearance, departure which in a particular sum and harmony of them we call the world.*[134]

Describing Om intellectually is a daunting task for Om is not a subject for academic study but a theme for meditative contemplation and inner concentration. Analyzing Om intellectually is like dissecting a poem into structure and semantics to find out how it is composed instead of plunging your mind and heart into it and letting it express itself through you. Analogies apart, this is what Om does: if we give ourselves wholly to it, immerse our minds and hearts in it, it comes alive in us, reveals and expresses itself through our consciousness, making our consciousness its own manifest field. This is the mantric power of Om.

The syllable Om itself is composed of three seed syllables—or letters as phonemes—A, U, and M,[135] and when pronounced together, give rise to the sound of OM or AUM, and it is this three-syllabled sound that the Yogi intones and meditates upon. There are layers of occult and mystical meanings involved with each of these three syllables, as with the integrated sound of Aum.

As Sri Aurobindo explains—*OM is the symbol of the triple Brahman, the outward-looking, the inward or subtle and the superconscient causal Purusha. Each letter A, U, M indicates one of these three in ascending order, and the syllable as a whole brings out the fourth state, Turiya, which rises to the Absolute. OM is the*

---

134 Excerpted from Sri Aurobindo's notes on the *Chhandogya Upanishads*.
135 A—अ, U—उ, and M—म.

*initiating syllable pronounced at the outset as a benedictory prelude
and sanction to all acts of sacrifice, all acts of giving, and all acts of
askesis; it is a reminder that our work should be made an expression
of the triple Divine in our inner being and turned towards him in
the idea and motive.*

Om is thus the vehicle of the highest meditations. By
meditating on each of the letters of AUM, the Yogi can access
and master the planes associated with each of the letters—the
waking, the subtle, the atmic or the inmost; and by meditating
on the integrated sound of AUM, the Yogi can enter the
integral Turiya[136] state that not only transcends but subsumes
the other three.

The *Mandukya Upanishad* opens with the declaration that
Om is the eternal, imperishable word. All other words, being
descriptors of transient subjects and objects of the universe,
perish; but Om being the descriptor of the Eternal, is itself
eternal and imperishable. The Hindus regard Om as the very
name of the Divine.

Let's reflect briefly on Om as the name of the Divine. All
manifestation consists of namarupa, the mind-body of all beings
in existence. The process of naming is essential for a complete
mental cognition of reality, as the senses, cognizing only form,
are unable by themselves to form a complete picture of reality.
The mind grasps or realizes—that is, makes real to itself—a
thing or being only by perceiving the form in conjunction with
the name, thus associating form with identifiable attributes.
Naming, therefore, gives the consciousness the power to recall
and invoke the entity that is named and perceived.

Thus, the name, in Sanatan Dharma, possesses enormous
power. We can perceive form but not be able to relate to the
form without recalling and invoking the name associated with

---

136 *Turiya* is the consciousness of our pure self-existence or our absolute being according to Sri
   Aurobindo. Sri Ramana refers to it as a state of wakeful sleep.

the form; a relationship is established and maintained only through namarupa, but in consciousness, a relationship doesn't need the form, the name alone is sufficient—the name can recall the form perfectly to mind even without the form being present. Form is impermanent and perishable since it depends on physical presence in space and time, but name, as a reality of consciousness, is imperishable and timeless. Thus, there are traditions in Hindu Dharma based solely on the name of the Divine, dispensing altogether with form. This is particularly true for some Vedantins who accept only the formless aspect of the Divine, for the formless Divine can only be invoked and recalled through the *nama* or the power of the *nama*. Anyone in love can readily testify to this power of the name—one only needs to recall the name of the beloved to be immediately in touch with them in one's consciousness, even to the exclusion of the entire world.

Om, then, is the seed-name of the Divine: Brahman, Atman, Ishvara are only descriptions of the attributes of the Divine, but Om is the name itself, the name that has the power to immediately recall and invoke the Divine. Meditating, therefore, on Om as the name of the Divine is held to be the most direct way to the realization of the Divine. The name leads to that which is named; the symbol leads to the symbolized. If Om is the living and direct symbol of the Divine, then the Divine, as the symbolized, is present in the name as its inmost vibration.

Om is thus not only the way but also the destination concealed in the way. To chant Om is to immediately connect in consciousness with all that Om represents, symbolizes, reveals, and conceals. Om is the surest, and perhaps the quickest, way to penetrate the multiple layers of the outer being and the outer universe and drill ever deeper into the inner and inmost layers of self and cosmic existence; it is indeed to return to one's spiritual source in Brahman.

As a mantra, Om is supreme, the *beej* or seed-mantra of all other mantras. Indeed, all mantras known to Yogis through the ages arise out of this one beej-mantra. Sri Krishna declares in the Bhagavad Gita, *Om iti ekaksharam brahman*—the single syllable Om is the supreme Brahman, and then goes on to establish his own identity with it: *pranavah sarva vedeshu*—within all the Vedas, I am the Aum; *giram asmi ekam aksaram*—of vibrations, I am the transcendental Aum. For those who know who Sri Krishna is, and what he represents, these three statements read together are the signature and seal of the Divine on Om.

In Sri Aurobindo's words again—*Om is the mantra, the expressive sound-symbol of the Brahman Consciousness in its four domains from the Turiya to the external or material plane. The function of a mantra is to create vibrations in the inner consciousness that will prepare it for the realisation of what the mantra symbolizes and is supposed indeed to carry within itself. The mantra OM should therefore lead towards the opening of the consciousness to the sight and feeling of the One Consciousness in all material things, in the inner being and in the supraphysical worlds, in the causal plane above now superconscient to us and, finally, the supreme liberated transcendence above all cosmic existence.*

And in the words of that other maharshi of the last century, Sri Ramakrishna—*Some sages ask what will you gain by merely hearing this sound of Om? You hear the roar of the ocean from a distance. By following the roar you can reach the ocean. As long as there is the roar, there must also be the ocean. By following the trail of Om you attain Brahman, of which the Word is the symbol. That Brahman has been described by the Vedas as the ultimate goal.*

Om is also known as *pranava*—the designator, *vachak*, of Ishvara, the Supreme Self.[137] By the *japa* or constant repetition of pranav with profound bhava or devotion, all obstacles in life and sadhana will disappear, and the consciousness will

---

137 Rishi Patanjali.

turn inward. The *Shiva Purana* describes Om as an excellent boat to cross the ocean of samsara or worldly existence, playing on an interesting etymology of the word pranav, the root *pra* from prakriti or manifestation, and *navam varam*, meaning excellent boat.

In the words of the Mother, *with the help of Om one can realize the Divine. Om has a transforming power. Om represents the Divine. You will recall this Om, Om, that's all. It must be manifested. If anything goes wrong, repeat Om, all will go well.*

The Guru in Sanatan Dharma

The Guru is one who personally leads you from the darkness of ignorance and unconsciousness to the light of Truth and Immortality. The Guru is the mother who nourishes the spirit even as the biological mother nourishes the body; the Guru is the father who disciplines, teaches, and instructs; he is the friend and guide who walks beside you, pace to pace, without judgment or expectation. But more than all that, the Guru is the living embodiment and representative of the Divine.

The Guru is the true anchor of Sanatan Dharma—not the priest, not the preacher, nor even the scripture. It is the Guru who is the source of all light and knowledge, the unfailing hand that steadies the difficult climb, the rock upon which you can stand, secure and safe. The Guru, in the Hindu tradition, is regarded as equal to God, *acharya devo bhava*—the *acharya*, one who teaches and transforms, is the divine.

There is an interesting fable. A long time ago, four wise men, seeking deeper answers to their existential queries, were wandering from place to place, looking for someone who could give them the key to the understanding they needed. Amongst these, the first wanted to find the secret to immutable bliss, permanent liberation from suffering. The second wanted the secret of prosperity and well-being—how to be permanently free of scarcity and insecurity. The third wanted to understand the meaning and significance of life. The fourth was a man of knowledge and wisdom but felt incomplete as his wisdom still did not have the transforming touch of the Supreme Truth that can come only through the living Guru. He did not know how to get to that.

So these four seekers came to an old banyan tree in a remote village and found there a young man sitting quite still, with a beatific smile on his face. Looking at his face, they all had the same thought simultaneously: that this young person would give them the key. So they sat down before him quietly and waited for him to open his eyes. The mysterious young man opened his eyes after what seemed an eternity and looked at the four of them. His smile became more radiant, and his eyes looked as if into the very depths of their hearts. But he said nothing. He just made a strange gesture, a *mudra*.[138] And, as if by some occult transmission, the four wise men understood, got their answers, their enlightenment. The first understood the root of human suffering; the second understood the root of fear and scarcity; the third understood the true value and significance of human existence; and the fourth realized *sannidhya*—the proximity to the living source, the deep inner contact with the Guru.

This is known as the first transmission of Yogic Knowledge from Guru to *shishya*, the disciple, and marked the birth of the Guru-Shishya tradition of Sanatan Dharma, a much-revered tradition that continues unbroken to this day. This tradition—*parampara* in Sanskrit—of transmission of Knowledge from Guru to disciple is indeed the backbone of Sanatan Dharma, for through this tradition, it is not just the knowledge and wisdom that is carried from generation to generation but the living inspiration and power of the Guru. This transmission may happen through the spoken or the written word, through inner inspiration—*prerna*—and insight, or, in rarer cases, through silence, *mauna*.

Adi Shankaracharya composed a beautiful verse to mark this first transmission of Knowledge from the first Guru to

---

138 A symbolic hand gesture used commonly in yoga and dance. In higher yoga practices, the mudra has the power to transmit a state of being, understanding, or occult knowledge.

the first disciples—*Praise and salutation to that Dakshinamurti* (one who faces the south), *who explains the true nature of the supreme Brahman, through his perfect silence, who is young in looks, surrounded by disciples who are old Sages, whose minds are fixed on Brahman, who is the greatest of teachers, who shows the Chinmudra* by his hand, *who is the personification of happiness, in the state of bliss within himself.*[139] Sri Ramana, also known as Dakshinamurti by his closest disciples, often used mauna to transmit spiritual knowledge to some of his disciples.

The disciple, too, must be worthy of the Guru. Not every person can become a true disciple. Traditionally, it is said that the Guru finds the disciple when the latter is spiritually ripe enough to receive the higher knowledge. But once the disciple finds the Guru one way or the other, the first thing is to surrender oneself to the Guru, to consecrate oneself. Consecration is the act of giving oneself integrally to the Guru, and by giving oneself, making oneself worthy of receiving the Guru's grace and force, preparing oneself in mind, heart, and body for the new inner life. Coming to the Guru implies severing one's emotional ties with the old life and identity and giving oneself to the life of the Spirit. At that point, the traditional practice for the disciple is to offer themselves, in a formal act of obeisance, to the Guru for life. Once the Guru formally accepts the obeisance, the initiation into the yogic or spiritual life is complete.

But obeisance and self-surrender are the initial steps—these must deepen into sannidhya, inner living contact and intimacy. To be in spiritual proximity of the Guru, in their living presence, is the essence of the Guru-shishya relationship. It does not matter if the Guru is physically near or far; it does not even matter whether the Guru is still in the physical body or not. Sannidhya transcends space, time, and form—the Guru

---

139 मौनव्याख्या प्रकटित परब्रह्मतत्त्वं युवानं, वर्षिष्ठांते वसद् ऋषिगणैः आवृतं ब्रह्मनिष्ठैः। आचार्येन्द्रं करकलित चिन्मुद्रमानंदमूर्तिं, स्वात्मारामं मुदितवदनं दक्षिणामूर्तिमीडे॥

who has realized the Self has gone beyond birth and death and can manifest as easily in the supraphysical planes as on the physical.

But the disciple must learn how to keep themselves open to the Guru and receive inwardly from the Guru, for the work of the Guru is in the consciousness—what the Guru transmits in words or gestures is only a mere fraction of what is transmitted through sannidhya. The whole weight of the teaching comes through the Guru's presence, and it is through his silence that the Truth is transmitted in all its force and purity. What is needed of the disciple is a state of deep receptive silence that can absorb the wordless influence of the Guru.

The Guru is the mediator between the human and the Divine, between Atman and the Paramatman, and the bridge between the mortal and the Eternal. The disciple must remember that there is no difference between the Guru and God. The Guru stands in the middle ground between the invisible and the visible, the manifest and the unmanifest, the high peaks of Self-realization and the base camp of our human aspiration our human sadhana. Without the Guru, our ascent would be enormously difficult and may take years of sadhana; with the Guru, we can fly and compress in a few years the sadhana of a lifetime. Such is the power of the Guru.

It is for this reason that Sanatan Dharma equates the Guru with the highest gods, and indeed, to Brahman itself—*guru sakshat param brahman*, the Guru himself is the supreme Brahman.[140]

---

140 गुरुर्ब्रह्मा गुरुर्विष्णुर्गुरुर्देवो महेश्वरः । गुरु साक्षात् परं ब्रह्म तस्मै श्रीगुरवे नमः — The Guru is Brahma, the creator; the Guru is Vishnu, the Preserver; the Guru is Maheshwara, the destroyer. The Guru himself is the living Supreme Brahman; my obeisance to that divine Guru.

The Gita,
the Essence of Dharma

The Upadesh of the Gita

If anyone wishes to know how exactly to live the Sanatan Dharma within oneself and in the situations and circumstances of everyday life, it is to the Bhagavad Gita that we must turn, for in its *upadesh*—the Vedic word for higher teaching—we find the most precise formulations of the Dharma. The Gita is a supremely pragmatic guidance on how to live an integral spiritual life in the world and how to apply the most profound truths of existence in the psychological and transactional details of our existence. There is no trace of speculative philosophy or reasoned theory in the Gita's upadesh; what the teacher gives to the disciple is an eminently practicable roadmap to the Eternal. The tone of the upadesh is neither didactic nor tentative: Krishna, the divine teacher, is telling Arjuna, the very down-to-earth and human disciple, how things are, with an authority of absolute knowledge and the profound tenderness of an elder brother.

Reflect on how their dialogue opens. Arjuna is despairing, and he is in no mood to fight his own family and kinsmen—

> *…if we slay*
> *Kinsfolk and friends for love of earthly power,*
> *Ahovat! what an evil fault it were!*
> *Better I deem it, if my kinsmen strike,*
> *To face them weaponless, and bare my breast*
> *To shaft and spear, than answer blow with blow.*[141]

---

141 From Edwin Arnold's *Song Celestial*, Chapter 1.

Krishna, quite the elder cousin, listens to Arjuna's desperate plea for peace, and, one would imagine smiling somewhat indulgently, replies—

> *How hath this weakness taken thee? Whence springs*
> *The inglorious trouble, shameful to the brave,*
> *Barring the path of virtue? Nay, Arjun!*
> *Forbid thyself to feebleness! it mars*
> *Thy warrior-name! cast off the coward-fit!*
> *Wake! Be thyself!*[142]

So far, the tone is familiar, friendly, an expression of emotional concern and support, but within the next few minutes, the tone shifts to the Upanishadic—

> *Thou grievest where no grief should be! thou speak'st*
> *Words lacking wisdom! for the wise in heart*
> *Mourn not for those that live, nor those that die.*
> *Nor I, nor thou, nor any one of these,*
> *Ever was not, nor ever will not be,*
> *For ever and for ever afterwards.*
> *All, that doth live, lives always!*[143]

The Upanishadic tone is not one of intellectual reasoning but of inner knowing, the assured tone of the maharshis, unarguably authoritative and yet deeply compassionate, the voice of someone who knows and is perfectly at ease with his knowledge; there is no hesitation, speculation, or exaggeration in this tone, nor any arrogance or humility. The tone is matter of fact—*this is how it is and this is how it shall be!*

---

142 From Edwin Arnold's *Song Celestial*, Chapter 2.
143 From Edwin Arnold's *Song Celestial*, Chapter 2.

This Upanishadic tone of the Bhagavad Gita is irresistible, and it puts all reasoning to rest and brings the mind to a kind of silence that is wonderfully conducive to sruti, for sruti is also meditative listening, absorbing the word—*vak*—in deep inner silence where it can explode in its fulness of meaning and significance. To come to sruti, it is important that the mind is not engaged in any kind of intellectual activity, and it must be open to what is being received as vak or bhava. It is through sruti that the highest knowledge is given and received.

The Gita reveals, sloka by sloka,[144] the inner mysteries of the self and life in the universe and builds up to a crescendo that reveals the highest, the secret of all secrets, the *rahasyam uttamam*[145] of the Gita. Many search for this supreme secret in the final chapters of the Gita, perhaps in the final verses where Sri Krishna seems to be wrapping up the great Wisdom. But the supreme secret or mystery is to be found not in a single sloka or series of slokas of the Gita but in the whole of it, in the entirety of its knowledge-body. The whole of the Gita is the mantra of the great Yoga that Sri Krishna imparts, through the instrumentality of Arjuna, to the whole of humanity.

For the Knowledge or the Secret was not imparted to Arjuna alone. As the great Teacher himself declares, in a somewhat mystical strain—*This imperishable Yoga I gave to Vivasvan, the Sun-God, Vivasvan gave it to Manu, the father of men, Manu gave it to Ikshvaku, head of the Solar line.*[146] Whatever the profound meaning of this mystical verse, it indicates one thing very clearly: the Gita's knowledge is eternal, timeless. It does not begin with Arjuna on the battlefield of Kurukshetra nor does it end with

---

144 Śloka (श्लोक) from the root *śru*, to hear, the same root for śruti, that which is heard. Generally, the word *sloka* is used for verse in any Sanskrit composition but the word has several technical and metrical definitions as well, which do not concern us here.

145 Literally, the supreme (*uttamam*) secret or mystery (*rahasyam*).

146 इमं विवस्वते योगं प्रोक्तवानहमव्ययम् । विवस्वान्मनवे प्राह मनुरिक्ष्वाकवेऽब्रवीत् ॥—Bhagvad Gita, 4.1.

Arjuna's enlightenment and his going into the great battle. Going by Sri Krishna's words, it begins before human civilization, with the Sun-God receiving it from Sri Krishna, perhaps at the dawn of cosmic Time, and continues to this day, an unbroken, and perhaps unbreakable, chain of transmission because the source is Divine.

The Symbol Battle

The Bhagavad Gita—also known as the upadesh of the Gita—is an episode in the epic poem Mahabharata and is symbolically set in the middle of the battlefield of Kurukshetra, just as a battle is about to begin between the clans of the Kauravas and the Pandavas. On the surface, in the visible earthly plane, the battle is about politics and military conquest—the Pandavas, who represent the forces of dharma, fighting the Kauravas, who represent the forces of adharma, for a piece of the kingdom that was rightfully theirs. Whoever would win this battle would rule the kingdom of Kuru. But on a deeper spiritual plane, where most of the Mahabharata is played out, this is a *dharmayuddha*—a battle for dharma, for righteousness, for the good and the true. And still deeper, at a cosmic level, this dharmayuddha is the manifestation of a primordial struggle between the forces of evolution and entropy, or what is symbolically known in most human mythologies as Light and Darkness. In the Vedic narrative of the Rishis, *prakasa* or Light represents evolution, and *tamas*, or darkness and inertia, represents entropy. Kurukshetra, more than the physical, is the inner—or yogic—battlefield where this primordial struggle between prakasa and tamas is brought to a climactic intensity.

In the Vedic narrative of the maharshis, the dynamic interplay of prakasa and tamas is the very nature of manifestation. Prakasa is not the physical but the supernal and supramental True Light—*rtam-jyotih*—of *Surya*, the supreme Sun, which is the living symbol of Brahman in the manifestation. Surya represents both Brahman and Rta—the divine cosmic order.[147] Therefore, the prakasa of Surya is the creative force—hailed by the Vedic Rishis as the Golden Ray that pulls ever upward—pulling cosmic existence towards Sat and Rta, the Truth, and the Cosmic order leading to the Truth. This very movement represents Dharma, as Dharma is the ascending movement towards Satyam and Ritam, the expression and actualization of Sat in cosmic manifestation.

Tamas, on the other hand, is the complete absence of prakasa and Surya, a primordial darkness of dense sleep, or deep trance, where prakasa lies coiled up in itself, like a black hole at the heart of a nebula.[148] Tamas then naturally pulls ever downward, back towards chaos, darkness, unconsciousness, and death— tamas is indeed the genesis of death, for death is the movement of life towards timeless sleep and trance, the closing of the inner eye to Surya and to the inner devas, those shining ones born of Surya who bring forth the awakening ray into the darkness of eternal Night.

The dharmayuddha then, in this deepest sense, is the human struggle for dharma, the upward pull towards Rta, the eternal cosmic order, led by Sri Krishna himself, against the dense pull of tamas downward into the abyss of sleep and death.

Each of us is given this dharmayuddha, where we must fight our own inner demons of adharma, counter that constant downward pull of tamas in all our thoughts and acts, and pave the upward path to Rta, to Dharma, to the radiance of Surya. This is undoubtedly the dharma of the hero-warrior, the Arjuna in all of us, and this obviously cannot be accomplished without the living presence of Krishna, the Ishvara in all of us. Thus, both the yuddha of the Mahabharata and the upadesh of the Gita

---

147 *Surya* in the Veda represents Brahman and Brahman's illuminating revelatory knowledge; the Light of Surya is also known as the true Light, *rtam-jyotih*, or the Vast Light, *brh jyoti*. —Sri Aurobindo, *The Secret of the Veda*.

148 This is not poetic imagery; these are the real-symbols of the Vedic narrative. In the vision of the maharshis, cosmic forms and processes are themselves symbolic of the inner processes of the 'evolution' of Surya in earthly mind and matter.

are within us, the constant background of all our psychological, social, and political existence on this earth, the background too of all our inner struggles, conflicts, contradictions, our desires and dreams, our little joys and sorrows, our trials and tribulations.

The symbolic significance of the Gita opening with Arjuna's bewilderment and despair on the battlefield of Kurukshetra should now be obvious—Arjuna is not just the hero-warrior of the Mahabharata, he is also, and much more, the representative human, the prototype, who is chosen to receive the highest wisdom from the incarnate godhead on a battlefield that represents the epic battle of the ages. His *adhikara*[149] to represent humanity extends far beyond the battlefields and kingdoms of the Mahabharata—it goes back, so to speak, to the origins of human time, an epoch before the dawn of humanity when the earth plane was peopled by gods and Rishis. Sri Krishna was then Narayana, the first of the divine seers, and Arjuna was Nara, Narayana's soulmate, his inseparable twin-soul. Together they undertook to perform severe *tapasya*—'askesis' is the nearest English equivalent of this word—to consume the *asuras*[150] who threatened to seize the earth-plane and tilt the balance of evolution.[151] The Mahabharata's dharmayuddha is the selfsame extension of this old battle against the asuras—and the bone of contention, as always, is the domination of the earth and, therefore, the universe. It is against this cosmic backdrop that the upadesh of the Gita must be read and understood.

---

149 This is one of the expressions of Sanskrit that has no equivalence in English. The closest rendering would be a moral, spiritual, intellectual, or social authority or right; in the Gita's context, it would be *the right to know or receive* the supreme knowledge.

150 Beings who represent the adverse forces that oppose the devas or divine beings. In Vedic mythology, the asuras are always fighting the devas for the domination of the universe and especially the conquest of the earth which is the only plane of existence that allows evolution.

151 According to Vedic mythology, the earth-plane, known as *mrityu-loka* in Sanskrit (literally, the mortal plane), is the only plane where any kind of evolution of life and consciousness is possible and thus, whichever force or principle, *daivic* or *asuric*, dominates this plane will determine the direction of the evolution towards itself.

The Question of Death

At the heart of Arjuna's despair is the question of death, of killing those who are his friends, kinsmen, and teachers—*if we slay kinsfolk and friends for love of earthly power, what an evil fault it were!* Being a hero-warrior, a noble kshatriya, Arjuna's concern is killing the other, but were he to be a lesser man, more ordinary in his temperament, his chief concern, most likely, would have been getting killed rather than killing. Behind all our fears and anxieties, our selfishness and greed, our attachments and possessions, is always the stated or unstated, conscious or unconscious, thought of death. Death, indeed, is the 'mother of all our fears', and by ridding our hearts of this one fear, we can soar beyond all others. It is thus said in the Dharma, he who does not know death cannot know life.

Thus, Sri Krishna begins his upadesh by confronting the ever-vexing question of death itself, for without first surpassing the fear of death, no yoga or upward climb is possible.

You grieve for those that should not be grieved for, yet speak words of wisdom, says Krishna to Arjuna, *the enlightened man does not mourn either for the living or for the dead. It is not true that at any time I was not, nor you, nor these kings of men; nor is it true that any of us shall ever cease to be hereafter.*

This is the first key to the profound mystery—there was never a time I was not, nor you, nor is it true that any of us will ever cease to be hereafter. No one dies. Only the Atman changes forms—*as the soul passes physically through childhood and youth and age, so it passes on to the changing of the body.* Only those who do not understand this simple fact of being will tremble at the thought of death, one's own or others'. But this 'simple' fact is not so simple, it seems, for how is one to really know, in experience, that what Krishna says is true? Krishna understands this and thankfully does not ask Arjuna to accept what he says unquestioningly. That is why the tone of the upadesh is dialogic and not didactic.

Krishna then defines the Real, and the Atman as that which represents the Real. *Nasato vidyate bhavo*, Krishna states, *nabhaavo vidyate satah*: that which really is—*Sat*—cannot go out of existence, just as that which is non-existent—*asat*—cannot come into being.[152] Krishna invokes here the knowledge of the maharshis: Sat, the Real, is that which abides eternally, is immutable, never changes or ceases to be, while the not-real, asat, is that which is impermanent and constantly changing. To know and understand this through self-reflection, observation in inner and outer experience, is the beginning of the upward ascent. When we observe carefully, we begin to clearly see that everything we are aware of through the mind and senses is impermanent, *anityam*. To know the impermanent as impermanent is really the beginning of wisdom, for how would it be possible to get attached to that which is in the passing, which will cease to be, in a moment or in an hour or even in a year or a decade? The great teachers of dharma exhort us always to look beyond the immediacy of the experience or the event, to widen our perspective, to look at life from a cosmic standpoint, and to know in our minds that nothing that we see, touch, or feel will last, and everything will pass into the fathomless silence of eternal time. And that which passes, as Krishna says, is asat, non-real; only that which abides, does not cease to be, that which is immutable and eternal—*akshara* and *nityam*—is the Real.

---

152 नासतो विद्यते भावो नाभावो विद्यते सतः।उभयोरपि दृष्टोऽन्तस्त्वनयोस्तत्त्वदर्शिभिः। — That which really is, cannot go out of existence, just as that which is non-existent cannot come into being. The end of this opposition of 'is' and 'is not' has been perceived by the seers of essential truths. —Bhagavad Gita, 2.16.

This whole phenomenal world that we know outwardly and the psychological world we know inwardly, by this definition, are not real. So why identify with the not real? Why grieve for that which shall, in the cosmic scheme of things, anyway pass?

Asato ma sadgamaya, as the maharshis prayed to the eternal Spirit in themselves, *tamaso ma jyotirgamaya, mrtyorma amritam gamaya*—lead me forth from Unreality to Reality, lead me forth from Darkness to Light, lead me forth from Death to Immortality.[153] To know that in us which is already and eternally immortal, beyond birth, decay, and death, the Atman, the eternal Spirit, therefore, is the first step of our ascent.

---

153 ॐ असतो मा सद्गमय।तमसो मा ज्योतिर्गमय।मृत्योर्मा अमृतं गमय। ॐ शान्ति: शान्ति: शान्ति: —
Om asato ma sad gamaya, tamaso ma jyotir gamaya, mrtyor ma amritam gamaya. Om shantih shantih shantih. —*Brihadaranyaka Upanishad*, 1.3.28.

No One Dies

The first great secret of the Gita is thus unveiled by Sri Krishna to Arjuna: that eternal Spirit, that Sat, which has become all this, is imperishable, immortal, and cannot be slain, for who can slay the immortal, imperishable Self? The body is finite and decays, and has an end, but that which shines through the body, possesses, and uses the body, is ananta—illimitable, eternal—and thus, indestructible. Whosoever regards this Self as slayer or slain is ignorant of the truth of being, for neither does the Self slay and nor can it be slain. This Self, this eternal atman, does not take birth, nor does it die, nor is it a thing that comes into being once and on passing away will never come into being again—atman is unborn, ancient, eternal, and does not die with the death of the body.

Whoever knows this atman as the real, immortal, eternal, imperishable spiritual existence cannot slay or cause to be slain. For the embodied soul casts away old and takes up new bodies as a man changes worn-out garments for new. Weapons do not cleave the atman, and fire does not burn it, water does not drench it, the wind does not dry it, eternally stable, immobile, all-pervading, it is for ever and ever. This atman is unmanifest, it is unthinkable, it is immutable, so it is described by the Srutis; therefore, knowing it as such, you should not grieve its passing or rejoice its coming. Even if you were to think of the atman as being constantly subject to birth and death, still, you should not grieve for certain is death for the born, and certain is birth for the dead. Therefore, what is inevitable ought not to be a cause of sorrow.[154]

---

154 Sankhya Yoga, Bhagavad Gita, 2. 17–27.

But this great secret, even when unveiled by Krishna himself, is not so easy to live, for the knowledge of the buddhi is no substitute for anubhava. But of death, there cannot be anubhava, only intuitive glimpses and insights which demand profound reflection, meditation, inner silence, and concentration. The true understanding of this secret comes only through atmajnana, atmachetana, for only by knowing the atman directly will we know the truth of Krishna's upadesh. This is why Krishna himself says—*One sees it as a mystery or one speaks of it or hears of it as a mystery, but none knows it. That—the Self, the One, the Divine—we look on and speak and hear of as the wonderful beyond our comprehension, for after all our learning from those who have knowledge, no human mind has ever known this Absolute.*[155]

The only assured way of resolving this 'mystery' is by identifying ourselves with the Atman and not the namarupa or the body-mind complex: of this, we have spoken earlier. We are not the body, for the body is ever-changing, though its continuous changing may not register on us moment to moment; and also, the body—or its awareness—comes and goes, as during deep sleep, deep meditative or comatose states, the body for all practical purposes, disappears. It comes back to consciousness only when its awareness returns to the conscious mind. Also, through atma-vichara, we can clearly see that the body is an object in our awareness, and whatever we are aware of cannot be ourselves. Through steady contemplation and reflection, it is quite possible to break the mind's habitual identification with the body.

But the mind, too, is not what we are. The identification with the mind goes deeper and is subtler, but through steady self-reflection and observation of the mind's activities, we can disengage and detach from the mind and regard it as something quite outside of us; and more and more the sense of being

---

155 Bhagavad Gita, 2.29.

an impersonal witness, sakshi, of the mind will grow till the identification shifts decisively from mental activities to pure witnessing. Once the consciousness stabilizes in the witnessing, we can take it still deeper within till we begin to sense the psychic or the Atman.

Whosoever becomes conscious of the Atman becomes conscious too of the eternal, the timeless. But, going deeper into Krishna's upadesh, we realize that the consciousness of the Atman and its immortality is perhaps only the initiation of the great Yoga of the Gita—we must pass eventually beyond time and universe into the supreme rta-chit, the truth-consciousness. To attain that height of Yoga, we have first to become fully conscious of ourselves as Atman, beyond the limitations of body and mind; and then we have to heighten and widen into cosmic consciousness and begin to live there as naturally and comfortably as we live in our present personal consciousness. To know oneself as Atman, and to know all existence as Atman, is the characteristic feature of cosmic consciousness.

Dharma as Ascension

In the evolutionary sense of the Gita, we may regard dharma as any movement of consciousness or life that ascends and widens towards Satyam and Brihat—the true and the vast—and any contrary movement of life or consciousness that falls back towards tamas and ego, or refuses to rise from the ego, may be regarded as adharma. In the Dharmic idiom, dharma is *urdhvagati*,[156] and adharma is *adhogati*[157]—dharma pulls the consciousness upward, towards the higher chakras, or centers of consciousness, and adharma either keeps the consciousness tied to the lower chakras or always tends to fall back towards them; Dharma tends inevitably towards the *Sahasrara*, the thousand-petalled Lotus blooming above the head, opening naturally to cosmic consciousness, a high and wide knowledge, freedom, and peace; and adharma equally inevitably tends to shrink into the small ego-consciousness and fall back towards the *muladhara*, the very base and root of existence.

Urdhvagati, in the context of the Gita's Yoga, is our heavenward ascent into the timeless vast of Brihat, and adhogati is our fall into the hellhole of misery, greed, and lust. One is the upward path of dharma—ritsya panthah—and the other of adharma, and this is the eternal choice that drives the evolution of life and consciousness on earth: Dharma is the invocation of the *daivic*—the divine, and adharma is the invocation of the

---

156 *Ūrdhvagati* (ऊर्ध्वगति) from *urdhva* meaning upward and *gati* meaning movement: upward soaring, heavenward.
157 *Adhogati* (अधोगति) from *adhas* meaning downward and *gati,* movement: downward going, degeneration, relapse.

asuric—the undivine, the darkness at the heart of things. Both of these are equally strong tendencies or possibilities in every one of us, and, at any moment, in any circumstance, we can go either way. The upadesh of the Gita, with Sri Krishna himself as the Teacher, precisely occurs when Arjuna is poised delicately between the two ends of the consciousness-spectrum: he can rise into dharma as easily as he can fall into adharma.

Even for the best of us, this is always an extremely subtle and difficult choice. Our inner Arjuna, facing myriad dharmic dilemmas, tends to fall too readily and frequently into adharma— all bodies, as physics tells us, tend to fall earthwards.

The Conflict and the Resolution

Every age, every form of conscious life, every individual existence possesses, to some degree, its own *swadharma*[158]—its natural truth and law of being, its own dharma. To find and live our swadharma is the first duty enjoined by Dharma upon us. Those who cannot or do not live their swadharma fall easily into adharma. This is important to grasp. Arjuna stands upon the brink of adharma when he refuses to bear arms against the Kauravas on the battlefield. Ironically, this moment of Dharmic crisis comes upon him not because he abandons Dharma but because he feels the awakening of what he believes to be a higher or deeper dharma in him. This is what makes Dharma subtle and complex. Unlike simplistic moral or religious commandments of *thou shalt* and *thou shalt not*, the conundrums of Dharma go far deeper into the human psyche and evoke a far deeper and more complex response.

Reflect on Arjuna's dharmic crisis with which he turns to his divine charioteer and companion: the great battle is about to commence; the armies of the Kauravas and the Pandavas are ranged on both sides of the battlefield; the chariot in which Arjuna sits and which Sri Krishna steers is in the very middle. The hero-warrior looks upon the enemy and sees those whom he loves, reveres, and cares for, his kin, his friends, his teachers, and mentors. Despair broods upon his heart, and in a moment, he is reduced to pathetic helplessness. Turning to his friend and philosopher, he says—*Nay, I cannot bear arms against those who*

---

158 Swadharma (स्वधर्म), literally one's own (*swa*) dharma or law or truth of being.

are mine! For amongst these hordes are my own kinsmen, my own teachers, my own grandsire. To fight and kill them for a mere earthly kingdom, nay, I shall not, for my soul refuses such a sinful act. It is better that I renounce and retire into the forests than rule at the cost of losing my soul!

This surely is not a sentiment that may be called adharmic. Not wanting to kill those whom you love and revere for the sake of an earthly kingdom is certainly not adharmic, for what can be nobler than forgiveness, renunciation of ambition and worldly claim? For many, this would be the case of a higher dharma overriding a lower, more selfish one. Perhaps a Gandhi would have loved this conversion of Arjuna,[159] but Sri Krishna is not taken in. He quietly dismisses Arjuna's moral trepidation and high-sounding sentiment and tells him, in so many words—*You will lose your soul not by action, Arjuna, but precisely by avoiding action. To fight and win on this battlefield is your dharma, that which is enjoined upon you by your highest nature and your deepest values. Fight you must, and not because you personally stand to gain or lose, not because this is right in this given scheme of things, not even because you are a warrior and must delight in the battle and the victory, but only because this is the act to which you are brought by Me, because this is My command to you. Fight for Me, Arjuna, and be perfectly calm knowing that it is for Me, and by My force, that you fight!*

Two clear insights here—one, that the true motive and purpose of all action is the Divine's will and not our own; all that we think, feel, will, desire, or fear to do, is to be given up to the Divine in a spirit of sacrifice and surrender, yajna, and yoga. *Yajna*[160] is a central idea of the Gita, an idea that keeps

---

159 Gandhi had said, 'Hindus should never be angry against the Muslims even if the latter might make up their minds to undo even their existence.'

160 Yajña (यज्ञ) pronounced yag-ya, refers to an act or process by which one offers or surrenders something of value to oneself for the sake of the Divine or the gods or deities. The sacrifice of oneself is considered the highest of sacrifices. Yajna is also used in the sense of *tapas* or askesis, any sustained and intense discipline or process to attain a high, usually spiritual, goal.

developing throughout the upadesh till it culminates in the final sacrifice, the abandonment of all dharmas, of Dharma itself, in an absolute self-giving to Sri Krishna. And two, the truth behind all our dharmas and karmas is the Divine; it is he who governs, wills, shapes, and directs the destinies and actions of individuals and nations, it is he alone who pulls all the strings while we believe that it is our desires, duties, and ambitions that move us to action.

This may seem to be some kind of divine determinism, but it is not. As we understand the deeper dimensions of Krishna's teachings, we begin to see that there is a truth deeper than the superficial duality of free will and determinism. As long as we live in our lower natures, moved by prakriti and karma, by our fears, compulsions, and desires, we obviously do not have any free will, and it is all determined and conditioned; and when we have given ourselves entirely to Sri Krishna, have become instruments of his will, then free will becomes irrelevant.

All conflicts then are essentially conflicts of ego, self-interest, self-preservation, whatever the psychological or material manifestation of the conflict may be, and the resolution is only one—surrender to the will of the Divine. But because the will of the Divine is not directly revealed or known to all, it is not easy to come to this resolution. So, for those of us who do not know the Divine will yet, there is the upadesh that contains in precise detail the guidance necessary not only for our deeper dharmic struggles but even for the living of our daily lives in samsara.

Yajna

Sacrifice, *yajna*, and instrumentality, *nimitta bhava*, are the two leitmotifs of the Gita.[161] No practice of the Gita is possible without understanding these two concepts—the idea of *yajna* runs deep through the Gita, and indeed, the whole of Vedic Dharma, and may be regarded as the key to unlocking the secret of the Gita. *It is through sacrifice*, the Rishis declare, *that one attains the nectar of Immortality*. Sri Krishna himself declares to Arjuna—*they who enjoy the nectar of immortality left over from the Sacrifice attain the eternal Brahman.*[162]

The *Sacrifice* here refers not to an act of renunciation but a process of transformation, almost like inner alchemy. We give up first, gradually or rapidly, all that we regard or believe to be ours; we willingly, even joyfully, 'sacrifice' all that we possess in the knowledge that whatever is sacrificed to the Divine is already his, and we are only giving to him what was never ours, so that, as the fruits of the sacrifice, we may be restored that which is rightfully ours. But this is the first *ahuti*[163] only.

We quickly realize that renouncing or sacrificing objects we possess is pointless if we do not sacrifice possessiveness itself, that deep-seated idea of me and mine, *mamatva*. So the deeper ahuti that must follow is of possessiveness itself, of mamatva, of the me and mine. But how are we to purify ourselves of possessiveness—*mine*-ness, if we will—without first purifying ourselves of the

---

161 Nimitta-bhava (निमित्त भाव) or nimittatva (निमित्तत्व)—instrumentality, from nimitta, instrument or cause. From the line—निमित्तमात्रं भव सव्यसाचिन्—be an instrument only. —Bhagavad Gita, 11.33.

162 यज्ञशिष्टामृतभुजो यान्ति ब्रह्म सनातनम् —Bhagavad Gita, 4.31.

163 Āhuti (आहुति), offering, oblation at one level; calling or invoking at another. Often used synonymously with sacrifice, *ahuti* is what one offers in the process of sacrifice.

idea of *me*? And this is the crux: *ahambhava*,[164] that inherent unshakeable sense of being a person and a personality, is at the root of all sense of possessing and belonging. So the Yajna cannot be completed without the sacrifice of selfhood, ahambhava, for that is the essential offering demanded.

The real sacrifice, of which the rest is a symbol, is of the aham with its associated worlds at the altar of the Atman. Symbolically, the head has to be cut off and offered to the Divine—the head, which represents the ego, the mental and vital personality, the seat of the *buddhi*[165] and *chitta*.[166] Thus, if the head were to go, one's mental and cognitive faculties would go, one's reasoning and knowledge would go, and what would remain, symbolically, would be the heart and the body. The heart and the body, then, would be the next offerings at the altar.

The body, which represents the very base, *adhara*, of the manifestation, is not a major issue. The body is a docile and plastic instrument of the mind and heart. The body, willy-nilly, goes where the mind and heart lead. This is a fact experienced every day and by everyone. The body's problems are inevitably rooted in the head or the heart. Left to itself, the body has no desires or fears, no violence or greed. Even the body's illnesses and diseases have their roots in the mind or the vital.

It is the heart, the seat of the *prana* or the life force, that represents the roots and knots of personal identification, the most stubborn knots of personal identity. It is here that one's *ahambhava*, the ego-sense, is situated. Even when one manages to purify oneself of the ego in the buddhi and the chitta, it remains

---

164 Literally, the I-sense: *aham*, I, *bhava*, sense, state of being, attitude, feeling, awareness.

165 *Buddhi* (बुद्धि) from *budh* (बुध्), meaning to be awake, aware, conscious. Buddhi is the power of forming and retaining conceptions and general notions, intelligence, reason, intellect, mind, discernment, judgment; also, comprehension, apprehension, understanding — Sir Monier-Williams, *A Sanskrit-English Dictionary*.

166 *Chitta* (चित्त) is mental consciousness, the mind stuff. Patanjali's famous expression *chitta vritti* refers to the waves or modifications of this *chitta*. (*Yogas chittavritti nirodh*: Yoga is the cessation of the waves of the chitta — Yoga Aphorisms of Patanjali).

stubbornly in the prana, refusing to budge. This is indeed the crux of the whole yogic issue: the essential ego-sense is almost inseparable from the prana and the feelings. Trying to get out of the ego in the prana is like trying to get out of one's skin.

But the heart center, the seat of the ego-self, is not just that: it is also the opening to the deeper self in us, the true individual, the spiritual or the psychic self—*chaitya purusha*, the one who is conscious within of its spiritual truth of being, its origin, and purpose.[167] Thus, if the heart is the seat of the chief resistance, it is also the key to the decisive conquest only if we can find our way into the cave of the heart, the hridaye guhayam of the Vedas.

The ahuti or offering of the heart that is asked of us is of the ego-self, the surface heart, and the purohit, the one that offers from the front, the leader of the Yajna, is the Will in the heart, symbolized by the divine agni, the psychic flame that burns ever upward and clears the way for the upward ascent of the being. When Sri Krishna tells Arjuna that he is seated as the Self in the heart, *ahamatma sarva bhutashayasthita*,[168] he is invoking that divine agni, the psychic self, in Arjuna, beyond all the noise and confusion of the outer mind and heart, and this indeed is the progression of the great Yajna in each one of us—the sacrifice of the self to the Self, the rising upward of the agni in the heart from the 'subterranean caves' of unconsciousness to the peaks of perfect truth-consciousness, rta-chit.

---

167 Chaitya purusha means the portion of the Divine which guides and governs from within, the chaitya Guru, the indwelling teacher and guide. In Sri Aurobindo's Integral Yoga, chaitya purusha represents the psychic being, the Purusha in the heart. The psychic being is the soul developing in evolution. (From A.B. Purani's *Evening Talk with Sri Aurobindo*.)

168 अहमात्मा सर्वभूताशयस्थितः — I am the Self, which abides within all beings. —Bhagvad Gita, 10.20.

Sraddha

But the indispensable ingredient for the Yajna, the fuel that will ignite the psychic agni, is neither knowledge nor devotion but *sraddha,* which is the very basis of all knowledge and devotion. *Sraddha,*[169] a difficult word to translate, implies faith, but a knowing, intuitive faith, almost a foreknowledge, a faith that is also our deepest aspiration and a firm holding of it in the mind and heart, in all conditions.[170] Krishna reveals the significance of such   sraddha to Arjuna—*shraddhamayoyam purusho yo yacchraddhah sa eva sah:*[171] whatever is our sraddha, that is what we are and what we become.

Sraddha, then, is not just mental or vital faith but spiritual, the soul's prefiguration of truth that it contains within itself as the seed of future realization, an intuitive knowing that comes long before mental knowledge. It is by sraddha that one can have an entirely effective and all-embracing faith in the Divine without having the realization. In fact, sraddha is the soul-force that precipitates realizations by transforming what is held as thought or belief into the living reality of experience. Without sraddha, as the teachers of the Dharma say, no spiritual realization is possible; and with sraddha, no realization is impossible. Sraddha is a force of self-becoming: we can spiritually will ourselves to

---

169 From the root *srat*, meaning truth, or whatever is true to one's aspiration, and *dha* implying holding, placing, or establishing.

170 As indicated by Sri Aurobindo.

171 सत्त्वानुरूपा सर्वस्य श्रद्धा भवति भारत।श्रद्धामयोऽयं पुरुषो यो यच्छ्रद्धः स एव सः। — The faith of each man takes the shape given to it by his stuff of being, O Bharata. This Purusha, this soul in man, is, as it were, made of shraddha, a faith, a will to be, a belief in itself and existence, and whatever is that will, faith or constituting belief in him, he is that and that is he. —Bhagavad Gita, 17.3.

become whatever we want or need to become, and eventually, at the pinnacle of our consciousness, become the Divine even as the Divine has become us. *Sraddha mayoyam purushso*, as Krishna explains—the Purusha, the conscious self in us, is made up of sraddha, and that is why we, the outer person, can become whatever we will to become because all becoming is finally by the creative will of Purusha in us. Therefore, the transformative power of sraddha.

In the buddhi, sraddha transforms knowledge into truth—jnana into satyam—and in the heart, sraddha transforms devotion—*bhakti*—into pure love—*prema*—and love into complete identification with the one we love—*sayujya*. This is why sraddha is regarded as the single most important condition for living the Sanatan Dharma. Sraddha is what makes all the difference between belief and reality, religion and Yoga.

The Inmost Secret

By Me, all this universe has been extended in the ineffable mystery of My being; all existences are situated in Me, not I in them[172]— declares Krishna to Arjuna. This is the divine seal Krishna places on the upadesh of the Gita, delivering the most sacred of his secrets to humanity: you don't have to go anywhere or do anything to find me—I am everywhere, in everyone and everything, and everyone and everything is in me—*by Me, all this universe has been extended.*

This revelation is the kernel of the Gita, that this universe is a self-extension of Krishna, who is the supreme being, *Purushottama* in the language of the Gita. Krishna is not a potter creating an artifact, he is a poet, a *kavi*, who extends himself into his creation, and thus nothing here is not him, and nothing here exists that is not in him. There are verses upon verses of the Gita echoing this same thought in various contexts and situations. The specific bhava may differ, but the import is always the same—all that we are, become, know, and feel, now or ever, is Krishna. There is none other, and there is no division or diversity in that one being: *neha nanasti kincana*, as the Upanishad declares.[173]

Anyone who grasps the significance of these statements will immediately realize that Sri Krishna is not an abstract, remote, and unreachable entity but the living substance of what we are and what everything is. He is literally the breath and stuff of

---

172 मया ततम् इदम् सर्वम् जगत् अव्यक्त-मूर्तिना। मत्-स्थानि सर्व-भूतानि न च अहम् तेषु अवस्थितः॥
— *Bhagavad Gita,* 9.4.
173 मनसैवानुद्रष्टव्यं नेह नानास्ति किंचन—Through the mind alone is the Divine to be realized. There is in It no diversity. —*Brihadaryanka Upanishad* 4.11.

which all of us and everything is made—in his various aspects, he is Atman, Purusha, Ishvara, and in the substance of our minds and hearts, he is sraddha.

This is Krishna's miracle that he shares all through his upadesh—that I am in your heart, in the very substance of your being, and not only am I the object of your inmost yearning, I am also the magnet that pulls you towards it. I am the sadhana, the sadhaka, the siddhi: the beginning, the middle, and the end in all things—*aham adish ca madhyam ca bhutanam anta eva ca.*[174]

The conclusion, thus, is overwhelming: finding Sri Krishna is not a matter of intellectual enquiry or yogic practice but of understanding, as deeply as possible, that Krishna resides in every fiber and vibration of our personal and universal being, and all we need to do is replace all doubt, striving, enquiry, and practice with that absolute inner knowing, sraddha, and never let go of that in any situation or circumstance.

---

174 अहमात्मा गुडाकेश सर्वभूताशयस्थितः। अहमादिश्च मध्यं च भूतानामन्त एव च। — I, O Gudakesha (Arjuna), am the Self, which abides within all beings. I am the beginning and middle and end of all beings. —Bhagavad Gita, 10.20.

The Three gunas of Prakriti

The fourteenth chapter of the Bhagavad Gita explains in detail the nature of the *gunas* of Prakriti. The gunas are the inherent attributes or qualities, modes and forces of nature that constitute and drive Prakriti and everything in Prakriti. What we regard and experience as Prakriti, is its gunas—*sattva, rajas, tamas*. These gunas or modes of Prakriti are not separate from Prakriti, but they are the very constituents of Prakriti. As Swami Krishnananda[175] explains, *they are not qualities like the whiteness of a cloth, which is different from the cloth, and the blueness of a flower, which is different from the flower, the gunas are qualities of prakriti in the same way as the three strands of a rope are qualities of the rope, they are the very substance of the rope.*

Sattva, from the root *sat*, or truth, represents illumination, balance, lightness, and purity; *rajas* represents passion, desire, and attachment; *tamas* represents darkness, inertness, and heaviness. These three gunas born of Prakriti bind in the body, declares Krishna to Arjuna—Of these sattva is by the purity of its quality a cause of light and illumination, and by virtue of that purity produces no disease or morbidity or suffering in the nature: it binds by attachment to knowledge and attachment to happiness; rajas has for its essence attraction of liking and longing, it is a child of the attachment of the soul to the desire of objects, it binds the embodied spirit by attachment to works. Tamas, born of ignorance, is the deluder of all embodied beings; it binds by negligence, indolence, and sleep.

---

175 Swami Krishnananda of the Divine Life Society.

Sattva attaches to happiness, rajas to action, tamas covers up the knowledge and attaches to the negligence of error and inaction. Now sattva leads, having overpowered rajas and tamas; now rajas, having overpowered sattva and tamas; and now tamas, having overpowered sattva and rajas. When into all the doors in the body there comes a flooding of light, a light of understanding, perception, and knowledge, one should understand that there has been a great increase and uprising of the sattvic guna in the nature. Greed, seeking impulsions, initiative of actions, unrest, desire—all this mounts in us when rajas increases.

Nescience, inertia, negligence, and delusion—these are born when tamas predominates. From sattva, knowledge is born, and greed from rajas; negligence, ignorance, and delusion are of tamas, and also ignorance. They rise upwards who are in sattva; those in rajas remain in the middle; the tamasic, those enveloped in ignorance and inertia, the effect of the lowest quality, go downwards. When the seer perceives that the modes of Nature are the whole agency and cause of works and knows and turns to That which is supreme above the gunas, he attains to *madbhava*—the movement and status of the Divine.[176]

---

176 Bhagavad Gita, 14.5–13, 18, 19.

Udasina, Above the Play

The condition of *udasinata*—from *udasina*, seated above or apart—is of profound importance to the Yoga of the Gita, indispensable for anyone who aspires to practice the Gita's nishkama karmayoga. The word udasina, most commonly translated as indifference, means one who is seated or situated above or apart, detached, neutral, unmoved by the play of dualities, above the gunas of prakriti, free from the pulls and pushes of ordinary human nature. To be udasina in all circumstances and conditions is a high yogic state—*He who, established in a position as of one seated high above, is unshaken by the gunas; who seeing that it is the gunas that are in process of action stands apart immovable.*[177]

What binds us to ordinary human nature and all its strains and stresses is the play of the gunas, and because the mind is entirely identified with the gunas, we move as the gunas move us. It is by constant inner witnessing that we can begin to see the play of the gunas as something separate from us, happening outside of us. From an involved and identified state, we must learn to stand apart and witness the play of the mind, as if we are watching a movie but refusing to get involved in it or identified with its narrative and its characters, detached, impersonal. This is known as the sakshi in the Gita—*He who sees that all action is verily done by Prakriti, and that the Self is the inactive witness, he sees.*[178] Therefore, when we see that

---

177 उदासीनवदासीनो गुणैर्यो न विचाल्यते । गुणा वर्तन्त इत्येव योऽवतिष्ठति नेङ्गते ॥ —Bhagavad Gita, 14.23.

178 प्रकृत्यैव च कर्माणि क्रियमाणानि सर्वशः। यः पश्यति तथात्मानमकर्तारं स पश्यति ॥ —Bhagavad Gita, 13.30.

everything, everywhere and in everyone, is being done by Prakriti and its gunas, and the Atman, is the passive, uninvolved witness, we come to the pure seeing of the yogi, and then alone is liberation in the divine consciousness possible. *When the seer perceives that the modes of Nature are the whole agency and cause of works and knows and turns to That which is supreme above the gunas, he attains to the movement and status of the Divine.*[179]

Whosoever is established in the witnessing mode, the sakshi bhava, has attained the udasina state, for such a one is above the buffeting of the gunas, high above the play of Prakriti, secure in the inner calm and peace of Yoga. It may be somewhat difficult to practice all this in real life, with real people and in the real circumstances of everyday existence, but that is precisely the message of the Gita—do not be taken in by appearances, the surface play of the storm and the waves, become quiet and dive within, into the depths of the soul, where no wave or wind disturbs the stillness of the sea.

---

179 नान्यं गुणेभ्यः कर्तारं यदा द्रष्टानुपश्यति। गुणेभ्यश्च परं वेत्ति मद्भावं सोऽधिगच्छति ॥ —Bhagavad Gita, 14.19.

The Witnessing Mode

The inner journey to the Self, the awareness that I am, must begin with a clear understanding of the self we are not or the self we mistakenly believe ourselves to be. Identified naturally with the body and world, we quite easily forget the substratum or the background of our being—awareness itself. It's very much like a person absorbedly watching a movie and forgetting that the whole cinematic experience is simply a quick succession of picture frames projected onto a white screen. The white screen, the background, is the reality, not the motion picture.

Suppose I were to point out this simple and obvious fact to you while you were watching a movie. Your attention would then suddenly shift from the succession of movie images to the screen. If I then were to ask you to keep watching the movie but remain aware of the background screen, you would have a somewhat surreal experience: a part of your mind watching the movie and another part aware of the screen. If you could manage to hold this double watching for a while, the movie would lose its hold on you, and the succession of the moving images would lose their coherence. You would become increasingly aware of the screen and less and less spellbound by the movie. And very soon, you would lose interest in the movie altogether and perhaps walk out to enjoy the fresh air.

This is what is happening in real life as well. The awareness, as would be obvious by now, is the background screen. The world that we are experiencing day to day is the movie. The self in us is absorbed by the movie, by the succession of moving images on the screen, and the screen itself, which makes the movie possible and real, is forgotten.

How does this happen? Reflect on this, and we will see at once that the root of this oblivion is our all-absorbing interest in the moving images. And the root of our all-absorbing interest is our identification with what we see in the images. Because what we are seeing is a reflection of our own existence—life, as it is happening or not happening to us, a reflection of our own fears and desires, hopes and frustrations, loves and hurts. Actually, it is always ourselves that we see on the screen, every character is a reflection of ourselves, as we are, or could be, or could never be. It is not a movie that we are watching, it is a mirror. The screen is a mirror. And the images being reflected, one after the other, are us—our dreams and nightmares. This is the root of all identification. We see ourselves in the other, and we get caught up in this magical hall of mirrors, everyone reflecting everyone, a thousand and one reflections, and we do not know which is the self and which is the other.

The starting point of the journey to self-knowledge and freedom is the conscious stepping out of identification and self-absorption in the world. The problem is not the world—there is nothing inherently wrong with the world, just as there is nothing inherently wrong with the movies we watch—but our complete self-absorption in the world.

Nishkama Karma and Nimittabhava

The mighty karmayoga of the Gita, perhaps its foundational teaching, rests on the idea of *nishkama karma,* action or work without personal preference or desire for outcomes, without attachment to results, doing to the best of one's ability whatever work needs to be done, *kartavyam karma,*[180] as an offering or sacrifice—yajna—to the Divine, and offering all of oneself, one's energies and capacities, to that yajna so that the offering is flawless—*srestha*—in all manner and aspects, worthy of the Divine.

Thus, Krishna tells Arjuna to concentrate on the action, not the outcome of the action—*You have a right to action, but only to action, never to its fruits; let not the fruits of your works be your motive, neither let there be in you any attachment to inactivity.*[181] But for the ordinary human mind, this is puzzling: how does one act if one is not concerned with the outcome of that act? If the fruits of the act are not important, then why would one act at all? And what exactly are the 'fruits' of action? What happens to the desire for excelling in work, for isn't excellence in action also a desire for outcome? This question becomes all the more acute in the light of Krishna's earlier statement to Arjuna that yoga is a skill in works—*yogah karmasu kaushalam.* How docs one attain to skillful action without concern for the fruits of action?

So, what exactly does Krishna mean by this injunction? To understand nishkama karma, we will first need to understand

---

180 Works or action that is done because it must be done.

181 कर्मण्येवाधिकारस्ते मा फलेषु कदाचन ।   मा कर्मफलहेतुर्भूर्मा ते संगोऽस्त्वकर्मणि ॥   —Bhagavad Gita, 2.47.

that in the context of the Gita, the objective of work and action is the Yajna—the sacrifice and consecration of action, of works, of will and energy, of the delight of action, to Krishna. It is the spirit of the Yajna alone that makes work and action meaningful and delightful to the soul, for without that spirit, action would be little more than compulsive activity driven by the force of rajas.

Human actions can either be driven by a sense of doership—kartabhava[182]—or a sense of instrumentality—nimittabhava. While kartabhava is essential for worldly action, including even philanthropy—and indeed, worldly action would simply collapse without kartabhava to drive it—nimittabhava is indispensable for Yajna and yogic action. The nishkama karma that Krishna teaches to Arjuna is yogic action in the spirit of Yajna—*Fixed in Yoga do your actions*, Krishna says, *having abandoned attachment, having become equal in failure and success; for it is equality that is meant by Yoga.*[183] And then, again, he expands the idea of yogic works through equality of mind and heart to excellence in action—*One whose intelligence has attained unity*, he says, *casts away, even here in this world of dualities, both good doing and evil doing. Therefore, strive to be in Yoga; Yoga is skill in works.*[184]

Samata, equality of mind and heart, is the condition that liberates from the action of dualities and the gunas, leading to the condition of *nirapeksha*—desirelessness, freedom from expectation, and detachment of spirit from action. Sri Krishna first introduces Arjuna to the idea of equality by stating that equality itself is yoga, *samatvam yoga uchayate*. The first level of equality comes with perfect contentment or *tripti*. Tripti, in yoga,

---

182 *Kartabhava* (करता भाव) means sense of doership, of being a doer, agent; also means the sense of separation or distinction as used in the *Bhagavat Purana* (Ref. Monier Williams).

183 योगस्थः कुरु कर्माणि संगं त्यक्त्वा धनंजय । सिद्ध्यसिद्ध्योः समो भूत्वा समत्वं योग उच्यते—Fixed in Yoga do your actions, having abandoned attachment, having become equal in failure and success; for it is equality that is meant by Yoga. —Bhagavad Gita, 2.48.

184 बुद्धियुक्तो जहातीह उभे सुकृतदुष्कृते । तस्माद्योगाय युज्यस्व योगः कर्मसु कौशलम् —Bhagavad Gita, 2.50.

implies perfect contentment with whatever we have, whatever
is given to us in the cosmic dispensation, when the spirit seems
sated, and nothing more is needed, and what is needed outwardly
and inwardly is exactly what is given to us; if more than needed
is given, that is grace—and we must be grateful for that grace—
and if less than needed is given, that too is grace, for the Divine
sometimes leads us through privation and struggle to greater
riches and fulfillment. In plenty and prosperity, we must remain
equal and unmoved, knowing that all comes from the Divine; in
scarcity and suffering, there should be no misgiving, repining,
nirananda, for the Atman in us knows best what is needed at
what stage of our life and yoga; and in loss, there should be no
sorrow or regret for whatever goes from us, returns to the Divine.

But there is still deeper equality that comes from an inner
sense of the Divine, from a growing sense of Krishna in the
heart. Once we come to this, samata becomes a delightful
acceptance of Krishna's will in the heart and mind, and in
the most transactional details of life. This is the bhava of an
integral and joyful submission and surrender to Krishna's will
in everything that happens or does not happen, everything that
comes or goes, good or bad, fortunate or unfortunate, pleasant
or unpleasant, in the play of the universe. Nothing touches the
inner consciousness, and in all, we sense the hand of the Divine,

Nirapeksh is desirelessness, being without expectation,
detached. Sri Krishna tells Arjuna that one who is free of desire,
anapeksha, pure and skillful in action, *suchirdaksha*, unaffected by
whatever comes or happens, *udasina*, beyond pain and suffering,
gatvyathah, one who has given up all personal initiative of action,
sarvarambha parityagi, such a one is dear to him.[185] In this sloka,
Krishna summarizes the qualities needed for nimittabhava, the
psychological and spiritual basis for the Gita's nishkama karma.

---

185 अनपेक्षः शुचिर्दक्ष उदासीनो गतव्यथः।सर्वारम्भपरित्यागी यो मद्भक्तः स मे प्रियः ॥ —Bhagavad
     Gita, 12.16.

Nimittabhava is a state of being, a settled attitude when we feel that we are not in control, nothing is in our hands, we do nothing—all is done by the Divine, overtly or secretly, it is the Divine that governs all actions and outcome of actions in the universe, guides and moves us through our volition, feelings, and thoughts, and through all the actions and circumstances of life. There is no sense of personal will or motivation in action, no sense of personal doership, no personal claim over what we are, think, or do. From nimittabhava, once firmly and deeply established in the mind and heart, we progress to identification with Krishna, with his will and action through us, and more and more, we become like Krishna—*madbhava*, of his essence.

Krishna Lila

There are two established ways in Sanatan Dharma of regarding human life—as Maya or as Lila. The Maya worldview, or *mayavada*, based on a recurrent misunderstanding of the vedantic concept of Maya, regards life as illusory and unreal and escape from worldly existence as the highest objective of life. The Lila, or *lilamaya*, worldview regards the universe as a playfield of the Divine and all existence as divine play—*Krishna Lila*—to be celebrated, lived fully, in Krishna's consciousness. In Sri Aurobindo's words, *the crowning realization (of yoga) is when you become aware of the whole world as the expression, play or Lila of an infinite divine personality.*[186]

The divine play or Lila is not to be confused with the human understanding of play as frivolous and childish, without any higher purpose. The divine Lila is neither serious, in our human sense of seriousness, nor frivolous—it is playful, an outpouring of infinite energy in infinite forms and movements for the sheer delight, *rasa* and *ananda*, of existence. There is no external purpose in the Lila, the Lila is its own purpose. We play with Krishna, and Krishna himself is the play. But without grasping the anandmaya nature of Sri Krishna, which in itself is impossible to understand without experiencing, in some form, the divine ananda, it may not be easy to grasp the purpose and truth of the divine Lila. It is the divine delight of existence that truly explains Lila—*all exist here, no doubt, for the delight of existence,* writes Sri Aurobindo, *all is a game or Lila, but a game too carries within*

---

186 Sri Aurobindo is referring here to a particular level of Yoga that he calls 'adhyatmik yoga'.

itself an object to be accomplished and without the fulfillment of that object would have no completeness of significance.

What would be the object, and its fulfillment, of Krishna Lila? Krishna tells Arjuna that he incarnates as an avatar to restore the evolutionary balance on earth whenever the forces of adharma threaten to overcome the forces of Dharma.[187] But this is the stated object of Krishna's incarnation. There is a deeper, unstated but implied object which is to attract souls caught up on the 'turning wheel of samsara' to himself, the symbolism of Krishna's Lila with the *gopis* or the milkmaids. What Krishna does with Arjuna—bring him out of delusion and ignorance through his direct intervention and turn him towards the highest truth of being—he would do through Arjuna with every embodied being on earth, and this is the deeper object of his Lila, to bring humanity to himself through his ananda and his Lila. This is the approach of the heart, but a heart touched and transformed by the delight of the Atman, for it is in the Atman that one touches the eternal ananda of the Divine and draws closer to Krishna's Lila.

But those who do not understand, or have not experienced, the lilamaya aspect of the Divine cannot believe that the Divine is playful—how can the Divine be at play when there is real suffering on earth, real evil, death, and tragedy? And if it is all a play, then does that not make the Divine cruel? These are legitimate questions, no doubt, but they all arise from the perspective of existence as Maya, while the Gita takes us beyond this perspective towards a higher and more profound truth of being. Also, we must not forget that this whole perspective of existence as Maya itself arises from an incomplete or incorrect understanding of the vedantic concept of Maya. Once the truth of Maya is understood—and we have spoken of this earlier—

---

187 यदा यदा हि धर्मस्य ग्लानिर्भवति भारत। अभ्युत्थानमधर्मस्य तदात्मानं सृजाम्यहम् ॥ —Whensoever there is the fading of the dharma and the uprising of unrighteousness, then I loose myself forth into birth. —Bhagavad Gita, 4.7.

then it is Maya itself that leads to Lila. These two perspectives are not irreconcilable or even disparate, and they merge into one single vedantic worldview once we have attained a certain height of consciousness from where we can see how Maya itself is the Lila, and how all our human existential issues are beautifully resolved in the eternally anandamaya Brahman. The key to this resolution is in attaining to that eternal delight of the self, *atma ratih—but the man whose delight is in the Self and who is satisfied with the enjoyment of the Self and in the Self he is content, for him there exists no work that needs to be done.*[188]

In the Gita's light, the secret of existence is the progressive recovery of our divine truth of being. In this progressive self-recovery, we will find the truth of perfect will and action, and of perfect love and delight, and of perfect self-becoming in Krishna's consciousness. This finding of perfect will and action is the siddhi of karmayoga, the finding of perfect love and delight is the siddhi of bhaktiyoga, and the perfect self-becoming in Sri Krishna's consciousness is the siddhi of jnanayoga. Whosoever attains these siddhis attains Krishna too.[189]

---

188 यस्त्वात्मरतिरेव स्यादात्मतृप्तश्च मानवः । आत्मन्येव च संतुष्टस्तस्य कार्यं न विद्यते ॥ —Bhagavad Gita, 3.17.

189 Siddhi, in this context, means complete practical understanding, a complete possession and living of these truths in mind, life, and body.

Sthitaprajna

The literal meaning of the word *sthitaprajna* is established—*sthita*—in wisdom—*prajna*.[190] But beyond its literal meaning, there are several other meanings and implications of this word. Sthitaprajna refers to one who is stable in the higher wisdom, calm and unaffected by the changing circumstances of the world.

Arjuna asks Krishna about the visible signs of one who has attained this condition of sthitaprajna or samadhi[191]—how would such a person speak, sit, or walk? Krishna then explains to him the characteristics of a person who is established in the highest wisdom of the Self.

Such a being is free of desire, Krishna declares, and is content in the completeness of the self by the self;[192] whose mind is undisturbed in the midst of sorrows and amid pleasures is free from desire, from whom liking and fear and wrath have passed away. Such a being, established in the wisdom of the Self, has attained the perfect equality of the soul, and in all things, he is unattached, unmoved by good or evil, neither hating nor rejoicing in the change of circumstances. The one settled in wisdom draws in his senses from sense-objects as the tortoise draws in his limbs into its shell. He who would be settled in the wisdom of the self would have to be in yoga, wholly given up

---

190 Sthitaprajna (स्थितप्रज्ञ) from sthita (स्थित) and prajna (प्रज्ञ, pronounced pragya).
191 Samadhi, in this context, means the state of perfect equality and equilibrium, a state that cannot be disturbed by any external or internal stimuli or movement, a state of perfect equipoise and calm.
192 प्रजहाति यदा कामान् सर्वान् पार्थ मनो-गतान् । आत्मन्य् एवात्मना तुष्टः स्थित-प्रज्ञस् तदोच्यते ॥
—Bhagavad Gita, 2.55.

to Krishna, his senses under complete control, not excited by the touch of the objects of sense, firmly founded in the calm of self-knowledge.

A being established in the highest wisdom and knowledge of the Self becomes like a wide ocean of consciousness that remains motionless even while all the desires of the world enter it as waters enter the sea; such a one is not disturbed by any inrush of desire. Such a being abandons all desires and lives and acts free from longing, who has no 'I' or 'mine', has extinguished his individual ego in the One and lives in that unity and attains the great peace of Brahman, for he is indeed settled in *brahmisthiti*— the condition of Brahman.[193]

But again, how to attain such a state? Is there a method of transcendence and liberation that the Gita provides? Having touched on some of the most fundamental ideas of the Gita, we can see that there is a method, a definite roadmap. One must begin with the *sankalpa*—determination, will—for perfection, for without a steady and unrelenting will for perfection, nothing will move, so heavy and resistant is the tamas of human nature. And the sankalpa has to be rooted in sraddha, that deep and dynamic faith and power of aspiration. The first step is always to invoke Krishna for the ascent, call him unwaveringly, till one finds a response in the being, first very subtle and intuitive, and then clearer to the conscious mind.

After the sraddha must come the practice of self-reflection and observation, a stepping back from the action, the play of the gunas, a progressive loosening of the identifications with mind, ego, life, and body. Witnessing is the first condition that must be established in the mind, for witnessing is what frees us from the habitual identifications of mind and heart. As the sakshibhava grows, one begins to see with growing clarity the movements and modes of nature separate from the sakshi, the witnessing

---

193 Slokas 57, 58, 61, 68, 70 of Chapter 2, Bhagavad Gita.

self. This is an indispensable yogic movement of separating the witnessing self, Purusha, from the play and field of Prakriti. Once that is more or less accomplished, the desires and passion of the mind and heart fall away or become irrelevant as one identifies increasingly with the Purusha or the Atman. And through all this, the Yajna—the self-consecration and sacrifice to the Divine—must continue in spirit and action, in bhava, karma, and kriya. As the Yajna progresses and perfects itself in the details of one's life and work, one grows more and more conscious of the workings and will of Krishna. One begins to sense Krishna everywhere, behind everything, within everyone, moving all things and beings, moving the universe itself. One begins then to live in what the Vaishnava monks call Krishna consciousness or Krishna-chaitanya.[194]

---

194 This is a gist based on the previous notes. There is, of course, much more to the Bhagavad Gita and its roadmap to self-perfection but that would make for a separate book on the Gita.

Sanatan Dharma and Our Times

Restoring the Dharma

There are two kinds of Sanatan Dharma in a manner of speaking. One may be called the Sanatan Dharma of the scholar and priest, the *pandit* and *purohit*; the other, the Dharma of the Rishi and Yogi. There are some superficial similarities between these, but the differences are deep and wide. The Dharma of the pundit and the purohit tends to be prescriptive, dogmatic, ritualistic, and largely symbolic, while the Dharma of the Rishi is necessarily open-ended, dialogic, contemplative, based on self-enquiry and the quest for truth and self-realization.

The Dharma of the pundit and the purohit stands with the other religions of the world—there are gods and goddesses, temples and priesthood, scriptural authority and dogma, ritualistic worship and sacrifice, symbol and representation. The Dharma of the Rishi is not a religion but a yoga, a spiritual discipline and inner seeking. When Sri Aurobindo said that the Sanatan Dharma is *life itself, a thing that has not so much to be believed as lived*, it was to the Dharma of the Rishi he was referring to. While the purohit insists on rituals and worship, and the scholar insists on enunciation and interpretation, the Seer insists only on Truth—*satyam paramo dharma*, truth is the highest dharma. *Seek Truth alone*, says the Rishi, *no scripture, no teacher or teaching, not even the gods and goddesses.*

While the Dharma of the priest tends inevitably to conservatism, the Dharma of the scholar tends equally inevitably to intellectual conservatism. But this was not always so. The Sanatan Dharma of the Hindus was originally the path of the seers and sages, and it was always the *godward endeavor of the human spirit*, a vast and intense self-searching that gave birth to the Vedas and the Upanishads. But, over time, as is perhaps inevitable in the meandering course of human history, this Dharma was appropriated by the brahmin, the high-caste scholar and priest, the thought-leader. The brahmin embodied the scholar and the priest in himself and was, therefore, powerful, charismatic, and a wielder of unquestioned authority. He was the teacher, the interpreter, and the shaman, all rolled into one. And there was a reason for this.

In those ancient times when Dharma was strong and dominant, the brahmin was first and foremost a knower of Brahman, the Supreme Truth. One couldn't be a brahmin without being a knower of Brahman. It was much later, when Dharma was receding from individual lives and communities, that one could be known as a brahmin just by virtue of being born into a brahmin family, so long as one would pass through the symbolical rites of passage. With every passing generation, as the living influence of Dharma in individuals and societies waned, and rituals and traditions became more important, the brahmin too became less of a knower of Brahman and more of a scholar, a knower of theories and systems.

Eventually, as the spirit of Dharma receded almost entirely from the masses, society slid comfortably into the easy zones of ritualism and symbolism, and the brahmin became more and more a dry scholar, a conventional priest, no longer in touch with the great and exacting living traditions of the Rishis and Yogis and became more interested in concentrating power in himself rather than pursuing the Truth. This led to an inevitable brahmanization of Hindu Dharma. The priest and the scholar appropriated the great traditions of the Rishis and Yogis, and the *sadhak*, the disciple of Truth, was replaced by the religious, superstitious, and simple-minded Hindu who came to passionately believe that Dharma was all about what you eat, what you wear, how you bathe, how you pray and recite your hymns. Sri Aurobindo once wrote—*there are two Hinduisms, one which takes its stand on the kitchen and seeks its Paradise by cleaning the body; another which seeks God, not through the cooking pot and the social convention, but in the soul.*

The pernicious caste system, with its unconscionable practice of untouchability, is a direct outcome of the gradual brahmanization of the Dharma. In the vedantic worldview of the Rishis, any kind of division or inequality amongst humans would be a violation of the first principle of Dharma—ekam Sat.

It is imperative that every true Hindu understands the difference between these two kinds of Dharma and chooses the Dharma of the Rishis over the Dharma of the purohit and the pundit, and makes this choice known as vocally as possible. There needs to be a visible and vocal movement against the dogmatic thinking and practices of the orthodox Hindu. Sanatan Dharma can be a universal religion only if we keep it free from all sectarian and reactionary influences of the past and do not allow it to be appropriated or hijacked by any clan or community, however entrenched or powerful they may be.

What is commonly practiced today as the Hindu religion is a superficial, ritualistic rendering of the Sanatan Dharma of the Rishis. This is a historical anomaly that, unfortunately, has become fairly widespread among Hindus, with many believing that this is how it has always been. This needs to be widely understood and promptly rectified. Much of what the present generation has inherited as the Hindu religion needs to be revisited, revised, and reformulated in an idiom aligned and more faithful to the original Dharma. Hindu religion needs to be freed from the many layers of dogma, practices, beliefs, and superstitions that have settled upon it through the ages and restored to its original Sanatan form—pristine and radiant in its mystical simplicity. It must now be returned consciously to its spiritual and philosophical roots and must be known and practiced again as the Dharma of the Rishis.

It is this thought that needs to be rekindled in every Hindu mind and heart, and it is this that must become again the engine of our great civilization and culture and the reawakened soul of our nation. But to do this effectively, we will need to reorient and re-educate Hindus worldwide, especially the young and the skeptical. Skepticism is healthy and, if positively managed and channeled in the right direction, can lead to new openings and understanding. Unfortunately, as I have observed, the orthodox believers of the Dharma do not know how to deal with religious skepticism, and as a result, those who would genuinely question and challenge the Dharma for their own good are pushed even farther away from it. We need teachers and guides today who can explain Dharma in modern scientific language, even in a secular idiom, if need be, and demonstrate through their own lives and understanding the relevance of Dharma for the twenty-first century.

What Sanatan Dharma Is Not

Sanatan Dharma is not religion—this is the first thing we must resolutely bear in mind. It has never had an established clergy or a central authority, and there has never been any final arbiter in the interpretation or application of the Dharma, no single scripture or theology, no prescribed rites and rituals, and whatever rituals that do exist in the day-to-day living of the Dharma are highly symbolic in nature.

The second important thing to remember is that Dharma has never been about mandatory or prescribed rules for ethical and religious behavior; it does not posit absolute rights or wrongs and holds that everything is relative and contextual and the sense of right and wrong must arise only from one's inner understanding, guided by the higher buddhi or the Atman. Therefore, in Sanatan Dharma, the most important practice is to awaken and cultivate the atman and the buddhi of which spiritual discrimination—*viveka*—is an essential part.

Sanatan Dharma does not tell us what to eat or not to eat, what to wear or not to wear, how to live and behave. It is not a set of dos and don'ts—for Sanatan Dharma, the only thing of spiritual, social, and moral significance is the development of consciousness: the height or depth of one's consciousness is incomparably more significant than a set of moral and social rules and laws. In fact, of what good use would all our ethical and social rules be without any development of consciousness?

We must also bear in mind that Sanatan Dharma is not just the Vedas, the Bhagavad Gita, or the Upanishads, nor the Mahabharata or the Ramayana, nor even the Puranas—these texts do not in any way define or limit the Dharma. However, these texts do align the buddhi to Dharma, making Dharma more accessible to the mind of humanity. A deep understanding of the Vedas, the Gita, and the Upanishads, for example, can be of immense importance to one who wishes to live the Dharmic life, but they are not the only sources or guides. The ultimate source of the Dharma, and the only infallible guide, is the eternal Wisdom within, the secret Veda in the heart. This is the only grand scripture and temple of Sanatan Dharma. Therefore, the finding of the Atman is the only fundamental and indispensable practice of Sanatan Dharma—all else is of secondary or peripheral interest.

A Dharmic Alternative

This erring race of human beings dreams always of perfecting their environment by the machinery of government and society; but it is only by the perfection of the soul within that the outer environment can be perfected. What thou art within, that outside thee thou shalt enjoy; no machinery can rescue thee from the law of thy being.

—Sri Aurobindo

The fundamental crisis of this century is spiritual and not social or moral, political or economic. As Sri Aurobindo suggests, it is only by 'the perfection of the soul within' that humanity can find and manifest lasting unity, peace, equality, and brotherhood as naturally as it now manifests fear, greed, and violence. Political leaders and organizations around the world have worked for peace, equality, and brotherhood, but nothing really has changed, and nothing will, as long as we focus only on fixing outer systems and structures, ignoring the Spirit itself. It is not by changing governments or political systems that we will find a long-lasting solution to our human problems but by changing consciousness, changing ourselves, our attitudes, and beliefs. This is the Dharmic alternative.

Writing of the future evolution of humanity, Sri Aurobindo states that *a true spiritual age will come only if the idea becomes strong in the intellectual life of humanity that the Spirit is the true Reality standing behind our physical existence, and to realise the Spirit and express it outwardly in mental, vital, and physical terms is the real meaning and aim of human existence.*

It is a straight and simple argument—our true human reality is spiritual, dharmic. It is by finding Dharma within, and uniting and identifying with it, that we can remold and reorder our external existence in the light of a higher truth of being and a deeper consciousness. In Sri Aurobindo's words, *It is only when human societies make the revealing and finding of the divine Self in man the whole first aim of all its activities, its education, its knowledge, its science, its ethics, its art, its economical and political structure that the crises will pass and humanity will awaken to its true destiny.*[195] The finding and living of the 'divine Self' that Sri Aurobindo mentions here is the pivot of Dharma.

Dharma is the principle and force that binds and prevents dissolution and disintegration, and   must therefore be established as the practical foundation of all our systems—educational, social, judicial, political, and financial. But most urgently, the educational. The coming generations must not lose the opportunity of a truly modern and Dharmic education. They must learn to look deeper into the foundational truths and values that have shaped and guided their civilization and nation through the ages, awaken to a deeper and truer reality of life, and reject all that is shallow, petty, and superficial; they must learn to do good not for the sake of reward but for the sake of the good itself, and without fear of punishment; to live a life guided by the inner law of Dharma—satyam vada, dharmam chara.

.

195 *The Human Cycle*, Sri Aurobindo.

A Dharmic Rashtra

For a true Dharmic resurgence in India, Dharma will have to be made the principle and motive-force of politics and the foundation of economics. No social or political movement can succeed without philosophical underpinnings, and no cultural or political narrative can be built and sustained without a deeper spiritual worldview and values. The philosophical framework for India was, and will always be, Sanatan Dharma. India's struggle for national identity has always been, in a fundamental sense, a struggle for Dharma, her sovereign law of being. India must recover that essential Sanatan character, her Hindutva,[196] and stand unapologetically as a Dharmic Rashtra[197] to fulfill her true role amongst the nations of the world. Without the Sanatan Dharma, which is her swadharma, India will remain weak and vulnerable.

The idea of a Dharmic Rashtra, based on the foundations of Sanatan Dharma, does not in any way violate the idea of secularism, as the Leftist-liberals mistakenly believe and propagate, and this mistaken belief arises from the fact that few among them really care to understand Sanatan Dharma. Sanatan Dharma is secular by its very nature. All belief systems, faiths, philosophies, and schools of thought are included in the universal sweep of Sanatan Dharma. Nothing that is human is outside the scope of the Dharma, and even the asura and his evil find a rightful place in the cosmic scheme of things.

The prevalent political understanding of secularism itself is deeply flawed and should be revised in terms of Sanatan Dharma.

---

196 The essence of being Hindu or Hinduness.
197 Rashtra, nation; thus, a Dharmic Nation.

Secularism, an idea essentially imported from Europe,[198] implies the separation of religion and state, the principle that the state shall follow no religion or creed. This does not apply in any sense to India because the Indian mind, nurtured by the worldview and values of Sanatan Dharma, has no concept of religion—it understands only Dharma as the eternal cosmic order based on spiritual truth and harmony inherent in the very nature of existence and shaping and influencing every aspect and movement of personal, social, and national life.

Indian nationalism, in fact, is shot through with the fervor and might of the Dharma. Indian civilization, with its origins in the Vedic religion and culture, is Dharmic in warp and woof. To attempt a secular political and social culture in India is untenable in the long run and destined to collapse.

True secularism can work only on the condition that the state accepts or acknowledges no religion or religious belief and does not allow any kind of discrimination or favor based on these concepts. Religion is left to the individual and does not in any way influence the politics or governance of the nation. Very straight and simple. But this is not how secularism panned out in independent India. For nearly seven decades of post-Independent India, secularism had become an excuse for marginalizing Dharma and Dharmic values. Almost everything openly Dharmic in identity and value was quickly labeled communal and dismissed for the sake of promoting secularism. The conflation of Dharma and communalism was disingenuous and was used to the hilt as a political tool by the former Congress governments and the Left-liberal cabal in India.

The Dharmic equivalent of secularism, but much more profound and wider in meaning and scope, is the idea of *vasudhaiva kutumbakam*[199]—the world is but one family. This

---

198 'A product of the Protestant Reformation and the Enlightenment', as historian Ian Copland writes.
199 See the chapter on Vasudhaiva Kutumbakam.

is not platitudinous idealism but an essential characteristic of Dharma, a fundamental civilizational value based on the declaration of Vedic seers who had realized in their cosmic consciousness the oneness of existence. There are no distinctions or divisions in cosmic consciousness, and the oneness of existence is not an ideal but a fact, a lived truth. The full verse from the Upanishad[200] means that the distinction between self and the other, the thought that this person is mine and that one is not, is characteristic of only the narrow-minded, egotistical individual who still lives in ignorance and duality; for those who are noble and vast in their being, those who have realized the truth of unity in multiplicity, this whole world is but one community.

Now consider, if one were to live the true Dharmic life and strive to attain its ideals and goals, why on earth would one need secularism? Ironically, secularism in India has translated into a denial of Dharma. The Hindi word for secular is *dharma-nirapeksha*. The word 'nirapeksha', amongst its other meanings, also means disregard, indifference, detachment. It is a beautiful word when used in its Yogic or spiritual sense,[201] but when used in conjunction with Dharma, it turns on its head—it immediately implies an indifference to Dharma, which doesn't make sense.

The immediate need is to bring Dharma back to the national center stage without creating an imbalance of political forces. If we were to keep politics entirely out of the play, a rashtra based on Dharma would not be a challenge at all. It is politics that has polarized India and not culture or Dharma, and therefore, we need to de-polarize India by de-politicizing Dharma. The one sure way of de-politicizing Dharma is to strengthen Dharma from within.

---

200 अयं निजः परो वेति गणना लघुचेतसाम्। उदारचरितानां तु वसुधैव कुटुम्बकम् —*Maha Upanishad* 6.71–75. See Footnote 47.

201 Nirapeksha, in the Dharmic and yogic sense, means to be above and beyond all desire and expectation, to have no preferences or points of view, to be above all differences, indifferent to the play of the ignorant world. To be nirapeksha is one of the ideals of the Gita.

It is by strengthening Dharma that India will stand tall and firm as a truly secular nation in the Dharmic sense, where all religions and cultures will be regarded equally as the play of the One Divine. It is also by strengthening Dharma that the threats of intolerant Gods, infallible scriptures, chosen prophets and peoples can be effectively countered. Falsehoods or half-truths in any form, even in their varied religious garbs, cannot be destroyed by battle or resistance; they can only be countered by simply reducing them to complete irrelevance. This is what Dharma does—as it grows in strength, it reduces falsehood or half-truths to irrelevance. One doesn't need to snatch a stuffed toy out of a child's hands: one allows the child to discover something more real, and the stuffed toy simply becomes irrelevant.

Therefore, the need to strengthen Dharma. There is no other option. Preaching Dharma is of no use, for Dharma must be lived for it to become an effective force, lived in our minds, lives, and bodies, its jnana transformed into shakti, for Dharma is Truth in action, Satyam-Ritam. It is to this call that India must awaken. The aspiration to become a Dharmic Rashtra leading human civilization towards an age of unity and harmony must become a collective sankalpa, transcending divisive religions and politics, concerned only about the good of humanity—*jagat kalyana*. As this sankalpa becomes an active force in the subtle atmosphere of the nation, it will grow quietly and surely into a groundswell, sweeping aside all opposition and dissolving all obstacles.

But for the aspiration to become an active force and a groundswell, we will need to collectively recover the Dharma out of the past and bring it alive in the present so that it can become powerfully active again in our individual and collective lives and effectively shape the future of our nation and our civilization. In Vivekananda's words—*Many times have I been told that looking into the past only degenerates and leads to nothing, and that we should look to the future. That is true. But out of the past is built the future. Look back, therefore, as far as you can, drink deep of the eternal fountains that are behind, and after that, look forward, march forward and make India brighter, greater, much higher than she ever was. Our ancestors were great. We must first recall that. We must learn the elements of our being, the blood that courses in our veins; we must have faith in that blood and what it did in the past; and out of that faith and consciousness of past greatness, we must build an India yet greater than what she has been.*

Juxtaposing this with Sri Aurobindo's words—*The recovery of the old spiritual knowledge and experience in all its splendor, depth and fullness is India's first, most essential work; the flowing of this spirituality into new forms of philosophy, literature, art, science and critical knowledge is the second; an original dealing with modern problems in the light of Indian spirit and the endeavor to formulate a greater synthesis of a spiritualized society is the third and most difficult. Its success on these three lines will be the measure of its help to the future of humanity.*

This, then, must be our collective sankalpa—to recover the depths and heights of consciousness we have lost over the generations, assimilate more deeply our heritage and our culture and make of it a force to mold our future. This will happen when we, as Indians, begin to awaken in our own minds and hearts the force and light of the tapasya that lives timelessly in the soul of our nation as Sanatan Dharma.

The Need for Dharmic Education

What the present generation of teachers and proponents of the Dharma will need to evoke in the masses is the higher intelligence, the buddhi, to balance the excess of the vital-emotional energies most dominant amongst present-day followers of the Dharma. Vital-emotional energies without the subtler discernment of the buddhi can very easily lead to aggressiveness and lumpenization, just as the buddhi without the vital energies can as easily lead to ineffectual idealism. We have experienced both these extremes in contemporary India.

In reaching out to a wider population, we will inevitably meet many already entrenched in their beliefs and ideologies, even opposed or hostile to Sanatan thought. We must not turn away from them, for none can be left out. There must always be space for debate and dialogue. A truly Dharmic society must be tolerant of dissent and debate, must be respectful of all worldviews, all thoughts and beliefs, and must allow for healthy disagreement. The rigidity of belief and thought, intolerance, and supremacist attitudes can have no place or relevance in Dharmic society. A genuine Dharmic discourse must necessarily be free of political and cultural prejudice. Dharma can and should inspire and guide politics but must never be subservient to politics.

Thus, the sore need of the hour is a deeper Dharmic narrative and discourse interwoven into the fabric of mainstream education in the country. It is obvious that Dharmic education cannot be exclusive to any community or caste, and it must be accessible to all. For Dharmic education is not, contrary to popular thinking, religious or moral education but spiritual. *Dharmic is spiritual—* this equation must be clearly understood, and wherever it is not, we can be sure that Dharma is being incorrectly or incompletely interpreted and applied. In fact, a Dharmic education, being spiritual, would be scrupulously 'secular' for the Spirit, and spiritual truths, are cosmic and universal. Whoever does not understand this does not understand Dharma.

A Dharmic education, by its very nature, must lead necessarily to truth and freedom. *Sa vidya ya vimuktaye*[202]—that alone is learning that leads to freedom—is the mantra of all Dharmic education. That which leads to fixity, rigidity, narrowness, exclusivity, bigotry, prejudice, or indoctrination is not education at all, let alone Dharmic education. The truth that education and learning must necessarily lead to freedom of mind and spirit, *sa vidya ya vimuktaye*, applies equally in all human contexts, across cultures and civilizations, to all humans everywhere.

The cardinal values of Dharma—truth, justice, equality, and freedom—are also the determining principles and forces behind all our civilizational pursuits and aspirations. Behind all our philosophies and sciences is the quest for truth, behind our laws and policies is the quest for justice, behind our economics and politics is the quest for equality, and behind human civilization itself is the quest for freedom. These cardinal values are sanatan—eternal and universal.

Yet, if we look back and take stock of our civilization and our collective human condition, we find that we live an antithesis of the defining civilizational values—we live not truth and justice but a travesty of truth and a mockery of justice; we are still too spiritually immature to understand spiritual equality and go on reinforcing separation and divide, the advantaged get more advantaged while the disadvantaged grow more disadvantaged. Instead of growing towards global oneness and freedom, we are

---

202 तत्कर्म यन्न बन्धाय सा विद्या या विमुक्तये।—That indeed is work that does not lead to bondage, and that indeed is learning that leads to freedom.

falling deeper into our collective prejudices, greed, and fears. The fundamental civilizational challenge today is not political or social but spiritual, and it is this alone that a twenty-first-century Dharmic education will need to address.

As our world becomes global, so must our education. Globalization is not just a socio-economic or a technological process—at the root, it is a consciousness process. *For the first time in human history*, as the Mother of Sri Aurobindo Ashram pointed out years ago, *a world consciousness is beginning to emerge, a consciousness that will drive people across the world to an imperative unity and harmony far beyond the politics and the governments of this world.* It is in this wider context that we will need a new generation of teachers and thinkers—truly, acharyas—to revisit the idea of how we humans live individually and collectively on earth and to understand what is missing. This may need an intuitive understanding of human evolution instead of textbook history. We need visionaries and philosophers, thought leaders and seers, to lead humanity to the next level of civilization, a Dharmic civilization based on truth and freedom.

And it does not matter whether we call it 'Dharmic' in Sanskrit, Latin, Greek, or Persian, as long as we understand the idea of 'Dharma'. Call a rose by any other name.

Towards Dharmic Capitalism

The question of money and wealth is perhaps the most vexing of all issues confronted by those who aspire to a Dharmic way of life. Money has a subtle corrupting influence, even on the best of minds. It is for this reason that money is amongst the first things to be rejected by the spiritually inclined. Most spiritual disciplines celebrate poverty because of a deeply ingrained fear of money. But wealth is indispensable to life on earth, and any spirituality that dismisses wealth will have to, by that very logic, dismiss life itself, which is why most spiritual disciplines have been life-negating.

According to Mother and Sri Aurobindo, money is not just a medium of exchange but a powerful force at work on earth. This force can be harnessed and used consciously and creatively for human welfare and wellbeing, to generate physical, material, and vital abundance for all humans everywhere, or it can be used for personal and collective aggrandizement. Being a force, money by itself is neither good nor bad: it is what we make of it and how we use it.

The Vedic seers knew the wealth force to be an essentially divine force to be used for the establishment of Dharma on earth. But, in the present scheme of things, this wealth force happens to be under the control of the Asuras—beings ruled by greed and ego and bitterly opposed to Truth and Dharma. Those influenced and ruled by the Asuras tend to concentrate wealth and power in their own hands for their selfish use, while those influenced and guided by the daivic forces tend to distribute, circulate, and share their material and intellectual resources so that everyone prospers together, following wider and deeper laws of universal oneness and harmony. The Asuras, or the demonic forces, represent the exaggerated and unbalanced ego that typically needs to devour others to grow and thrive.

The fact that the Asuric forces rule most of the wealth and resources on earth explains the present state of affairs in the world—the irrational imbalance of wealth, the inequality of distribution of resources, the rampant greed and corruption of spirit that marks most businesses and money-making ventures. Because the forces controlling wealth are Asuric in origin, the all-around consequences are equally Asuric—our work and business culture, which is based on a cultural obsession with making money at all costs, is obviously self-destructive. Hardly anyone in our contemporary corporate and business environment loves or enjoys the work they do, or grows inwardly through it. Most—at least below the top-level leadership—work like donkeys in disempowering psychological environments for overtly utilitarian aims. The objective of work should be inner fulfillment, the ananda of creative and productive work that generates individual well-being and global prosperity. But few ever come to such delight of work in their lifetimes.

Consider the fact that we are living in a world where the richest 1 percent own 44 percent of the world's wealth and resources. If that's not bad enough, consider further that adults with less than $10,000 in wealth make up 56.6 percent of the world's population but hold less than 2 percent of global wealth. If this is what we have achieved over millennia of civilization and economic planning, then we seriously need to check our premises.

This is what the Asuric influence is doing—pushing human civilization inexorably towards a collapse of internal harmony and external order. Human societies are sitting on a powder keg. Such glaring Asuric inequality is bound to implode. It is a question of time. The socialist model failed because human consciousness, dominated by the Asuric ego, was not ready for it, and those who drove the system were themselves driven by the Asuric. The capitalist model, too, is failing because of the same reason—Asuric domination. The way we work, earn money, and live is a reflection and expression of Asuric greed and insecurity: corporate systems and governance are based on mutual distrust, and the corporate and social machinery is ruthless, exploitative, and transactional.

Self-interest is the defining attribute of the Asura, and it is self-interest that has largely defined us as communities, organizations, and nations. We act compulsively out of self-interest, and this is what makes us and our systems exploitative. This is inevitable, and we don't need a Marx to tell us that. If we act out of self-interest, we will inevitably end up exploiting each other.

In an ideal world, where the wealth force is possessed by the daivic and Dharmic forces, those with a higher and wider consciousness would have access to the wealth force; only the enlightened would be given the power over wealth and resources. The most privileged would also be the most responsible, conscious, compassionate, and, therefore, the most grateful and generous. Generosity is the defining attribute of the Deva, just as self-interest is the defining attribute of the Asura. But an ideal world will be created only under certain ideal conditions—the balance of forces will have to be restored, the Asuric influences have to be replaced by the daivic, the generation of wealth will have to be aligned to Dharma: the True, the Right, the Just.

The first condition for reversing the balance of forces would be to ensure that the spiritually conscious are the ones who take up the task of generating wealth. There is a cosmic law that governs the flow of wealth force—wealth flows towards its votaries and not towards those who resist or reject it. It has been the great tragedy of our civilization for millennia that those who should wield control over the wealth force are the ones who have deeply resisted or completely rejected it. This must change. The old idea of poverty as a condition for spiritual life must be rejected for what it is, a life-negating belief; wealth is a divine force and must be used for the service of the Divine. And this can best be done by those who seek the higher Light and Truth in their lives, those who aspire for Dharma. Dharma is not to be found in forests and monasteries but in the active field of life. Wealth is not a thing to be rejected but to be possessed by the mighty in spirit and used for the welfare of humanity.

We must remember that the ancient Indians did not reject human desire, Kama, or wealth, Artha, in their pursuit of spiritual Truth and liberation, Moksha—they harmonized and synthesized fulfillment of desire, generation of wealth, the pursuit of Dharma and Moksha, in a wide integral embrace of the whole field and scope of human existence. Kama, Artha, Dharma, and Moksha were interwoven in the very fabric of everyday life in the world. This is the principle to which our modern civilization must return, for this is the true resolution of our conflicts and crises.

The second condition would be to bring back the Rishi and the Yogi to the center stage of our collective life. We need to discover amongst ourselves the votaries of the higher Truth and not the votaries of money and power; we need to find and value those men and women of consciousness, those enlightened masters, who can be our new thought leaders and role models. We must collectively realize that possessing wealth, power, and fame does not mean anything if one does not possess consciousness, wisdom, and compassion. We must collectively understand that the rich, the powerful, and the famous are not necessarily the true and the wise—quite on the contrary. We must insist on the values of consciousness, integrity, and responsibility and must collectively and vigorously reject the self-indulgent, the false, and the hypocritical; we must, with great vigor and passion, reject pettiness and falsehood and celebrate truth and wideness;

we must learn to discern the most conscious amongst us and honor them, value them, celebrate them.

Those of us who can see through the guises of greed and corruption must begin to speak up like the little child in the fable who publicly asks why the emperor was not wearing clothes. We must learn to see truly, without filters; we must learn to stand for truth, whatever we may possess of it; we must learn to speak for the true and the right, call a spade a spade, and live with integrity and courage. The poverty of consciousness must end, and we must grow rich in mind, spirit, and body. The old division between wealth and spirit must go. The next generation should learn this invaluable lesson: that to possess true wealth force, one must possess true consciousness.

These, then, would be the indispensable conditions for establishing the next capitalism on earth. A conscious and enlightened capitalism created and sustained by groups of conscious and enlightened thought leaders wielding the wealth-force will open the possibilities of a new and enlightened socio-economic order. Only such a conscious and enlightened capitalism based on Dharma, or a dharmic capitalism, will bring about crucial changes in the way we collectively work and live on this planet. A dharmic capitalism will naturally encourage the principles of justice, fair play, and equal opportunity as much as the values of hard work and excellence. Unfair wealth generation, crony capitalism, unbridled greed and corruption do not make for a healthy and sane society, and the aim of wealth is to create a healthy and sane society. This is a spiritual truth, a truth of Dharma.

Dharma in the Twenty-First Century

The twenty-first-century post-pandemic world is going to be markedly different from the twentieth-century one. The twenty-first century, in all likelihood, will be the century of artificial intelligence, machine learning, technological singularity,[203] and transhumanism. Observing current trends worldwide, I have little doubt about this. Ironically, the objectives of transhumanism, specifically the enhancement of human cognitive and physical capacities, increasing longevity, and overcoming biological and psychological limitations of the human condition, are remarkably similar to those of Dharma. Dharma, too, through Yoga, seeks to enhance human cognitive abilities, overcome physical and psychological limitations, and extend the natural human lifespan.

There are, of course, obvious and critical differences: to begin with, transhumanism depends on the use of technology while Dharma seeks growth of consciousness; transhumanism will be machine-driven while Dharma is consciousness-driven. Transhumanism, even in the best-case scenario, will only make the human smarter, more informed, more distracted, and certainly not wiser or more conscious, while Dharma will, and can, only make the human wiser, more conscious, more spiritual.

The human species is fast approaching a critical evolutionary bifurcation, with one curve moving swiftly towards singularity

---

203 Popularized by mathematician and computer scientist Vernor Vinge in the 1980s and further explored by futurist Ray Kurzweil, technological singularity refers to a hypothetical future point in time when technological progress, specifically in artificial intelligence (AI) and machine learning, reaches a stage where it surpasses human intelligence and understanding.

and transhumanism (almost as a new religion) and another moving, perhaps much slower, towards a decisive change of consciousness and spirituality. While the former curve would logically lead to an eventual emergence of a hybrid species of human and machine, the latter may lead to a possible emergence of spiritual or psychic humans, a kind of higher-consciousness sapiens. This kind of an evolutionary bifurcation is not such a far-fetched idea; on the contrary, I feel it is an inevitable outcome of several interpenetrating civilizational and global consciousness trends. The way we humans live on earth today is simply not tenable anymore, and it's just a matter of time before life as we know it collapses altogether. Sri Aurobindo, who foresaw the present civilizational crisis at multiple levels, had said that the real crisis is one of consciousness, and unless there is a global change of consciousness, there is no escaping a civilizational collapse.

And maybe it is a good thing that collapse is imminent. Without a catastrophe hitting us, it is difficult to wake up. The Mother[204] wrote in 1964—*The future of the earth depends on a change of consciousness. The only hope for the future is in a change of man's consciousness and the change is bound to come. But it is left to men to decide if they will collaborate for this change or if it will have to be enforced upon them by the power of crashing circumstances.*

These 'crashing circumstances' are all around us. Some we are battling right now, others still hidden beneath the surface, waiting to break out. And these waves of calamities and crises will continue coming at us till we, at least in our higher parts, begin to acknowledge that our civilization, our collective way of being, is no longer working, that we are at an evolutionary dead-end, that we need to reimagine and redesign our future, and that we are running out of time and options. In many fundamental

---

204 The Mother of Sri Aurobindo Ashram, Pondicherry. This was written as a message for the First World Conference of the Sri Aurobindo Society (August 1964).

ways, our species is being gently nudged to look within for the next solution. Nature is compelling us to delve within, deeper into our own bodies and minds, to see beyond the immediate and the expedient and penetrate the layers of obscurity and figure out, each on our own, what we are all about. And if, as a species, we can learn from the circumstances around us and intuit from the present what is likely to happen in the near future, we may well be saved from calamities, and our awakening be made gentler. That, indeed, would be a coming of age for our species.

All the more reason we need a restoration of the Sanatan Dharma, the dharma of the Rishis. As the world slowly but surely moves away from religions altogether, the need for Dharma grows more intense and more widespread. Those who need Dharma the most want it the least, and those who want it do not know how to come to it. Most of those who teach the Dharma today teach it in the old idiom, still wedded to ideas and conventions that have outlived their purpose. We need young teachers and proponents of the Dharma who can effectively express the Dharma in the language of the twenty-first century and can approach this task with the zeal of an entrepreneur and the commitment of a commando.

A Symbolic Restoration

The ongoing construction of the Ram Janmabhoomi Temple at Ayodhya in India is a profound symbolic victory for Dharma: it is the culmination of a 490-odd years struggle for restoring Sri Ram, the seventh avatar in the line of Vishnu in Sanatan Dharma, to his rightful birthplace in the fabled city of his birth.[205] Whether or not he was actually born in this exact location matters little, for Sri Ram is not just a historical being for Hindus but a Divine incarnation, and Divine incarnations transcend the birth and death of mortal bodies.

The struggle through several generations to rebuild the temple at Ayodhya and restore Sri Ram to his birthplace was never a religious or political issue for the Hindus—it was always a question of Dharma. Sri Ram, for the common Hindu, is at once a complete embodiment and a shining representation of the Dharma itself; to displace Sri Ram and destroy his temple was a direct attack on the very fabric of Hindu Dharma.

Sri Ram had to be restored and the temple rebuilt—this was inevitable, a historical necessity. But it took a long time, seventy-three years even after India's political independence, and perhaps, had the Hindus not become assertive against the domineering narrative of the Islamist and Left-liberal forces, it would have taken even longer.

It must have been a deeply fulfilling moment for many a Sanatani when they beheld the leader of the nation himself presiding over the *bhumi-poojan*[206] of the Ram Mandir at

---

205 He had been, in fact, installed for years in a tent!
206 Consecration of the land upon which the structure would be built.

Ayodhya—it was undoubtedly an important symbolic victory, but also something much wider and more significant, for it marked the reversal of a national narrative. But however significant symbolically, the battle of narratives is far from over. There are other such symbolic and real battles to be taken up and won—nationally and globally.

Sri Ram has indeed been restored but let us not forget that Sri Ram stands for Dharma, Satya, and *Ram Rajya*.[207] This goes beyond symbols to the very heart of the matter. Satya is the core of Dharma, and Dharma is the core of Ram Rajya. Ram Rajya is neither a metaphor nor a utopian ideal: it is the natural culmination of Dharmic politics and the Dharmic way of life. When the life of the individual and the life of the collective become natural expressions of Dharma and Satya, when Dharma and Satya are used as the cohesive forces for nation-building, then Ram Rajya is established. Ram Rajya is not just a political theory but a growing spiritual need in the lives of men and nations. Ram Rajya is the kingdom of Truth on earth, and to establish Ram Rajya—however we may choose to designate it—in India must be Hindutva's aim and objective. Anything short of this and India's struggle for a Dharmic rashtra will not be complete.

We must remember that the real challenge to establishing Ram Rajya will not be political but social and intellectual. Though India is a young country, with 50 percent of its population under the age of thirty-five, a large section of our urban youth has been culturally and spiritually alienated from Dharma through generations, convinced that Western values and culture are superior to their own and that their Dharma is regressive, superstitious, in need of systemic reform; and that a large number of these youth believe all this unquestioningly is the real tragedy.

---

207 The rule of Rama, widely representative of Dharmic rule.

Thanks to a particularly decrepit and lackluster education system in India—arguably the worst case of an imperialist hangover in independent India—we, as a nation, have learnt to live comfortably with mediocrity and inefficiency at all levels, with most of our systems and institutions infected with this malaise. An alien education—where alien does not mean foreign but devoid of Dharma—has made us a society of well-read imitators, half-baked liberals, and petty-minded cynics. We have lost the depths and widenesses of Sanatan Dharma, and if that is not bad enough, we have learnt to criticize our Dharma in the language of our erstwhile colonial masters. We have lost the courage to stand for Dharma and to fight for what is right and true and just—we have become weak and selfish over the generations, our very life force has been sapped by the forces of adharma.

These are the challenges we must be mindful of. It is not the proselytizing religions and greedy nations that should worry us but our own incompetence, selfishness, falsehood, and deception. These are the deeper and more dangerous forces of adharma. Let us make no mistake about this—if we do not or cannot overcome the forces of adharma in ourselves and our systems and institutions, fighting anything else will be of little value. But, on the other hand, if we vanquish the inner foes, we will become towering forces of Dharma that no outer force or foe can shake or weaken.

This alone is the way to Ram Rajya, to the rule of Satya. In the inspiring words of the Indologist Koenraad Elst—*What Hindus will have to learn is that the essence of Hindu Dharma is not 'tolerance' or 'equal respect for all religions' but Satya, Truth. It is to this Truth that the Hindu raises temples and installs deities; the outer names and forms are mere contexts.*

Maharshi Sri Aurobindo

Rarely in the history of nations has a single person's spiritual influence shaped so profoundly a nation's destiny as Sri Aurobindo's has shaped India's. Yet, this is not a widely known or understood fact, as the modern Indian mind has lost its connection with the spiritual dimension of life. This is somewhat ironic because the Indian civilization has been influenced and shaped through millennia by some of the greatest spiritual seers ever to have walked the earth. Before Sri Aurobindo, and in recent history, the redoubtable Swami Vivekananda caused seismic shifts in Indian civilization through his enormous spiritual force.

Indians are no strangers to spiritual and Yogic phenomena. Some of the greatest influencers and architects of Indian civilization and culture have been the Rishis and the Yogis, the great preceptors of the Sanatan Dharma. It is because of this that the Indian civilization has always been nurtured by the perennial streams of living Dharma. Dharma has thrived in India and grown in power because of these legendary seers and prophets. Most of these seers lived and worked in complete seclusion and anonymity, influencing a million lives and events from their mountain caves or forest ashrams.

Sri Aurobindo was amongst the last Maharshis of the Sanatan Dharma who occultly influenced and shaped India's destiny from his seclusion in Pondicherry. His life and his Yoga were not for all to see or know. What he himself revealed to disciples of his Yoga was only the tip of a massive iceberg. What he did for humanity, and what he did for India, will take several centuries to unfold, for the results of a Yogic mission such as his become embedded in the very fabric of universal time and evolution.

Yet, Sri Aurobindo remains a peripheral, somewhat mythical, figure of Indian history for most educated Indians. This has been the unutterable tragedy of modern India—generations of educated Indians have been kept away from their own Dharma and civilizational values first by the British and then by our own political leadership driven by an agenda heavily shaped by the foreign influences of Western liberalism, secularism, and socialism. As a consequence, generations of Indians have grown up with little or no knowledge of their own heritage or destiny.

Most young Indians do not learn much of Sri Aurobindo from their history books. The most that they are taught is that he was a political revolutionary who quit politics and retired to Pondicherry to do Yoga. But then, they are not given any further knowledge of India's vast Yogic tradition or of the rich national politics of those times either. They have no idea why Sri Aurobindo left politics and what he did after leaving politics. The history of Indian nationalism, within years of Sri Aurobindo's retirement, became overshadowed by Gandhi, and most other luminaries of the freedom struggle were reduced to footnotes.

Few amongst us would know that Sri Aurobindo was the first political leader to proclaim that India was not merely a landmass but a living consciousness, a Divine Shakti, that needs to be awakened; he was indeed the High Priest who lit the sacrificial fires of the great Yajna for India's freedom. He was the first to invoke India as Shakti, as the divine Bhawani Bharati—*What is our mother-country? It is not a piece of earth, nor a figure of speech, nor a fiction of the mind. It is a mighty Shakti, composed of the Shaktis of all the millions of units that make up the nation, just as Bhawani Mahisha Mardini sprang into being from the Shakti of all the millions of gods assembled in one mass of force and welded into unity. The Shakti we call India, Bhawani Bharati, is the living unity of the Shaktis of three hundred million people.*

Sri Aurobindo's own deeper Yoga began with his quest for spiritual power that he could place at the service of his motherland. For Sri Aurobindo, the fight for India's freedom was spiritual first and then political, for political freedom would mean little without spiritual freedom. Only as a spiritually free nation would India be able to fulfill her destined role as jagat-guru, universal teacher, amongst the nations of the world. This was Sri Aurobindo's dream for India, and this was the seed of future greatness that was planted in the very bosom of India, the truth that India had borne in her soul since the beginning of her ancient civilization. India's freedom as a nation and a civilization was thus inevitable in the divine scheme of things, but what still had to be worked out was the way, the process, and the details of the great Yajna. Sri Aurobindo, as the great devas and maharshis of old, spoke of India's future from the highest planes of truth-consciousness—*India cannot perish, our race cannot become extinct, because among all the divisions of mankind it is to India that is reserved the highest and the most splendid destiny, the most essential to the future of the human race. It is she who must send forth from herself the future religion of the entire world, the Eternal Religion which is to harmonize all religion, science and philosophies and make mankind one soul.*

It is for this ultimate purpose of world transformation that India has birthed and nurtured through millennia the Sanatan Dharma, and it is for this that Sri Aurobindo himself embodied the Sanatan Dharma and brought it into the collective consciousness of Indians in those formative years of India's nationhood and established the Sanatan Dharma as the true basis and framework for a pan-Indian spiritual nationalism or *Dharmic nationalism* if you will.

Let us recall those profound and mighty words from his Uttarpara speech—*I say that it is the Sanatan Dharma which for us is nationalism. This Hindu nation was born with the Sanatan Dharma, with it, it moves and with it, it grows. When the Sanatan*

Dharma declines, then the nation declines, and if the Sanatan Dharma were capable of perishing, with the Sanatan Dharma it would perish. The Sanatan Dharma, that is nationalism.

Sri Aurobindo, thus, was the first prophet of spiritual or Dharmic nationalism. He, by his work, his speeches and writings, and his own active leadership, spiritualized Indian nationalism and politics; and in doing so, he also paved the way for Dharmic politics and economics in India, the old concept of Ram Rajya, the kingdom of God on earth. The culmination of political governance will have to be in a Ram Rajya of the future, and the culmination of economics and business will have to be a Dharmic or spiritual blend of capitalism and communism, purified of the distortions of the unregenerate human nature driven by egoistic fear and greed. This is yet another aspect of Sri Aurobindo's creative vision for India and the world. It must be remembered that spiritual nationalism is not the same as the self-limiting, self-aggrandizing exclusivist nationalism the world is used to; being spiritual, this form of nationalism will be an expression of a nation's soul, its spiritual and civilizational essence, and will necessarily be in harmony with all other nationalistic expressions and aspirations, even as various notes of music blend to create a symphony. As Sri Aurobindo would say, harmony is the law of spiritual life.

Sri Aurobindo saw clearly that India, of all nations in the world, with her enormous cultural heritage and spiritual and Yogic knowledge, would be the best equipped to lead this change to a new and more conscious world order. But spiritual nationalism must be founded on spiritual consciousness, for it cannot be an intellectual ideal or a mere philosophical system. The individual, therefore, must first find in themselves the spiritual consciousness and truth and then make that the basis for a wider social and national life. In other words, the framework and basis for the individual, the society, and the nation will have to become increasingly Dharmic, or spiritual, and therefore, Sri Aurobindo's insistence on spiritual freedom and truth-consciousness as the foundation for social and national existence.

How many of us today realize the enormous significance of spirituality and Dharma in our daily lives and actions? Spirituality, once the vital life force of Indian civilization, has now shrunk to facile new age practices and the psychobabble of self-proclaimed and self-marketed gurus, or worse, has been reduced to practices and mindless rituals. In our social and national life, spirituality has all but disappeared. From the high ideals of Dharmic politics and governance that Sri Aurobindo held in his vision for a future India, we have been reduced to intractable systemic corruption that has sapped the lifeblood of our nation. A return to some semblance of Dharma in the nation's political life has just started, but there is still a long way to go. It is now, in these circumstances raging around us, that we need to return to Sri Aurobindo's Truth and Light. Each of us needs to do this, for each of us individually will add to the gathering force of the Truth. Small waves make a tsunami.

Again, in Sri Aurobindo's words: *India of the ages is not dead nor has she spoken her last creative word; she lives and has still something to do for herself and the human peoples... That which must seek now to awake is still the ancient immemorable Shakti recovering her deepest self, lifting her head higher towards the supreme source of light and strength and turning to discover the complete meaning and a vaster form of her Dharma.*

In a very real sense, Sri Aurobindo is the custodian of India's eternal Dharma; he, more than anyone else, saw how absolutely indispensable India's Dharma was to India's future and proclaimed the urgent necessity to recover and rejuvenate India's Dharma. But, in an ironical twist of fate, even as Sri Aurobindo labored to awaken the nation's Shakti, the then political leaders of our nation and the arbiters of her destiny were turning away from the Dharma and vigorously replacing it with newfangled notions of social justice, economic equality, and political sophistication, overlooking the simple fact that without a Dharmic base and framework, no political, economic, or social edifice would stand for too long. Unbeknownst to most Indians of that time, our national leaders were steering India away from her essential Indianness towards an indeterminate universalism.

Contemporary India continues to live through the malaise of economic reservations, minority appeasement, communalism, and corruption, all of which could have been avoided had India's leadership aligned itself with the true Dharma when it mattered most. However, all nations, like individuals, have a certain karma that even the Divine cannot alter. But we can learn and grow more conscious. As Sri Aurobindo says, *by our stumbling, the world is perfected.* So we need to grow conscious not only of our strengths but also of our frailties, not only of our high destiny but also of all the forces ranged against us, determined to thwart that destiny. The resistance to a Dharmic India is still strong and adamant. Much more needs to be done if India has to awaken to her truth. Indians, or at least those who carry India in their hearts and minds, must turn to the highest truth, the highest Dharma, that they can access. And that which they can access, with only a little labor of love, is the Truth that Sri Aurobindo embodies and represents.

Sri Aurobindo needs to be read, researched, discussed, debated, understood, and applied, widely across the country. Sri Aurobindo's vast vision and work have still not found a place in Indian public or academic discourse, even decades after Independence. Our schools and universities hardly touch Sri Aurobindo at any depth. Only a superficial and cursory mention is made of him as the freedom fighter who renounced political life. Hardly anything beyond that. Few students of Indian history today know of Sri Aurobindo as the prophet of Indian nationalism, as the first radical revolutionary in India's struggle for freedom, as a poet and writer of rare eminence, and as a

Mahayogi and Maharshi of Indian spirituality. This is a historical anomaly that needs to be vigorously corrected.

We need to learn and understand how Sri Aurobindo, from the 1870s to 1950, right through the critical formative years of India, shaped India's destiny through his Yogic force and will This may be difficult to grasp for most, but we owe ourselves this knowledge and understanding. Sri Aurobindo is India's inestimable heritage, and he must be presented to the educated Indian and to the Indian youth objectively, rationally, and cogently.

Let us recall Sri Aurobindo's message to the Indian youth— *Our first necessity, if India is to survive and do her appointed work in the world, is that the youth of India should learn to think, – to think on all subjects, to think independently, fruitfully, going to the heart of things, not stopped by their surface, free of prejudgments, shearing sophism and prejudice asunder as with a sharp sword, smiting down obscurantism of all kinds as with the mace of Bhima.*

These are not mere words. This is an invocation of *yuvashakti*—the creative force of the youth, and not just the young in age but the young in mind and spirit. To understand and live Sri Aurobindo's Truth, we need to be clear as crystal in the mind and strong as a lion in the heart and ageless in spirit; we need to make ourselves the true hero-warriors of the Divine Shakti.

In the words of the Mother, Sri Aurobindo's divine collaborator in his Work and Yoga—*Sri Aurobindo always loved deeply his Motherland. But he wished her to be great, noble, pure and worthy of her big mission in the world. He refused to let her sink to the sordid and vulgar level of blind self-interests and ignorant prejudices. This is why, in full conformity to his will, we lift high the standard of truth, progress and transformation of mankind, without caring for those who, through ignorance, stupidity, envy or bad will, seek to soil it and drag it down into the mud. We carry it very high so that all who have a soul may see it and gather round it.*

It was obviously no coincidence that India's Independence Day fell on Sri Aurobindo's birthday, the 15th of August. In his message to the nation on 15th August, Sri Aurobindo said— *August 15th, 1947 is the birthday of free India. It marks for her the end of an old era, the beginning of a new age. But we can also make it by our life and acts as a free nation an important date in a new age opening for the whole world, for the political, social, cultural and spiritual future of humanity.*

Let us remember that though Sri Aurobindo struggled all his life for India and India's highest and widest freedom, he was not limited in his vision and will to India alone. For him, India was the starting point of a human transformation, the hub of a universal evolution of consciousness. *I have always held and said that India was rising, not to serve her own material interest only, to achieve expansion, greatness, power and prosperity, though these too she must not neglect, and certainly not like others to acquire domination of other peoples, but to live also for God and the world as a helper and a leader of the whole human race,* he had said in his message to the nation.

To limit Sri Aurobindo to India alone would be a disservice to his work and legacy. Sri Aurobindo labored for all humanity; all that he attempted and attained was for all humanity and for the Divine in humanity. If there is one who can be said to belong to the world, it is Sri Aurobindo. Sri Aurobindo's Truth is the future of the human species; it is the path to the true Kingdom of God on earth, and it is the Truth of the Divine still to be realized in the mind, life, and body of the earth. The world needs such a vision and an inspiration, and desperately so, and India, most of all.

Endnotes

Sanatan Dharma, the Cosmic Code

If Brahman—absolute being and consciousness—has become this universe by self-extension, as the Vedic Rishis declare, then this universe is living and conscious, and just as any living organism is programmed by its genetic coding, the universe too possesses a genetic code—a dynamic blueprint that determines its structure, evolution, and workings. This genetic code is the Dharma, the cosmic principle of order and harmony, embedded in the very fabric of the universe. This is an analogy that reveals a deeper mystical fact. The Vedic Rishis always referred to the human body as a microcosm of the cosmic body, *as above, so below.* The macrocosm, this universe with all its forms, formations, and forces that they called *brahmanda*, corresponds exactly to the human individual, the microcosm, that they called *kshudra-brahmanda.*[208]

The Vedic Rishis saw the human body, with its physical and subtle structures, its centers of consciousness or *chakras*, from the *muladhara* to the *sahasrara*,[209] with its play of the gunas and the forces, as the exact equivalence or reflection of the cosmic body—the *virat rupa*—of Purusha with each part and function of the body representing a dimension or aspect of the cosmic. As Sri Aurobindo describes: *Every being really holds in himself all that his outward vision perceives as if external to him. We have subjective*

---

208 *Brahmanda*, literally Brahman's egg, refers to the womb of Brahman; kshudra means small.
209 There are seven chakras or centers of consciousness in the subtle body, which, in ascending order, are the *muladhara*, the root chakra, *svadhisthana* or the sacral chakra, *manipura* or the solar plexus chakra, *anahata* or the heart chakra, *visuddha* or the throat chakra, *ajna* or the forehead (third eye) chakra, and the *sahasrara*, the crown chakra. These seven chakras correspond to the seven planes of the universe.

faculties hidden in us which correspond to all the tiers and strata of the objective cosmic system and these form for us so many planes of our possible existence... For as the Gods have built the series of the cosmic worlds, even so they labour to build up the same series of ordered states and ascending degrees in man's consciousness from the mortal condition to the crowning immortality... pure thought and feeling are man's sky, his heaven; this whole vitalistic existence of emotion, passions, affections of which desire is the pivot, forms for him a mid-world; body and material living are his earth...[210]

Thus, in the Vedic darshan, the human body is a living representation of the cosmos, the cosmos projecting itself into the human form just as it extends itself into the human psyche, and all that is in the cosmic body, the subtle and the gross worlds, the tattvas—*akasha, vayu, tejas, apas,* and *prithvi*[211]—and the gunas—sattva, rajas, and tamas—is as much in the human body, and so, every state and movement of the human mind-body system is deeply and inextricably connected with the cosmic system. Just as the genetic code that determines the development and functioning of all living organisms is embedded in the DNA, deep in the subtle cellular consciousness, so is the genetic code of the universe embedded in its Dharma. To grasp this, we must remember the word genetic derives from genesis or origin, and if we trace back our individual and cosmic existence to their origin, we will come to the same One Truth—ekam Sat—which expresses itself as the Dharma.

In a very fundamental and subtle sense, human consciousness affects and continuously shapes the universe as the universe affects and shapes the human—we are cosmic in more ways than

---

210 Sri Aurobindo, *Hymns to the Mystic Fire.*
211 Akasha or space tattva represents location and extension, vayu or air tattva gives movement, tejas (arising from agni) or fire tattva gives form and shape, apas or water tattva gives fluidity, prithvi or earth tattva gives solidity to the body. In all, there are thirty-six tattvas that form the cosmos, ranging from the subtlest suddha tattvas to the grossest material tattvas, mahabhutas. A complete description of the tattvas, though essential to understanding the entire idea of the correspondence, is beyond our present scope.

we can imagine. If we were to go deep down enough into our own DNA, in some quantum sense that we cannot at present entirely grasp, we would find in its subtlest layers the genetic code of the universe—or its Dharma. And this is perhaps what the Maharshis did—who knows?

In the final analysis, it's the same thing: DNA or Dharma. From the microcosmic perspective, we, as human individuals, are programmed by our DNA, and from the macrocosmic perspective, we, as cosmic existences, are programmed by the Dharma, the intertwining strands of Sat and Rta. It makes no difference what language or religious context we use—ultimately, it is all cosmic. The differences and divisions we carry in our minds are childish, and someday we will all outgrow them. Whether we call our cosmic code Sanatan Dharma or by any other name, it will always and inevitably refer to the same immutable reality of existence—that which has no name or description, that which is beyond thought and word. *Anirvachaniya.*

The Metaphor of Deepavali

Deepavali, meaning row of lights, is the annual festival of lights and fireworks in India, and now known the world over, wherever there are Indians. It is an old festival, its roots going far back in time.

The story that has come down through generations is that when Sri Rama returned to Ayodhya after completing fourteen years in exile, everyone in the city celebrated his return by lighting lamps. Light has always been an auspicious symbol in Sanatan Dharma and indeed in almost all religions.

But there is a deeper story here, a more evocative symbolism.

Sri Rama is the avatar, incarnation, of the Divine. And as all avatars, he resides as the inmost Light in all of us, deep in our hearts. This is the true meaning of *avataran*—the descent of the Divine into the human. Long before the outer form of the Avatar is visible to our eyes, he has already descended into the secret caves of our hearts and is preparing the grounds for his avataric work, a work that involves each one of us, whether we know it or not. But awareness of the Avatar within is always difficult for our sense-driven minds, habitually turned outward.

The lure of the sense objects and the charms of the outer world are strong, and the pull of the ego is irresistible. We cannot acknowledge the Lord in our hearts, we cannot revere the godhead in our souls, and so, unwittingly, sadly, we exile the Divine from our beings into the outer forests of our lives. So Sri Rama's exile is, in a much deeper sense, our own exile. It is we who go wandering into the forests, those thick and dark forests of our desires and fears.

And it is in those formidable forests that we lose Sita to Ravana. Sita, who always returns, age after age, lifetime after lifetime, into our hearts and souls, as the pure crystalline love for the Divine—Sri Rama in one epoch, Sri Krishna in another. How does it matter if the names and forms change? The inner, that which is the true and infallible base of all our existence here on earth, remains the same, ever, through the roll of time and ages.

Sita is the Divine love seated secret in our inmost being. Each time our hearts rise up to the Godhead, in this form or that, it is Sita, and it is Radha,[212] who rises in us as a pure flame of love and aspiration, quietly and blissfully, penetrating through all the outer layers and coverings of our unregenerate and stubborn earthly nature, drunk with the pride and arrogance of the ego.

Ravana is not out there, that ten-headed monstrosity that we burn each Dusshera. Ravana is that ego, the ten-headed asura, hidden deep in the folds of our own being, one head in the buddhi, another in the chitta, one in the heart, another in the prana, each head symbolizing a power of our own consciousness; Ravana plunges into our beings, in joyful abandon, and takes Sita captive, and this inner drama is repeated every time we surrender to the ego in us and exile the Divine. Ravana, mind you, does not look hideous at all. He looks charming, like a prince, which he indeed is, a veritable prince of darkness. His words enchant, and his voice mesmerizes. His eyes penetrate deep as if looking into your inmost secrets. Before you know it, you have lost your balance and have gone on a wild chase following a scent and a sight that you will never trace to the source. Such are the mysteries of the dark forests. And, in a trice, Sita is abducted. And all you hear is a soft whisper of prayer.

---

212 Sri Krishna's consort, celebrated in the Vaishnava tradition for her entire self-giving to Krishna. The Radha-Krishna love is also a profound symbol of divine love in human terms.

Rama's struggle, then, is against the forces of our own nature. Make no mistake, he doesn't fight the asura. He fights us, within ourselves. Each time. Repeatedly. The epic battle rages within us, in our hearts and souls, in our minds, in our bodies. Each part of our being is one front for the battle. On each front, we are fronted by one of the asura's heads. And we get taken in only because all those heads look so much like our own in that dim light of our hearts.

But the Divine cannot be defeated. The victory is assured, now or in another hundred years—what does it matter in cosmic time? When Sri Rama wills the victory, a victory it shall be, no matter how many Ravanas stand ranged against him. When Sri Krishna wills a victory, victory again it shall be, no matter how many Naraksuras rise against him. For the asuras rise and fall by the will of the Divine, and behind all those numerous risings of the asuras is a deeper mystery and purpose, something still to be unearthed from the pits of the forests that engulf us in our own exiles.

But the battle will be won. Eventually. Inevitably. The forests will burn, and the blaze will illumine the dark. Sri Rama will return from exile. Sri Krishna will return to his rightful throne in his rightful kingdom. The exile will end. For each exile returns the godhead to itself. And so, Sri Rama returns to Ayodhya, that real Ayodhya deep in our beings, that sacred invincible space that lives in each of us—*ayodhya*, which cannot be attacked or vanquished.

And when Sri Rama walks down the gold-paved path of this Ayodhya, deeper into our hearts, we light a lamp to express our gratitude, our prayer, and our love. And we seek to become that lamp, that *deepa*, that we must kindle with our own sacred Agni, that same Agni lit by our ancestors, our forefathers, our maharshis, age after age, that same Agni brought down by the ancient gods from those high regions that have now receded in time and consciousness.

And this lighting of the lamp must be understood for what it is—an act of profound reverence, an act that symbolically connects us in spirit to the primordial Agni, that first explosion of Light from the womb of the Unknown. It is thus that we can become the act and the symbol, embody consciously that illumination that cannot be extinguished. And, secure in that knowing, we bow in love and gratitude as Sri Rama returns with Sita beside him, for Sita, too, is eternal.

Do not misunderstand that ancient event, that beautiful metaphor, of Sita descending into the earth and disappearing. Sita does not disappear nor does she despair. Sita's love for Sri Rama is not subject to time or circumstances, politics or culture. Sita's love is sanatan—eternal and universal. She loves him not just for herself but for each one of us, for all embodied life that must live through a thousand *agni-parikshas*, a thousand trials by fire, where many shall burn to ash, and many shall be redeemed by fire. The fire that consumes is also the fire that purifies and restores.

When we burn in the living flames of our inner hells, it is that love of hers for Sri Rama that can keep us from burning to ash. And when the fire purifies and redeems, transforming a part of us into pure flame, it is that love of hers for Sri Rama that keeps us from melting into the transmuting furnace.

So, Sita's descent into earth is her secret descent into the terrestrial body—our bodies—for this body of earth is one. She does not disappear, for she who is born of fire and earth returns to fire and earth, resplendent with her love for Sri Rama.

And so, deepavali—the spiritual, the inner deepavali—the row of lamps signifying those inner states of being that must be brought to the light of consciousness in each of us—benevolence, humility, gratitude, purity, peace, and joy. These inner states are auspicious and divine, and to invoke these is to invoke *Sri*, the Divine's sweet grace and splendor. Sri, this grace and splendor of the Divine, is not outside of us; it arises from within, of itself, when we light those symbol lamps in our consciousness. One by one. Carefully, with sincerity that burns all the dross, with love that consumes the ego. One by one. Mindfully. Prayerfully.

Then deepavali happens. The real deepavali. The night lights up and dances with joy, the joy of divinity, the joy of utter self-giving. In that dance of joy, the Mother descends as Lakshmi, the godhead of prosperity and wealth. Wealth is always spiritual first, and so is prosperity. Material wealth and prosperity are but inevitable expressions of spiritual wealth, the spiritual grace. We have forgotten this over the ages. We have turned outward, and we invoke the Grace in external forms through external rituals.

The true deepavali is a reversal: a turning inward, lighting the lamps of consciousness with the inner Agni of our aspiration for the Divine—*Thou, thou alone, Mother*. The true invocation is not for wealth, not for health, not for *mangalam*, but for the Mother Herself, for Sri to descend into our lives. Then, no other mantra or worship is needed. Our call, ever so softly whispered in our own hearts, becomes the mantra; our love for Her, however delicate, however frail, becomes the worship, the puja. Then deepavali happens—in us, and in the world outside. The true Deepavali, then is our conscious offering to the Light, to that Light which is the foremost symbol of the Divine Truth, to that Light which returns us eternally to the very source of all life in the universe—and to that undying Light of godhead in us, may our prayers and offerings go forth.

How to Become a Hindu

(A Dialogue)

John Shotton used to be a professor of English at Oxford. He had given up all that and had come to India seeking enlightenment. While at Mirtola[213] for a few days, we became good friends and would often discuss philosophy and religion. One warm November afternoon, while sitting on the grassy lawn in front of the temple, he asked me how he could become a Hindu.

'Meditate.' I told him somewhat dismissively. 'That's the best way to become a Hindu.'

'No,' he said again. 'I mean formally. The way you can convert to Christianity. How do I convert to Hinduism?'

He was serious. So I had to reflect on his question and then answer. 'You cannot convert to Hinduism, John, because there is no religion, no ideology, or belief to convert to.'

'But you are a Hindu, aren't you? You belong to a religion!' He persisted.

I tried to answer as simply as I could. 'For me, being a Hindu or a Christian means nothing. It's all in the mind. Cultural conditioning. People convert from one belief to another, from one conditioning to another. It's all superficial and makes no difference. You only eat, dress, and live differently. Nothing essential changes.'

He didn't say anything for a while. So I asked him—'Why do you wish to become a Hindu, John?'

'So that I can read the Gita and dance for Krishna.'

---

213 A Vaishnav ashram about a couple of hours' drive from the town of Almora in Uttarakhand. The ashram has been built around a Radha-Krishna temple.

I smiled at him. 'But you can still read the Gita and sing for Krishna!'

'At the temple here? They won't allow.'

'But why should you need to go to a temple to sing to Krishna? You sing because you want to, because the song comes to you, it is your expression, between you and Krishna.'

John thought for a while. 'That may be true. But isn't there something to being a formal Hindu?'

'There are no formal Hindus, John,' I said. 'Hindu Dharma is not the same as religion, it is a process, not an end-product that you can label as formal religion.'

'And where does the process lead?'

'To Truth,' I said. 'Once you understand that, you will understand that the Hindu is simply someone who is seeking the Truth of being.'

'The Hindu is a disciple of Truth,' John said, 'not a disciple of any formal religion or a holy prophet. This is what Ashish told me once.'

'And I agree,' I said, 'and so you, John, can be a Hindu if you seek only the Truth and give all of your being and consciousness to it.'

'But I can seek Truth as a Christian too?' John asked.

'Of course, you can, provided you do not accept a given scriptural or theological truth to be the final one. The moment you accept such a truth, however on high that may be coming from, you cease to be a seeker, and you become a believer.'

'But the Truth comes from God, does it not?'

'How does one know?'

'One accepts on faith.'

'Precisely—faith, belief. But a follower of Truth accepts nothing on faith.'

John looked pensive.

'Or...' I continued, 'let me say it in another way. A disciple of Truth has only one article of faith: that Truth is infinite and eternal, and no one single belief or thought system, no one single God or religion, can contain it. We can all catch glimpses of Truth, but none can claim that they or their religion possess the whole of the eternal and infinite Truth. If that were so, then Truth would not be eternal or infinite.'

'But Truth being eternal and infinite is a matter of faith too, as you are yourself acknowledging, no one knows for sure.'

'Yes, either way, no one knows for sure. So why not find out? See, the belief that there is a particular Truth, which is the Truth of this or that religion, kills my seeking. But the other belief, that Truth is infinite and cannot be known by any human religion or philosophy, adds fuel to the fire of my seeking and does not let me rest till I find the Truth myself, in whatever humble measure. So, left to myself, I would happily go with the latter belief.'

'So a Hindu does not believe in God? In Krishna?'

'A Hindu,' I said, 'does not believe. Period. The Hindu is a seeker, a disciple of the eternal Truth, and accepts no external authority. He may use scriptures and teachers as aids, markers along the way, but his final submission is to the eternal Truth that is beyond names, forms, and systems.'

'I understand,' John said quietly.

'So if being a Hindu is being a disciple of the eternal Truth, how do you convert to it?'

'You can't,' said John. 'But there must be people who have found this eternal Truth?'

'Yes, of course—the Rishis, yogis, mystics, perhaps even some of the sadhus and swamis!'

'Ah, yes! But do they not share the Truth? Pass it on to their disciples?'

'They do, I'm sure!'

'Then what happens to the seeking of the disciples? They get the Truth from their teachers, don't they?'

'What teaching or truth do they get, John?'

'That there is Brahman. Exactly like we say there is God, the Father and His only begotten Son.'

'What does Brahman mean?'

'God?'

'No,' I said. 'Brahman does not mean God. It refers to the infinite ultimate reality—that which is the best, the supreme, the most auspicious, and that which is everything and everyone. And so on. Brahman means a lot of things.'

'So, who is Krishna, then?' John asked. 'Isn't he God?'

'Good question to ask, John,' I said. 'See, you are already becoming a Hindu! This questioning is what will open your mind and heart to Dharma. You cannot be born into this seeking; none can convert you to it. You yourself have to be drawn to it, you have to come to it, like a true disciple, and give all of yourself to it.'

'Hmm. I understand that.'

'And then alone will Truth come to you,' I continued. 'In measures you can take within yourself and assimilate. Truth is in no hurry; it is eternal and can wait for lifetimes.'

After a long silence, John asked again. 'Is there a method? Some process, some path?'

'Yes, there is,' I said. We call it Sanatan Dharma.'

Levels of Relation with the Guru

The Guru can teach, initiate, or lead in several ways and at several levels. Just as there are many kinds of spiritual traditions, disciples, and disciplines, so are there several kinds of gurus. The Sanatan tradition recognizes at least seven kinds of gurus.

The Guru who imparts knowledge, advises, or suggests spiritual or yogic practices to the disciple is called the *suchak* guru—suchak implies indication or suggestion. When such a guru uses his influence to inspire the disciple—for inspiration in Yoga is always a living and animating force—to sadhana and truth, he is also a *prerak* guru—prerak from *prerna*, meaning inspiration.

Similarly, a *vachak* guru informs, describes, explains, elaborates: vachak comes from vak, speech, and therefore, the guru who engages in oral teachings, discussions, and debates is the vachak guru. But a *bodhak* guru is one who awakens bodh or awareness. He initiates the disciple into sadhana. Such a guru may be a guide and a philosopher and may even be known as a *darshak* guru—darshak from darshan, philosophy. A bodhak or darshak guru may go deeper, revealing to the disciple the mysteries of avidya and suffering in order to awaken the buddhi to something higher; in that case, the bodhak or the darshak guru can be a *karan* or *karanyakya* guru. A karanyakya guru may even initiate the disciple into sannyasa, the life of renunciation. Such a guru leads the disciple into the deeper spiritual or occult causes—*karan*—of things.

At a deeper level of sadhana, we come to the *paramguru*, also known in certain traditions as *paratpara* guru. The paramguru can take the disciple's spiritual responsibility upon himself and guide the disciple in their sadhana and show the path to liberation, moksha. A paramguru is a remover or dispeller of doubts and delusions and is also known as *sadguru* or *mahaguru.* A sadguru or mahaguru can lead the disciple to adhyatmik jnana or spiritual knowledge and liberation. But for this, the guru himself must be self-realized, a *Jnani.* Without self-realization, the guru does not have the adhikara to be a paramguru, sadguru, or mahaguru.

Gurus in the Sanatan tradition are generally shiksha or diksha gurus. A shiksha guru imparts knowledge to the disciple—*shiksha* means knowledge or learning; a diksha guru initiates the disciple into Yoga, spiritual practice, or a specific spiritual or yogic lineage. *Diksha* means initiation. Therefore, the suchak, prerak, bodhak, and darshak gurus are shiksha gurus, while the paramguru, sadguru, or mahaguru are diksha gurus.

These are, of course, not watertight compartments. A shiksha guru may also be a diksha guru; a prerak or bodhak guru may have the capacity or adhikara to be a sadguru or paramguru but may not choose to play that role. Or they may be a suchak guru to one disciple, a bodhak guru to another, and a sadguru to a third. On the other hand, a lower adhikari guru may have the pretenses of being a higher adhikari guru and may even believe that they are higher in consciousness than they actually are. There is indeed a kind of guru called nisiddha guru—nisiddha means forbidden. Such a guru may give incomplete or even false knowledge to the unsuspecting disciple and can cause much damage to the psyche. It may take a sensitive disciple several years to recover from a nisiddha guru. Even worse, such a guru may be a fraud, a false teacher deliberately leading disciples astray. Such gurus—and unfortunately, there are many today—seek only to exploit disciples for their own ends. These are the so-called gurus who want to be well-known, wealthy, and influential and would typically have mass followings and lavish lifestyles.

But how to differentiate the genuine from the fraudulent? For a disciple, it would be well-nigh impossible to judge from the outside, similar to a junior physics student trying to assess a Nobel laureate! But then, the Nobel laureate would have solid credentials to prove their worth, but a fraud guru wouldn't need any credentials. No one normally challenges such a guru—or any guru, for that matter. The old story of the emperor with no clothes.

Finally, of course, there is the *antarguru*—the inner Guru, the guru residing in the heart, one's own psychic presence, the living Veda in the heart. The antarguru is like the *ishta-deva*— one's chosen and beloved deva or godhead.

The Battle to the End

So long as Dharma is not incontrovertibly established on earth, the battle for Light and Truth will continue, and this battle, unlike other battles fought on the ground, will be mostly invisible and inaudible, waged in the depths of consciousness, engaging unseen forces that have always been on earth to resist the victory of Light and Truth. The forces of falsehood—the Asuric—have always seemed to triumph over the forces of Truth—the daivic—which have always struggled to maintain a foothold on earth. The battle for Dharma is really the battle for earth, for it is earth alone that is the decisive evolutionary plane where consciousness can either grow to its supreme heights or fall to its abysmal depths; and because earth is the only evolutionary plane, even the gods seek to be born here so that they can attain the heights of consciousness.

There are other planes of consciousness too besides earth, but those are all typal planes where consciousness neither evolves nor devolves: it is only earth-consciousness that possesses both the highest evolutionary potential and its exact antithesis. Therefore, this ageless struggle of the forces of Truth against those of Falsehood, of Light against Darkness, echoed in almost every religion and mythology on this planet. And whichever force dominates earth finally will dominate evolution. If falsehood were ever to dominate earth—and no, in spite of all contrary appearances, it still does not—this universe would be one of falsehood where the Asuras would grow in stature and become the godheads of this Cosmos. Instead of a Rama, we would have a Ravana presiding over the evolution of consciousness on earth.

Each time, in fact, an *avataran* or divine incarnation occurs on earth, and the forces of Truth come to the front, the asuric forces, too, intensify their energies and multiply their efforts to push back the Truth, perhaps destroy it altogether. However, Truth being what it is, it cannot be destroyed, but it can be pushed back, opposed, and resisted, even driven underground. And this is precisely what is happening today, all around us, from global religious and political platforms to our homes and hearts; wherever even a trace of falsehood exists, there the battle rages, unseen and unsounded.

Make no mistake about this: each one of us is an instrument, a nimitta, in this great battle for earth-life. Which way the battle will go depends on how much of ourselves we put into this battle, how much of our skin is in the game, and how conscious and silent we can remain even as the battle rages furiously on. But to fight, to be in the thick of this battle, to be effective and efficient instruments of the Truth in this pitched battle against cosmic, terrestrial, and psychological falsehoods, there is a necessary preparation that all have to undergo, a secret kshatriya training of old, a training as much spiritual as physical and psychological.

The warrior of Light must first be immersed in Light, he who fights for Truth must be immersed in Truth, and no shadow of doubt or falsehood must be cast on the mind or heart, and the fidelity to Truth must be constant and unrelenting. This is nothing short of tapasya, but a tapasya that needs to be enormously concentrated, hastened, intensified, and for this intensification and acceleration, two conditions are necessary—deep inner silence and equality of spirit, mind, and heart: no disturbance, agitation, or excitement can be allowed. The warrior of Light must always wear a luminous armor. As Sri Krishna tells Arjuna, *agitation obscures the Light*. Remember, this is exactly what the asuras around us want, to obscure our Light by contaminating our own inner state, by throwing into us their disturbances and excitements, their bitterness and grievances, their soul-sapping selfishness and fears. Remember, too, that there is no way an asuric being can directly attack an armor of Light—they can only attack by using our own consent and will, which we give too often and too willingly.

Samata—yogic equality—is a shield in this battle. No matter how disturbing or hostile the circumstances, our equality of spirit must be firm and unshakeable. It is this one shield that the Divine Master in us needs to wage this battle. Without this shield of samata, even the Lord cannot fight. But then, it is not too difficult to mount this shield, for all that is needed is faith and a vast surrender. Nothing else is needed. With faith and surrender, the warrior can go through any battle unscathed.

Faith, in the most practical sense, implies stillness, inner immobility: no thought must arise, no desire to destroy, and no fear of being destroyed. The mind and heart must remain immutably calm, the being quiet and concentrated. This is the inner condition demanded of the warrior.

Postscript—A Personal Context

Though I was born into the Hindu Dharma, it took me nearly three decades to come to any real understanding and appreciation of it. Like so many others of my generation, brought up in English public and Jesuit schools and elitist colleges, I was completely ignorant of Hindu Dharma and spirituality. My education was neither Indian nor Hindu nor even properly European. It was a superficial medley of Christian morality and anglicized post-colonial academic culture with its inherent civilizational biases against Indian culture and thought.

We learnt extensively about Shakespeare and Milton and were taught Eliot and Lawrence, but we never got to hear of Kalidas, Vyasa, Valmiki, Sayana, or Panini, except for some cursory passing references in history or Hindi classes. We learnt science and mathematics but were never told of our Vedic heritage in the sciences and mathematics, in the arts and music, in philosophy, logic, and grammar, except, again, for some cursory mentions in history classes. Even our history books told us more about the Mughals and the British than about India and India's traditions and culture. The great movements of the Buddha and Jain dharmas were dealt with in a couple of chapters, and I don't recall reading anything of Sikhism at all, except for a few paragraphs on the Sikh gurus, and that too in relation to the Mughals.

The profound religious and spiritual movements within Hindu Dharma were given just a few paragraphs, not even chapters. There was no in-depth enquiry or serious research into our own Dharma and Dharmic traditions and practices. No critical thought was expected of us. We were merely expected to 'learn up' a few facts and figures and answer a few dumbed-down questions in an examination. That was it—our venerable Indian schooling system!

Few of us managed to pass out of school unscathed by the mind-numbing effects of twelve years of enforced schooling of mind and soul. All I wanted at that time was to avoid the inevitability of university education—frying pan to fire kind of a thing. But by an inexplicable twist of fate, I found myself at St. Stephen's College of Delhi, not only one of the most prestigious colleges in the country at that time but perhaps the cream of Christian missionary education as well. And ironically enough, we had the Hindu College right across the road—it didn't matter that the Hindu College had nothing overtly Hindu about it, just as St. Stephen's had nothing overtly Christian about it.

The three years at college turned out to be quite a different experience. While I studied English literature for the university course, I engaged in deep personal study of philosophy and physics. I owed my passion for philosophy to Bernard Shaw and Herman Hesse—Shaw's *Back to Methuselah* and Hesse's *Siddhartha* gave to my mind and soul in less than a month what twelve years of schooling could not—and my pursuit of physics to a college senior, a brilliant but eccentric student of physics who would regularly get high on cannabis, play the flute, and unravel the mysteries of relativity and quantum physics as if he was unraveling the tapestry of the gods.

Philosophy and quantum physics—and specifically, the *Tao of Physics* by Fritjof Capra—led me to Hindu philosophy, and my first response to it was somewhat skeptical. It took some more years, and a fortuitous dream experience, to shake me out of my intellectual skepticism and open me to the possibilities of Hindu Dharma. I graduated with a university rank and record grades—a perfect candidate for higher education but with zero interest in pursuing any of it. There was something else pulling me like a powerful magnet in an entirely different direction, and I didn't know what that was. What I did know, without a doubt, was that academic education was of no further use to me, as I had exhausted that karma entirely in college. And I had also realized by then that formal education did not lead anywhere—it was far too utilitarian to serve any real evolutionary purpose. Perhaps what I needed at that time, more than ever, was to find a route to practical enlightenment, and if my school education had given me any grounding in Hindu Dharma, I would have found that route without much effort.

However, after about three years of inner struggle and search, that route was opened for me by Swami Vivekananda, that great Vedantic Seer, that lion of Hindu Dharma. He stood tall before me in a dream vision more vivid than any I'd ever known, and I bowed and touched his feet, and he placed his palm on my head, blessing me. That touch was electric.[214] A current went right through my body, from head to toe, and it woke me up with a start. That single touch changed my inner life and orientation forever. Within just a few weeks, I lost all interest in my outer life and plunged headlong into the study of Vedanta. I devoured almost every book on Vedanta I could find and drank of the wisdom as one would drink from a well in the middle of a hot and dry desert. Day by day, Vedanta poured itself into my mind and heart. I was not just reading it, I was rediscovering it, almost recovering it from some deep and unknown depth of being. Many years later, I would come to know that it was indeed recovering the knowledge from my inner depths, for the knowledge is always there, only waiting to be awakened and brought to the surface.[215]

---

214 Much later, I discovered that the touch of such beings actually did possess certain electricity and is called *vidyut* in Yoga—the same word for electricity in Sanskrit.

215 I share this personal experience with my readers to make an important point—that the truths of Sanatan Dharma are not abstract or spiritually remote but ever present, in seed-form, in our minds and hearts, and can be recovered, brought to the surface, experienced and realized, if only we want it that bad.

As I have mentioned throughout this book, it is this knowledge in our depths that is the real scripture of Hindu Dharma, the scripture that we must recover and bring back to life. As I myself realized, and now openly share, we do not become a Hindu by birth—that means nothing—we become a Hindu by Yoga, by deep and sustained aspiration, intellectual enquiry, spiritual discipline, and progressive self-realization. We do not become a Hindu by going to temples, keeping religious fasts, going on pilgrimages, or offering ritualistic prayers to gods and goddesses—for these are all childlike measures to possess a supremely sublime and subtle Truth, almost like a child trying to catch the moon by grasping at its reflection in the water. All religious practices, as I have come to understand, are like the moon's reflection in the water. We can go on gazing at the reflection for a lifetime without realizing that we are not looking at the moon at all—for the moon is not there in the water, it is up there in the sky. To catch a glimpse of the real moon, you have to raise your head and look up.

I realized this day by day, with every small step I took into the vastness of vedanta. The more I delved into vedanta, the more of the Dharma I recovered. It took me many years to understand the basics, to unravel just the first layers of the profound mysteries of Sanatan Dharma. But the more I unraveled, the more clearly I could see.

I often feel like a mountain trekker. I climb towards what looks like a beautiful peak, but when I stand upon that peak, I see higher peaks far more radiant in the sunlight, some quite clear and not too far, and some shrouded by mist because of the distance, but each as enchanting, as mysterious.

—iti—

Appendix

Appendix

Atman, Jivatman, and the Psychic

It is necessary to understand clearly the difference between the evolving soul (psychic being) and the pure Atman, self or spirit. The pure self is unborn, does not pass through death or birth, is independent of birth or body, mind or life or this manifested Nature. It is not bound by these things, not limited, not affected, even though it assumes and supports them. The soul, on the contrary, is something that comes down into birth and passes through death—although it does not itself die, for it is immortal—from one state to another, from the earth plane to other planes and back again to the earth-existence. It goes on with this progression from life to life through an evolution which leads it up to the human state and evolves through it all a being of itself which we call the psychic being that supports the evolution and develops a physical, a vital, a mental human consciousness as its instruments of world-experience and of a disguised, imperfect, but growing self-expression. All this it does from behind a veil showing something of its divine self only in so far as the imperfection of the instrumental being will allow it. But a time comes when it is able to prepare to come out from behind the veil, to take command and turn all the instrumental nature towards a divine fulfillment. This is the beginning of the true spiritual life. The soul is able now to make itself ready for a higher evolution of manifested consciousness than the mental human—it can pass from the mental to the spiritual and through degrees of the spiritual to the supramental state. Till then there is no reason why it should cease from birth, it cannot in fact do so. If having reached the spiritual state, it wills to pass out of the terrestrial manifestation, it may indeed do so—but there is also possible a higher manifestation, in the Knowledge and not in the Ignorance.

—*Letters on Yoga*, Sri Aurobindo

The Uttarpara Speech by Sri Aurobindo

May 30, 1909

When I was asked to speak to you at the annual meeting of your Sabha, it was my intention to say a few words about the subject chosen for today, the subject of the Hindu religion. I do not know now whether I shall fulfill that intention; for as I sat here, there came into my mind a word that I have to speak to you, a word that I have to speak to the whole of the Indian Nation. It was spoken first to myself in jail and I have come out of jail to speak it to my people.

It was more than a year ago that I came here last. When I came I was not alone; one of the mightiest prophets of Nationalism sat by my side. It was he who then came out of the seclusion to which God had sent him, so that in the silence and solitude of his cell he might hear the word that He had to say. It was he that you came in your hundreds to welcome. Now he is far away, separated from us by thousands of miles.

Others whom I was accustomed to find working beside me are absent. The storm that swept over the country has scattered them far and wide. It is I this time who have spent one year in seclusion, and now that I come out I find all changed. One who always sat by my side and was associated in my work is a prisoner in Burma; another is in the north rotting in detention.

I looked round when I came out, I looked round for those to whom I had been accustomed to look for counsel and inspiration. I did not find them. There was more than that. When I went to jail, the whole country was alive with the cry of Bande Mataram, alive with the hope of a nation, the hope of millions of men who had newly risen out of degradation. When I came out of jail I listened for that cry, but there was instead a silence.

A hush had fallen on the country and men seemed bewildered; for instead of God's bright heaven full of the vision of the future that had been before us, there seemed to be overhead a leaden sky from which human thunders and lightnings rained. No man seemed to know which way to move, and from all sides came the question, 'What shall we do next ? What is there that we can do?'

I too did not know which way to move, I too did not know what was next to be done. But one thing I knew, that as it was the Almighty Power of God which had raised that cry, that hope, so it was the same power which had sent down that silence. He who was in the shouting and the movement was also in the pause and the hush. He has sent it upon us, so that the nation might draw back for a moment and look into itself and know His will. I have not been disheartened by that silence, because I had been made familiar with silence in my prison and because I knew it was in the pause and the hush that I had myself learned this lesson through the long year of my detention.

When Bipin Chandra Pal came out of jail, he came with a message, and it was an inspired message. I remember the speech he made here. It was a speech not so much political as religious in its bearing and intention. He spoke of his realisation in jail, of God within us all, of the Lord within the nation, and in his subsequent speeches also he spoke of a greater than ordinary force in the movement and a greater than ordinary purpose before it.

Now I also meet you again, I also come out of jail, and again it is you of Uttarpara who are the first to welcome me, not at a political meeting but at a meeting of a society for the protection of our religion. That message which Bipin Chandra Pal received in Buxar jail, God gave to me in Alipore. That knowledge He gave to me day after day during my twelve months of imprisonment and it is that which He has commanded me to speak to you now that I have come out.

I knew I would come out. The year of detention was meant only for a year of seclusion and of training. How could anyone hold me in jail longer than was necessary for God's purpose? He had given me a word to speak and a work to do, and until that word was spoken I knew that no human power could hush me, until that work was done no human power could stop God's instrument, however weak that instrument might be or however small. Now that I have come out, even in these few minutes, a word has been suggested to me which I had no wish to speak. The thing I had in my mind He has thrown from it and what I speak is under an impulse and a compulsion.

When I was arrested and hurried to the Lal Bazar hajat I was shaken in faith for a while, for I could not look into the heart of His intention. Therefore I faltered for a moment and cried out in my heart to Him, 'What is this that has happened to me? I believed that I had a mission to work for the people of my country and until that work was done, I should have Thy protection. Why then am I here and on such a charge?'

A day passed and a second day and a third, when a voice came to me from within, 'Wait and see.' Then I grew calm and waited. I was taken from Lal Bazar to Alipore and was placed for one month in a solitary cell apart from men. There I waited day and night for the voice of God within me, to know what He had to say to me, to learn what I had to do. In this seclusion the earliest realisation, the first lesson came to me.

I remembered then that a month or more before my arrest, a call had come to me to put aside all activity, to go in seclusion and to look into myself, so that I might enter into closer communion with Him. I was weak and could not accept the call. My work was very dear to me and in the pride of my heart I thought that unless I was there, it would suffer or even fail and cease;

therefore I would not leave it. It seemed to me that He spoke to me again and said, 'The bonds you had not the strength to break, I have broken for you, because it is not my will nor was it ever my intention that that should continue. I have had another thing for you to do and it is for that I have brought you here, to teach you what you could not learn for yourself and to train you for my work.'

Then He placed the Gita in my hands. His strength entered into me and I was able to do the sadhana of the Gita. I was not only to understand intellectually but to realise what [Sri Krishna] demanded of Arjuna and what He demands of those who aspire to do His work, to be free from repulsion and desire, to do work for Him without the demand for fruit, to renounce self-will and become a passive and faithful instrument in His hands, to have an equal heart for high and low, friend and opponent, success and failure, yet not to do His work negligently.

I realised what the Hindu religion meant. We speak often of the Hindu religion, of the Sanatan Dharma, but few of us really know what that religion is. Other religions are preponderatingly religions of faith and profession, but the Sanatan Dharma is life itself; it is a thing that has not so much to be believed as lived.

This is the Dharma that for the salvation of humanity was cherished in the seclusion of this peninsula from of old. It is to give this religion that India is rising. She does not rise as other countries do, for self or when she is strong, to trample on the weak. She is rising to shed the eternal light entrusted to her over the world. India has always existed for humanity and not for herself and it is for humanity and not for herself that she must be great.

Therefore, this was the next thing He pointed out to me, He made me realise the central truth of the Hindu religion. He turned the hearts of my jailors to me and they spoke to the Englishman in charge of the jail, 'He is suffering in his confinement; let him at least walk outside his cell for half an hour in the morning and in the evening.' So it was arranged, and it was while I was walking that His strength again entered into me. I looked at the jail that secluded me from men and it was no longer by its high walls that I was imprisoned; no, it was Vasudeva who surrounded me.

I walked under the branches of the tree in front of my cell, but it was not the tree, I knew it was Vasudeva, it was Sri Krishna whom I saw standing there and holding over me his shade. I looked at the bars of my cell, the very grating that did duty for a door and again I saw Vasudeva. It was Narayana who was guarding and standing sentry over me. Or I lay on the coarse blankets that were given me for a couch and felt the arms of Sri Krishna around me, the arms of my Friend and lover. This was the first use of the deeper vision He gave me.

I looked at the prisoners in the jail, the thieves, the murderers, the swindlers, and as I looked at them I saw Vasudeva, it was Narayana whom I found in these darkened souls and misused bodies. Amongst these thieves and dacoits, there were many who put me to shame by their sympathy, their kindness, the humanity triumphant over such adverse circumstances.

One I saw among them especially, who seemed to me a saint, a peasant of my nation who did not know how to read and write, an alleged dacoit sentenced to ten years' rigorous imprisonment, one of those whom we look down upon in our Pharisaical pride of class as Chhotalok. Once more He spoke to me and said, 'Behold the people among whom I have sent you to do a little of my work. This is the nature of the nation I am raising up and the reason why I raise them.'

When the case opened in the lower court and we were brought before the Magistrate I was followed by the same insight. He said to me, 'When you were cast into jail, did not your heart fail and did you not cry out to me, where is Thy protection? Look now at the Magistrate, look now at the Prosecuting Counsel.'

I looked and it was not the Magistrate whom I saw, it was
Vasudeva, it was Narayana who was sitting there on the bench.
I looked at the Prosecuting Counsel and it was not the Counsel
for the prosecution that I saw; it was Sri Krishna who sat there,
it was my Lover and Friend who sat there and smiled. 'Now do
you fear?' He said, 'I am in all men and I overrule their actions
and their words. My protection is still with you and you shall
not fear. This case which is brought against you, leave it in my
hands. It is not for you. It was not for the trial that I brought
you here but for something else. The case itself is only a means
for my work and nothing more.'

Afterwards when the trial opened in the Sessions Court, I
began to write many instructions for my Counsel as to what
was false in the evidence against me and on what points the
witnesses might be cross-examined. Then something happened
which I had not expected.

The arrangements which had been made for my defence were
suddenly changed and another Counsel stood there to defend
me. He came unexpectedly, a friend of mine, but I did not know
he was coming. You have all heard the name of the man who
put away from him all other thoughts and abandoned all his
practice, who sat up half the night day after day for months and
broke his health to save me, Srijut Chittaranjan Das.

When I saw him, I was satisfied, but I still thought it
necessary to write instructions. Then all that was put away from
me and I had the message from within, 'This is the man who will
save you from the snares put around your feet. Put aside those
papers. It is not you who will instruct him. I will instruct him.'

From that time I did not of myself speak a word to my
Counsel about the case or give a single instruction and if ever
I was asked a question, I always found that my answer did not
help the case. I had left it to him and he took it entirely into his
hands, with what result you know. I knew all along what He
meant for me, for I heard it again and again, always I listened to

the voice within; 'I am guiding, therefore fear not. Turn to your own work for which I have brought you to jail and when you come out, remember never to fear, never to hesitate. Remember that it is I who am doing this, not you nor any other.

'Therefore whatever clouds may come, whatever dangers and sufferings, whatever difficulties, whatever impossibilities, there is nothing impossible, nothing difficult. I am in the nation and its uprising and I am Vasudeva, I am Narayana, and what I will, shall be, not what others will. What I choose to bring about, no human power can stay.'

Meanwhile He had brought me out of solitude and placed me among those who had been accused along with me. You have spoken much today of my self-sacrifice and devotion to my country. I have heard that kind of speech ever since I came out of jail, but I hear it with embarrassment, with something of pain.

For I know my weakness, I am a prey to my own faults and backslidings. I was not blind to them before and when they all rose up against me in seclusion, I felt them utterly. I knew then that I the man was a man of weakness, a faulty and imperfect instrument, strong only when a higher strength entered into me. Then I found myself among these young men and in many of them I discovered a mighty courage, a power of self-effacement in comparison with which I was simply nothing. I saw one or two who were not only superior to me in force and character— very many were that—but in the promise of that intellectual ability on which I prided myself.

He said to me, 'This is the young generation, the new and mighty nation that is arising at my command. They are greater than yourself. What have you to fear? If you stood aside or slept, the work would still be done. If you were cast aside tomorrow, here are the young men who will take up your work and do it more mightily than you have ever done. You have only got some strength from me to speak a word to this nation which will help to raise it.' This was the next thing He told me.

Then a thing happened suddenly and in a moment I was hurried away to the seclusion of a solitary cell. What happened to me during that period I am not impelled to say, but only that day after day, He showed me His wonders and made me realise the utter truth of the Hindu religion. I had many doubts before. I was brought up in England amongst foreign ideas and an atmosphere entirely foreign.

About many things in Hinduism I had once been inclined to believe that they were imagination; that there was much of dream in it, much that was delusion and Maya. But now day after day I realised in the mind, I realised in the heart, I realised in the body the truths of the Hindu religion. They became living experiences to me, and things were opened to me which no material science could explain. When I first approached Him, it was not entirely in the spirit of the... Jnani. I came to Him long ago in Baroda some years before the Swadeshi began and I was drawn into the public field.

When I approached God at that time, I hardly had a living faith in Him. The agnostic was in me, the atheist was in me, the sceptic was in me and I was not absolutely sure that there was a God at all. I did not feel His presence. Yet something drew me to the truth of the Vedas, the truth of the Gita, the truth of the Hindu religion. I felt there must be a mighty truth somewhere in this Yoga, a mighty truth in this religion based on the Vedanta.

So when I turned to the Yoga and resolved to practise it and find out if my idea was right, I did it in this spirit and with this prayer to Him, 'If Thou art, then Thou knowest my heart. Thou knowest that I do not ask for Mukti, I do not ask for anything which others ask for. I ask only for strength to uplift this nation, I ask only to be allowed to live and work for this people whom I love and to whom I pray that I may devote my life.'

I strove long for the realisation of Yoga and at last to some extent I had it, but in what I most desired I was not satisfied. Then in the seclusion of the jail, of the solitary cell I asked for it again. I said, 'Give me Thy Adesh. I do not know what work to do or how to do it. Give me a message.' In the communion of Yoga two messages came.

The first message said, 'I have given you a work and it is to help to uplift this nation. Before long the time will come when you will have to go out of jail; for it is not my will that this time either you should be convicted or that you should pass the time as others have to do, in suffering for their country. I have called you to work, and that is the Adesh for which you have asked. I give you the Adesh to go forth and do my work.'

The second message came and it said, 'Something has been shown to you in this year of seclusion, something about which you had your doubts and it is the truth of the Hindu religion. It is this religion that I am raising up before the world, it is this that I have perfected and developed through the Rishis, saints and avatars, and now it is going forth to do my work among the nations. I am raising up this nation to send forth my word. This is the Sanatan Dharma, this is the eternal religion which you did not really know before, but which I have now revealed to you.

'The agnostic and the sceptic in you have been answered, for I have given you proofs within and without you, physical and subjective, which have satisfied you. When you go forth, speak to your nation always this word, that it is for the Sanatan Dharma that they arise, it is for the world and not for themselves that they arise. I am giving them freedom for the service of the world. When therefore it is said that India shall rise, it is the Sanatan Dharma that shall be great.

'When it is said that India shall expand and extend herself, it is the Sanatan Dharma that shall expand and extend itself over the world. It is for the Dharma and by the Dharma that India exists. To magnify the religion means to magnify the country. I have shown you that I am everywhere and in all men and in all things, that I am in this movement and I am not only working in those who are striving for the country but I am working also in those who oppose them and stand in their path. I am working in everybody and whatever men may think or do, they can do nothing but help on my purpose.

'They also are doing my work; they are not my enemies but my instruments. In all your actions you are moving forward without knowing which way you move. You mean to do one thing and you do another. You aim at a result and your efforts subserve one that is different or contrary. It is Shakti that has gone forth and entered into the people. Since long ago I have been preparing this uprising and now the time has come and it is I who will lead it to its fulfilment.'

This then is what I have to say to you. The name of your society is 'Society for the Protection of Religion'. Well, the protection of the religion, the protection and upraising before the world of the Hindu religion, that is the work before us. But what is the Hindu religion? What is this religion which we call Sanatan, eternal? It is the Hindu religion only because the Hindu nation has kept it, because in this Peninsula it grew up in the seclusion of the sea and the Himalayas, because in this sacred and ancient land it was given as a charge to the Aryan race to preserve through the ages.

But it is not circumscribed by the confines of a single country, it does not belong peculiarly and for ever to a bounded part of the world. That which we call the Hindu religion is really the eternal religion, because it is the universal religion which embraces all others. If a religion is not universal, it cannot be eternal. A narrow religion, a sectarian religion, an exclusive religion can live only for a limited time and a limited purpose. This is the one religion that can triumph over materialism by including and anticipating the discoveries of science and the speculations of philosophy.

It is the one religion which impresses on mankind the closeness of God to us and embraces in its compass all the possible means by which man can approach God. It is the one religion which insists every moment on the truth which all religions acknowledge, that He is in all men and all things and that in Him we move and have our being. It is the one religion which enables us not only to understand and believe this truth but to realise it with every part of our being. It is the one religion which shows the world what the world is, that it is the Lila of Vasudeva. It is the one religion which shows us how we can best play our part in that Lila, its subtlest laws and its noblest rules. It is the one religion which does not separate life in any smallest detail from religion, which knows what immortality is and has utterly removed from us the reality of death.

This is the word that has been put into my mouth to speak to you today. What I intended to speak has been put away from me, and beyond what is given to me I have nothing to say. It is only the word that is put into me that I can speak to you. That word is now finished. I spoke once before with this force in me and I said then that this movement is not a political movement and that nationalism is not politics but a religion, a creed, a faith. I say it again today, but I put it in another way. I say no longer that nationalism is a creed, a religion, a faith; I say that it is the Sanatan Dharma which for us is nationalism. This Hindu nation was born with the Sanatan Dharma, with it it moves and with it it grows. When the Sanatan Dharma declines, then the nation declines, and if the Sanatan Dharma were capable of perishing, with the Sanatan Dharma it would perish.

The Sanatan Dharma, that is nationalism. This is the message that I have to speak to you.

The Rishi Tradition by Swami Vivekananda

This you have always to remember that because a little social custom is going to be changed you are not going to lose your religion, not at all. Remember these customs have already been changed.

There was a time in this very India when, without eating beef, no Brahmin could remain a Brahmin; you read in the Vedas how, when a Sannyasin, a king, or a great man came into a house, the best bullock was killed; how in time it was found that as we were an agricultural race, killing the best bulls meant annihilation of the race. Therefore the practice was stopped, and a voice was raised against the killing of cows.

Sometimes we find existing then what we now consider the most horrible customs. In course of time other laws had to be made. These in turn will have to go, and other Smritis will come. This is one fact we have to learn that the Vedas being eternal will be one and the same throughout all ages, but the Smritis will have an end. As time rolls on, more and more of the Smritis will go, sages will come, and they will change and direct society into better channels, into duties and into paths which accord with the necessity of the age, and without which it is impossible that society can live. Thus we have to guide our course, avoiding these two dangers; and I hope that every one of us here will have breadth enough, and at the same time faith enough, to understand what that means, which I suppose is the inclusion of everything, and not the exclusion. I want the intensity of the fanatic plus the extensity of the materialist. Deep as the ocean, broad as the infinite skies, that is the sort of heart we want. Let us be as progressive as any nation that ever existed, and at the same time as faithful and conservative towards our traditions as Hindus alone know how to be.

In plain words, we have first to learn the distinction between the essentials and the non-essentials in everything. The essentials are eternal, the non-essentials have value only for a certain time; and if after a time they are not replaced by something essential, they are positively dangerous. I do not mean that you should stand up and revile all your old customs and institutions.

Certainly not; you must not revile even the most evil one of them. Revile none. Even those customs that are now appearing to be positive evils, have been positively life-giving in times past; and if we have to remove these, we must not do so with curses, but with blessings and gratitude for the glorious work these customs have done for the preservation of our race. And we must also remember that the leaders of our societies have never been either generals or kings, but Rishis. And who are the Rishis?

The Rishi as he is called in the Upanishads is not an ordinary man, but a Mantra-drashta. He is a man who sees religion, to whom religion is not merely book-learning, not argumentation, nor speculation, nor much talking, but actual realisation, a coming face to face with truths which transcend the senses. This is Rishihood, and that Rishihood does not belong to any age, or time, or even to sects or caste. Vatsyayana says, truth must be realised; and we have to remember that you, and I, and every one of us will be called upon to become Rishis; and we must have faith in ourselves; we must become world-movers, for everything is in us. We must see Religion face to face, experience it, and thus solve our doubts about it; and then standing up in the glorious light of Rishihood each one of us will be a giant; and every word falling from our lips will carry behind it that infinite sanction of security; and before us evil will vanish by itself without the necessity of cursing any one, without the necessity of abusing any one, without the necessity of fighting any one in the world. May the Lord help us, each one of us here, to realise the Rishihood for our own salvation and for that of others!

This mass of writing called the Vedas is not the utterance of persons. Its date has never been fixed, can never be fixed, and, according to us, the Vedas are eternal. There is one salient point which I want you to remember, that all the other religions of the world claim their authority as being delivered by a Personal God or a number of personal beings, angels, or special messengers of God, unto certain persons; while the claim of the Hindus is that the Vedas do not owe their authority to anybody, they are themselves the authority, being eternal—the knowledge of God. They were never written, never created, they have existed throughout time; just as creation is infinite and eternal, without beginning and without end, so is the knowledge of God without beginning and without end. And this knowledge is what is meant by the Vedas (*Vid*, to know).

The mass of knowledge called the Vedanta was discovered by personages called Rishis, and the Rishi is defined as a Mantra-drashta, a seer of thought; not that the thought was his own. Whenever you hear that a certain passage of the Vedas came from a certain Rishi, never think that he wrote it or created it out of his mind; he was the seer of the thought which already existed; it existed in the universe eternally. This sage was the discoverer; the Rishis were spiritual discoverers.

Men found out ages ago that the soul is not bound or limited by the senses, no, not even by consciousness. We have to understand that this consciousness is only the name of one link in the infinite chain. Being is not identical with consciousness, but consciousness is only one part of Being. Beyond consciousness is where the bold search. Consciousness is bound by the senses. Beyond that, beyond the senses, men must go in order to arrive at truths of the spiritual world, and there are even now persons who succeed in going beyond the bounds of the senses. These are called Rishis, because they come face to face with spiritual truths.

The proof, therefore, of the Vedas is just the same as the proof of this table before me, Pratyaksha, direct perception. This I see with the senses, and the truths of spirituality we also see in a superconscious state of the human soul. This Rishi-state is not limited by time or place, by sex or race. Vatsyayana boldly declares that this Rishihood is the common property of the descendants of the sage, of the Aryan, of the non-Aryan, of even the Mlechchha.[216] This is the sageship of the Vedas, and constantly we ought to remember this ideal of religion in India, which I wish other nations of the world would also remember and learn, so that there may be less fight and less quarrel. Religion is not in books, nor in theories, nor in dogmas, nor in talking, not even in reasoning. It is being and becoming. Ay, my friends, until each one of you has become a Rishi and come face to face with spiritual facts, religious life has not begun for you. Until the superconscious opens for you, religion is mere talk, it is nothing but preparation.

You are talking second-hand, third-hand, and here applies that beautiful saying of Buddha when he had a discussion with some Brahmins. They came discussing about the nature of Brahman, and the great sage asked, 'Have you seen Brahman?' 'No', said the Brahmin; 'Or your father?' 'No, neither has he'; 'Or your grandfather?' 'I don't think even he saw Him.' 'My friend, how can you discuss about a person whom your father and grandfather never saw, and try to put each other down?' That is what the whole world is doing. Let us say in the language of the Vedanta, 'This Atman is not to be reached by too much

---

216 A term generally used for barbarians, foreigners, those who do not follow Vedic tradition. Also, the name of an ancient tribe in India.

talk, no, not even by the highest intellect, no, not even by the study of the Vedas themselves.'

When you have known God, your very face will be changed, your voice will be changed, your whole appearance will be changed. You will be a blessing to mankind; none will be able to resist the Rishi. This is the Rishihood, the ideal in our religion. The rest, all these talks and reasonings and philosophies and dualisms and monisms, and even the Vedas themselves are but preparations, secondary things. The other is primary. The Vedas, grammar, astronomy, etc., all these are secondary; that is supreme knowledge which makes us realise the Unchangeable One. Those who realised are the sages whom we find in the Vedas; and we understand how this Rishi is the name of a type, of a class, which every one of us, as true Hindus, is expected to become at some period of our life, and becoming which, to the Hindu, means salvation. Not belief in doctrines, not going to thousands of temples, nor bathing in all the rivers in the world, but becoming the Rishi, the Mantra-drashta—that is freedom, that is salvation.

But the truth came to the Rishis of India—the Mantra-drashtas, the seers of thought—and will come to all Rishis in the future, not to talkers, not to book-swallowers, not to scholars, not to philologists, but to seers of thought. The Self is not to be reached by too much talking, not even by the highest intellects, not even by the study of the scriptures. The scriptures themselves say so. Do you find in any other scripture such a bold assertion as that—not even by the study of the Vedas will you reach the Atman? You must open your heart. Religion is not going to church, or putting marks on the forehead, or dressing in a peculiar fashion; you may paint yourselves in all the colours of the rainbow, but if the heart has not been opened, if you have not realised God, it is all vain.

There are, therefore, many stages, and we need not quarrel about them even if there have been quarrels among the ancient commentators, whom all of us ought to revere; for there is no limitation to knowledge, there is no omniscience exclusively the property of any one in ancient or modern tunes. If there have been sages and Rishis in the past, be sure that there will be many now. If there have been Vyasas and Valmikis and Shankaracharyas in ancient times, why may not each one of you become a Shankaracharya? This is another point of our religion that you must always remember, that in all other scriptures inspiration is quoted as their authority, but this inspiration is limited to a very few persons, and through them the truth came to the masses, and we have all to obey them. Truth came to Jesus of Nazareth, and we must all obey him.

We must, therefore, remember that our religion lays down distinctly and clearly that every one who wants salvation must pass through the stage of Rishihood—must become a Mantra-drashta, must see God. That is salvation; that is the law laid down by our scriptures. Then it becomes easy to look into the scripture with our own eyes, understand the meaning for ourselves, to analyse just what we want, and to understand the truth for ourselves. This is what has to be done. At the same time we must pay all reverence to the ancient sages for their work. They were great, these ancients, but we want to be greater. They did great work in the past, but we must do greater work than they. They had hundreds of Rishis in ancient India. We will have millions—we are going to have, and the sooner every one of you believes in this, the better for India and the better for the world. Whatever you believe, that you will be. If you believe yourselves to be sages, sages you will be tomorrow. There is nothing to obstruct you. For if there is one common doctrine that runs through all our apparently fighting and contradictory sects, it is that all glory, power, and purity are within the soul already.

Our scriptures declare again and again that even the knowledge of the external senses is not religion. That is religion which makes us realise the Unchangeable One, and that is the religion for every one. He who realises transcendental truth, he who realises the Atman in his own nature, he who comes face to face with God, sees God alone in everything, has become a Rishi. And there is no religious life for you until you have become a Rishi. Then alone religion begins for you, now is only the preparation. Then religion dawns upon you, now you are only undergoing intellectual gymnastics and physical tortures.

So, be you all Rishis and sages; that is the secret. More or less we shall all be Rishis.

What is meant by a Rishi? The pure one. Be pure first, and you will have power. Simply saying, 'I am a Rishi', will not do; but when you are a Rishi you will find that others obey you instinctively. Something mysterious emanates from you, which makes them follow you, makes them hear you, makes them unconsciously, even against their will, carry out your plans. That is Rishihood.

Do not be in a hurry, do not go out to imitate anybody else. This is another great lesson we have to remember; imitation is not civilisation. I may deck myself out in a Raja's dress, but will that make me a Raja? An ass in a lion's skin never makes a lion. Imitation, cowardly imitation, never makes for progress. It is verily the sign of awful degradation in a man. Ay, when a man has begun to hate himself, then the last blow has come. When a man has begun to be ashamed of his ancestors, the end has come. Here am I, one of the least of the Hindu race, yet proud of my race, proud of my ancestors. I am proud to call myself a Hindu, I am proud that I am one of your unworthy servants. I am proud that I am a countryman of yours, you the descendants of the sages, you the descendants of the most glorious Rishis the world ever saw.

Therefore, have faith in yourselves, be proud of your ancestors, instead of being ashamed of them. And do not imitate, do not imitate! Whenever you are under the thumb of others, you lose your own independence. If you are working, even in spiritual things, at the dictation of others, slowly you lose all faculty, even of thought.

Bring out through your own exertions what you have, but do not imitate, yet take what is good from others. We have to learn from others. You put the seed in the ground, and give it plenty of earth, and air, and water to feed upon; when the seed grows into the plant and into a gigantic tree, does it become the earth, does it become the air, or does it become the water? It becomes the mighty plant, the mighty tree, after its own nature, having absorbed everything that was given to it. Let that be your position.

Who are these Rishis? Vatsyayana says, 'He who has attained through proper means the direct realisation of Dharma, he alone can be a Rishi even if he is a Mlechchha by birth.

Strive after that Rishihood, stop not till you have attained the goal, and the whole world will of itself bow at your feet! Be a Rishi—that is the secret of power.

In the remote past, our country made gigantic advances in spiritual ideas. Let us, today, bring before our mind's eye that ancient history. But the one great danger in meditating over long-past greatness is that we cease to exert ourselves for new things, and content ourselves with vegetating upon that bygone ancestral glory and priding ourselves upon it. We should guard against that. In ancient times there were, no doubt, many Rishis and Maharshis who came face to face with Truth. But if this recalling of our ancient greatness is to be of real benefit, we too must become Rishis like them. Ay, not only that, but it is my firm conviction that we shall be even greater Rishis than any that our history presents to us. In the past, signal were our attainments—I glory in them, and I feel proud in thinking of them. I am not even in despair at seeing the present degradation, and I am full of hope in picturing to my mind what is to come in the future. Why? Because I know the seed undergoes a complete transformation, ay, the seed as seed is seemingly destroyed before it develops into a tree. In the same way, in the midst of our present degradation lies, only dormant for a time, the potentiality of the future greatness of our religion, ready to spring up again, perhaps more mighty and glorious than ever before.

You must not merely learn what the Rishis taught. Those Rishis are gone, and their opinions are also gone with them. You must be Rishis yourselves. You are also men as much as the greatest men that were ever born—even our incarnations.[217]

217 From *The Complete Works of Swami Vivekananda*, Volume III.

About the Author

Partho is a disciple of Sri Aurobindo and the Mother. His inner journey started with a vision of Swami Vivekananda when he was 26, and it was Swami Vivekananda who brought him to Sri Aurobindo and the Mother.